Gastrostomy Care
A Guide to Practice

Other titles by Ausmed Publications

All of these titles are available from the publisher:
Ausmed Publications
277 Mt Alexander Road, Ascot Vale, Melbourne, Victoria 3032, Australia
website: <www.ausmed.com.au>
email: <ausmed@ausmed.com.au>

Gastrostomy Care

A Guide to Practice

Edited by Catherine Barrett

Foreword by Patsy Montgomery

AUSMED PUBLICATIONS
MELBOURNE – SAN FRANCISCO

Copyright ©Ausmed Publications Pty Ltd 2004

Ausmed Publications Pty Ltd
Melbourne – San Francisco

Melbourne office:
277 Mt Alexander Road
Ascot Vale, Melbourne, Victoria 3032, Australia
ABN 49 824 739 129
Telephone: + 61 3 9375 7311
Fax: + 61 3 9375 7299
email: <ausmed@ausmed.com.au>
website: <www.ausmed.com.au>

San Francisco office:
Martin P. Hill Consulting
870 Market Street, Suite 720
San Francisco, CA 94102
USA
Tel: 415-362-2331
Fax: 415-362-2333
Mobile: 415-309-2338
email: <mphill@pacbell.net>
website ref: <www.ausmedpublications.com>

Although the Publisher has taken every care to ensure the accuracy of the professional, clinical, and technical components of this publication, it accepts no responsibility for any loss or damage suffered by any person as a result of following the procedures described or acting on information set out in this publication. The Publisher reminds readers that the information in this publication is no substitute for individual medical and/or nursing assessment and treatment by professional staff.

Gastrostomy Care: A Guide to Practice
ISBN 0-9579876-1-7
First published by Ausmed Publications Pty Ltd, 2004.
Without limiting the rights under copyright reserved above, no part of this publication may be reproduced, stored in, or introduced into a retrieval system or transmitted in any form or by any means (electronic, mechanical, photocopying, recording, or otherwise) without the written permission of Ausmed Publications. Requests and enquiries concerning reproduction and rights should be addressed to the Publisher at the above address.

National Library of Australia Cataloguing-in-Publication data

Gastrostomy care : a guide to practice.
        Bibliography.
        Includes index.
        ISBN 0 9579876 1 7.

        1. Gastrostomy. 2. Tube feeding. 3.Stomach—Surgery—Nursing. 4. Stomach—Surgery—Patients—Care. I. Barrett, Catherine, 1960–

        617.553059

Produced by Ginross Publishing
Printed in Australia

Contents

Acknowledgments

A large number of people contributed to the development of this book. Thanks are extended to all who provided assistance, especially the following.

To the staff at Melbourne Extended Care and Rehabilitation Service (MECRS), particularly Anne Cassar and the staff in Gardenview House. Their commitment to best practice in aged care drove the development of the guidelines that were the impetus for this book.

To the residents, patients, and their families who taught us so much and waited patiently while we 'got it right'. In particular, to David and Di who worked hard to get us to understand how it was from their perspective.

To Majella Pugh, former librarian at MECRS, who maintained enthusiasm for the project over five years of literature searches; to Jenny Gough, former co-director of the Education Division of the National Ageing Research Institute for assisting in the development of a statewide training program on tube feeding and several ethics forums debating tube-feeding decisions; and to Robyn Sloane for coordinating and implemening the training program and ethics forums.

To Patsy Montgomery, clinical nurse consultant to Abbott Australasia, for her support in troubleshooting problems, her feedback on the book, and her provision of the Foreword to this book.

To Abbott Australasia for generously allowing its illustrations to be reproduced in this book.

To Tracey Bucknall, associate professor in the School of Nursing at the University of Melbourne, for her support in the review of the literature relating to tube-feeding decisions; and to Trisha Dunning, professor in the Department of Endocrinology and Diabetes at St Vincent's Hospital (Melbourne), for her editorial support and information relating to the special needs of people with a gastrostomy tube and diabetes.

To Cynthea Wellings and Ausmed Publications for recognising the value of the manuscript to health professionals and the people for whom they care.

Finally, special thanks to Brian Seaton for his exceptional love and support.

Foreword

Patsy Montgomery

I am delighted to write the Foreword for *Gastrostomy Care: A Guide to Practice*. A book such as this—dedicated to the care of those who require enteral feeding—provides an invaluable resource for all health professionals and carers working in this specialised area.

The ageing of the population represents a challenge to all health professionals. An increasing number of complex and difficult issues will arise—particularly in nutrition and enteral feeding. I remember my patients who suffered with dysphagia in the 1960s and 1970s. These people had surgical 'rubber hoses' kept in place with sutures, and were fed vitamised food through a funnel. Infection, blocked tubes, and skin excoriation were common. I do not care to think about what happened to these people when they were discharged into the community.

I became involved in this area as a specialty 20 years ago, and learnt gastrostomy management on the job. At least patients had good equipment and formulae to make their lives more bearable. But if only we had a book such as this—and all the wonderful contemporary information it contains—available to us then!

The advent and development of the relatively safe percutaneous endoscopic gastrostomy (PEG) procedure since 1980 has made enteral feeding available to many people who would not previously have received it. The PEG procedure has also expanded the roles of a range of health professionals who are responsible for caring for people with gastrostomy tubes in care facilities and in the wider community. However, many health professionals have little specific training in the specialty area of enteral feeding and gastrostomies. This textbook and audiobook package is therefore a most valuable resource.

Enteral feeding is more than stomas and formulae. It can be devastating for people to learn that eating and drinking will no longer be a pleasurable social interaction. Compassion and understanding are required if health professionals are to deal properly with this personal adjustment, and with the ongoing daily needs of these people. And when they are discharged into the community or home, people require equipment, formulae, and support. What happens if the tube falls out? Panic? Health professionals, carers, and family members must have answers at their fingertips if they are to cope with this or any other eventuality.

In bringing this book into being, Catherine Barrett has brought together an excellent team of authors from a range of disciplines. For many years these experienced professionals have worked successfully with people who have gastrostomies, and with their families. I have much pleasure in commending this textbook and audiobook package as a very valuable resource for all professionals and carers who work in stoma management.

Patsy Montgomery

Patsy Montgomery is a registered nurse, registered midwife, and stomal therapist who holds a bachelor's degree in educational studies. She is co-founder and consultant for the Gastrostomy Information Support Service, president of the Peninsula Ostomy Association (Melbourne, Australia), and the coordinator and clinical nurse consultant for the Abbott Nutrition Service, Victoria (Australia). Patsy's role is to provide a support service for tube-fed people, their families, and their carers when patients are discharged from hospital into the community. This includes information and help for managing enteral tubes and equipment, advice about methods of feeding and nursing care, and information regarding supplies of formula, equipment, and pumps. Patsy also provides education and practical 'hands-on training' for gastrostomy-fed people and carers. She also provides in-service training, workshops, videos, and literature for healthcare professionals.

Preface

Catherine Barrett

Background to this book

The insertion of a feeding tube into the stomach was once a complex surgical procedure that was inaccessible to many people. However, since the replacement of the open surgical procedure with an endoscopic technique in the early 1980s, tube feeding has become an option for many more people. Since the development of the endoscopic procedure, the number of gastrostomy tubes being inserted has increased significantly. For example, from 1990/91 until 1995/96, the number of gastrostomy tube insertions in public hospitals in Victoria (Australia) increased by a staggering 685% (DHS 1997).

> *'Most staff members had no formal training in caring for people with a gastrostomy tube ... we were unable to locate any comprehensive training programs or texts to assist us.'*

As the nurse manager of a residential aged-care unit, I had first-hand experience of this increase in the use of gastrostomy tubes. Before 1993 I had not cared for a person with a gastrostomy tube; two years later, more than half of the people in our unit had a gastrostomy tube. Providing appropriate care for these people was a challenge—given that most staff members in the unit had no formal training in caring for people with a gastrostomy tube. Furthermore, we were unable to locate any comprehensive training programs or texts to assist us to update our skills.

There was therefore an immediate need to develop guidelines for health professionals in the care of a person with a gastrostomy tube. It also became apparent that there was a need to develop these guidelines in a manner that supported patients by providing them with information and involving them in informed choices with regard to their tube feeding.

These guidelines had to take account of the fact that tube-feeding decisions are often complicated by the emotional states of the person and his or her family. Moreover, there is often confusion regarding the evidence about tube feeding and the roles of health professionals in the decision-making process. In addition, there is variability in the outcomes of tube feeding. For some people, tube feeding has clear benefits; it can provide nutritional support during recovery from an acute illness, or it can allow people to be discharged home more promptly. However, for a significant number of people, the benefits of tube feeding are less obvious.

'For some people, tube feeding has clear benefits ... However, for a significant number of people, the benefits of tube feeding are less obvious.'

In 1995, in response to these concerns, Ann Cassar (then a dietitian at Melbourne Extended Care and Rehabilitation Service) established a multidisciplinary working party to develop practical guidelines for staff. These guidelines were refined over a number of years before being used to develop a training program for staff in the unit. The training program was so well received by staff members that a decision was made to offer the program to health professionals across the state of Victoria in conjunction with the National Ageing Research Institute. A series of forums on the ethical implications of tube-feeding decisions was also developed and conducted. These forums generated passionate debate. The overwhelming interest in both the training program and the ethics forums confirmed the need for this book.

'The overwhelming interest confirmed the need for this book.'

Aims and authorship of this book

The primary aims of *Gastrostomy Care: A Guide to Practice* are:

- to assist health professionals in understanding the care needs of a person with a gastrostomy tube;
- to provide guidance in managing those needs appropriately; and
- to equip health professionals with the information necessary to assist people to make informed choices about their tube feeding.

This book draws primarily on the clinical expertise of health professionals working with people who have gastrostomy tubes. The chapter authors include experienced nurses, speech therapists, dietitians, and doctors. This wealth of practical clinical experience is enhanced with appropriate reference to the published literature—particularly with respect to issues that are contentious or poorly understood.

'... to assist in understanding the care needs of a person with a gastrostomy tube, to provide guidance in managing those needs appropriately, and to assist people to make informed choices about their tube feeding.'

Arrangement of this book

The arrangement of the book follows the experiences of a person with a gastrostomy tube. The book begins by discussing swallowing difficulties. It then accompanies the person as he or she works through decisions about tube feeding, has a tube inserted, assists in having nutritional needs assessed, and collaborates in planning a feeding regimen.

The book then examines the challenges faced by the person and his or family in adjusting to life with a gastrostomy tube. Innovative strategies are provided to facilitate adjustment—including reintroducing meal choices via the gastrostomy tube and (if possible) orally. Practical strategies are also provided for the care of the person's gastrostomy stoma, tube, and mouth.

'The arrangement of the book follows the experiences of a person with a gastrostomy tube.'

The book then provides strategies for managing common problems, before offering information on changing a gastrostomy tube and administration of medication. Although the focus of the book is on gastrostomy tube feeding, a chapter has also been included on feeding via a nasogastric tube. The book concludes with a chapter on the person's preparations for discharge into the wider community.

The informative text is enhanced with illustrative case studies, practical assessment tools, useful proformas, and explanatory diagrams. In keeping with the evidence-based nature of the text, the book concludes with a list of references and a comprehensive, cross-referenced index.

Guidance, support, and understanding

Gastrostomy Care: A Guide to Practice provides expert guidance to all health professionals who care for people with gastrostomy tubes. It also provides valuable support to those who are involved in helping people, and their families, to make informed decisions about tube feeding.

'In providing a better understanding of the experience of people with a gastrostomy tube, this important book will lead to better outcomes for all.'

In providing a better understanding of the experience of people with a gastrostomy tube, this important book will lead to better outcomes for all.

About the Authors

Michelle Allen
Chapter 3

Michelle Allen holds a diploma of nursing (St Bartholomew and Princess Alexandra College of Nursing and Midwifery, London, UK) and a certificate of middle management. Michelle worked at the Royal London Hospital for one year on an acute admissions ward before returning to Melbourne (Australia) where she began working at Melbourne Extended Care and Rehabilitation Service as associate nurse unit manager on a complex care unit. She participated in a falls research project as a nurse researcher for the National Ageing Research Institute. Michelle later served as a veterans project officer and now works for Lundbeck Australia Pty Ltd as a medical representative.

Jacqui Bailey
Chapters 4, 14

Jacqui Bailey is a dietitian who holds a master's degree in nutrition and dietetics, a bachelor's degree in science, and a graduate certificate in paediatric nutrition and dietetics. She is a member of the Australasian Society for Parenteral and Enteral Nutrition, and Nutrition Australia. Jacqui has worked as a clinical dietitian for eight years. She was responsible for establishing a home enteral nutrition service for Latrobe Regional Hospital (Victoria, Australia) and for designing educational materials relating to tube feeding at home. Jacqui understands the intricacies of caring for people at home, and is aware of the importance of communication among members of a healthcare team before and after discharge from hospital if care is to be optimised. She continues to work with gastrostomy patients both in hospital and after discharge from her current workplace, Monash Medical Centre (Melbourne, Victoria).

Catherine Barrett

Subject specialist editor, Chapters 2, 3, 6, 11, 13

Catherine Barrett is a registered nurse who holds a bachelor's degree in nursing science and certificates in gerontic nursing, advanced management, sexual and reproductive health, and assessment and workplace training. She is a member of Geriaction Victoria, the Australian Association of Gerontologists, and the Royal College of Nursing, Australia. Catherine has been working in aged care since 1982 as a nurse unit manager, an external assessor for the Standards and Accreditation Agency, a veterans' project officer, and a consultant nurse for the National Ageing Research Institute. Catherine is currently a PhD candidate at the University of Melbourne (Victoria, Australia). The subject of her thesis is practice change to enhance patient-centred care. Catherine's research interests include sexuality in aged care, person-centred care, organisational change, practice development, and action research. She is also co-director of Desirable Outcomes Pty Ltd, a business that is committed to promoting sexual and sensual health for adults in aged-care and disability services.

Sally Bowen

Chapter 6

Sally Bowen is a chef and food consultant, businesswoman, and sculptor who holds a bachelor of arts degree. As a qualified chef, Sally has worked in restaurants, catering businesses, and hospitals. She believes that food should be presented elegantly and simply, and that it should stir the senses with vibrant colours, aromatic smells, diverse textures, and stimulating flavours. Sally has worked with health professionals to develop exciting and stimulating foods for those in their care—both those who take their food orally and those who are fed via gastrostomy tubes. Sally is committed to improving the quality of life of her clients, customers, and colleagues. Sally is a co-director of Desirable Outcomes Pty Ltd, a business that is committed to promoting sexual health for adults in aged and disability services.

Alison Bowie

Chapter 10

Alison Bowie is an accredited practising dietitian who holds a bachelor's degree in science and a master's degrees in nutrition and dietetics. She is a member of the Dietitian's Association of Australia and is secretary of the Rehabilitation and Aged Care Interest Group of that association. Alison's work as a dietitian has been principally in the area of aged care, and she is currently employed as a dietitian at St Vincent's Hospital and St George's Hospital (Melbourne, Australia) servicing the geriatric evaluation and management unit. Before this she worked at Melbourne Extended Care and Rehabilitation Service where she was responsible for dietetic services in home enteral-nutrition gastrostomy care and rehabilitation.

Susan Camilleri

Chapter 13

Susan Camilleri is a registered nurse who holds a bachelor's degree in health science, a diploma of health science, a graduate diploma in gerontological nursing, and a certificate in workplace leadership. Susan has worked in aged care for the past 17 years, and was an associate nurse unit manager in a complex residential care unit. Susan's passions include the effect of culture on care, and quality outcomes for patients. Susan currently works on a surgical unit at Northern Hospital (Melbourne, Australia).

Leone Carroll

Chapter 1

Leone Carroll holds bachelor's degrees in social science (psychology) and applied science (speech pathology) and has worked as a speech pathologist for more than ten years. She has been involved in the management of communication and swallowing difficulties in adults in hospitals (both acute and rehabilitation) and in residential care. Leone has worked in a variety of capacities—including clinician, manager, and project officer. Most of her clinical work has been at Melbourne Extended Care and Rehabilitation Service (Victoria, Australia) where she worked on the Home Rehabilitation Service and the Complex Care Unit and was involved in developing a manual for activity workers in communication groups in residential-care facilities. Leone then managed the speech pathology departments at Broadmeadows Health Service (Sunshine Hospital) and Melbourne Extended Care and Rehabilitation Service for two years, before moving to Perth (Western Australia) in 2002. Leone is currently project officer with Speech Pathology Australia, the national professional association.

Peteris Darzins

Chapter 2

Dr Peteris Darzins is an academic geriatrician who holds bachelor's degrees in medicine and surgery, a PhD gained through epidemiological research, and fellowships in both the Australian and Canadian colleges of physicians. Peteris is consultant geriatrician to the Rehabilitation and Aged Services Program of Southern Health (Victoria, Australia) and associate professor of geriatric medicine at Monash University (Victoria, Australia). He conducts research through the Monash Ageing Research Centre where his research interests include the measurement of personal-care handicap, the assessment of people's decision-making capacity, and working as a methodologist for the research of others.

Catherine Edgar

Chapter 8

Catherine Edgar is a registered nurse who holds a diploma in applied science (nursing), a graduate diploma in neurosciences, and a master's degree in nursing studies. She is a member of the Royal College of Nursing, Australia. Catherine's professional background is in rehabilitation, education, and aged-care nursing. She has worked as a clinical nurse specialist, clinical consultant, quality manager, and unit manager. She has also been involved in nurse education as a clinical teacher and associate lecturer at RMIT University and Deakin University (both Victoria, Australia). Catherine is currently an adjunct lecturer at La Trobe University (Melbourne, Australia).

Julie Garreffa
Chapter 7

Julie Garreffa is a registered nurse who holds a graduate certificate in aged-services management, a certificate in health nursing, and a certificate in workplace training and assessment. Julie worked for eight years as hostel supervisor for the Anglican Homes for the Elderly in Melbourne (Australia). She has also served in private practice as an educational assessor, facilitator of learning, and quality consultant. Julie is a member of the Accreditation and Practice Committee of the Nurses Board of Victoria, and is currently undertaking a graduate diploma in industrial training and adult education at RMIT University (Melbourne, Victoria). In all her roles, Julie has actively pursued her professional goals of supporting health professionals in achieving quality outcomes for the recipients of health services. Julie is now a registered nurse course coordinator (community services and health) at Kangan Batman TAFE (Melbourne, Australia).

Clare Hetzel
Chapters 5, 6

Clare Hetzel is a psychologist, sexual health consultant, and visual artist. She holds a bachelor of arts degree (in psychology and anthropology), a diploma in educational psychology, and a diploma in visual arts. Clare has been involved in both private and public health care as a psychologist, educator, family counsellor, mediator, and consultant for the past twenty years. During this time she has developed and implemented a range of programs—including programs on sensual well-being and sexual health promotion, communication and conflict resolution, and grief and stress management. Clare spent four years working with the complex care unit at Melbourne Extended Care and Rehabilitation Service (Victoria, Australia), during which time one of her roles was supporting people and their families in adjusting to living with a gastrostomy tube. Clare is a co-director of Desirable Outcomes Pty Ltd, a business that is committed to promoting sexual health for adults in aged and disability services.

Jan Iskander
Chapter 12

Jan Iskander is a registered pharmacist who holds a bachelor's degree in pharmacy and a graduate diploma in clinical pharmacy. She is a member of the Society of Hospital Pharmacists of Australia. Jan has extensive experience in community and hospital pharmacy. She was previously manager of the pharmacy service at North West Hospital (Melbourne, Australia). In this role she was, at various times, responsible for the pharmacy departments at North West Hospital, Greenvale Centre, Royal Park Hospital, Essendon & District Hospital, and the Mental Health Services for the 'Kids & Youth Program'. She also managed the quality portfolio for the network pharmacy service of North Western Health. Jan is currently manager of the pharmacy department at Sandringham & District Memorial Hospital (Melbourne, Australia), a community-based public hospital with medical, surgical, obstetric, haemodialysis, and emergency services. Her interests are the safe use of medicines and quality-improvement processes.

Jane Panaccio
Chapter 1

Jane Panaccio holds a bachelor's degree in applied sciences (speech pathology) and a graduate diploma in rehabilitation studies. She has broad experience in rehabilitation and acute-care settings—specialising in the assistance of those who have swallowing and communication disorders. Jane has conducted many inservices for hospital staff on swallowing disorders, and has been involved in hospital committees established to review the appropriateness of foods for people experiencing these disorders. She has also worked in the Cognitive Dementia Assessment and Management Service at Melbourne Extended Care and Rehabilitation Service (Victoria, Australia) for many years. Jane is currently in private practice in Melbourne. She provides consultancy services to several private hospitals and to individuals in the community.

Raquel Rogers
Chapter 9

Raquel Rogers is a registered nurse who holds a diploma of health science in nursing, a graduate diploma of advanced nursing (gerontic nursing), an advanced certificate of leadership and management, a certificate of continence management, and a graduate diploma of advanced nursing (neurosciences). Raquel currently works at St Vincent's Hospital (Melbourne, Australia) as part of the neuroscience team. She has previously worked as a nurse unit manager of a 30-bed chronic neurological disorders unit and as acting nurse unit manager in a 30-bed psychogeriatric unit. Raquel has also worked as an associate nurse unit manager where she was an active participant in the development of procedures and policies for tube feeding.

Julie Ryan
Chapter 9

Julie Ryan is the senior nurse for the North-Western Aged Persons Mental Health Program in Melbourne (Australia). She holds a bachelor's degree in applied science (nursing), a graduate diploma in advanced nursing (gerontic nursing), an advanced certificate of leadership and management, and a certificate in psychiatric nursing. Julie is a member of the Royal College of Nursing, Australia. She has worked extensively with aged clients in general and psychiatric settings, including four years as manager of a 30-bed psychogeriatric facility. Julie's current role encompasses staff education, policy development, and monitoring of care standards and client outcomes. She is currently undertaking studies for a master's degree in nursing, majoring in dementia care.

Chapter 1
Indications for Tube Feeding
Jane Panaccio and Leone Carroll

Introduction

Tube feeding via a gastrostomy tube is one way of managing the nutrition and hydration needs of people experiencing dysphagia (difficulty with swallowing). Dysphagia can occur as a result of a neurological event, a carcinoma (of the mouth, pharynx, or larynx), or other disease processes. Tube feeding is also used for people with a decreased level of consciousness, severe weight loss, and inadequate nutrition.

This chapter discusses:

- the swallowing process in healthy individuals;
- the factors that can affect the swallowing process;
- the dangers of dysphagia;
- the management of dysphagia;
- the indications for tube feeding; and
- the contraindications to tube feeding.

Most people have had the experience of feeling something 'stuck in the throat' or 'going down the wrong way'. It is uncomfortable, and can be frightening. However, individuals who have difficulty swallowing because of an impaired swallowing reflex are at risk of choking, chest infections, and pneumonia—all of which can be fatal. The insertion of a percutaneous endoscopic gastrostomy (PEG) tube can decrease the risk of such complications.

The normal swallowing process

The normal swallowing process consists of three stages. These are:

- the oral stage;
- the velopharyngeal stage; and
- the pharyngeal stage.

  These are discussed below.

1. Oral stage

The oral stage of the swallowing process involves voluntary movements in the mouth. It involves the lips, jaw, tongue, and facial muscles in the following processes:

- the lips close (to hold food and fluid in the mouth);
- the teeth chew solids;
- saliva mixes with the solids and liquids;
- food is prepared into a bolus (ball); and
- the tongue and oral pressure propel the bolus towards the back of the throat.

2. Velopharyngeal stage

The velopharyngeal stage of the swallowing process is made up of both volitional (voluntary) and reflexive (involuntary) movements. The following processes occur:

- the bolus is held against the hard palate;
- the velum (soft palate) lifts to seal the mouth off from the nasopharynx;
- the bolus passes over the base of the tongue; and
- the swallowing reflex is triggered.

Stages in the swallowing process

A knowledge of the stages in the normal swallowing process is essential to understanding dysphagia and the indications for tube feeding. These stages are mentioned several times in the course of this chapter.

The normal swallowing process consists of three stages:

- the oral stage;
- the velopharyngeal stage; and
- the pharyngeal stage.

3. Pharyngeal stage

The pharyngeal stage occurs in the pharynx ('throat'). The following processes occur:

- the swallowing reflex is triggered;
- the pharyngeal muscles of the throat contract;
- the bolus moves down through the throat;
- the laryngeal muscles bring the larynx ('voice box') upwards and forwards;
- the epiglottis moves down to close over the trachea ('windpipe');
- the vocal folds (or cords) close;
- the cricopharyngeus muscle opens the upper oesophageal sphincter to allow the bolus to pass through into the oesophagus; and
- peristalsis moves the bolus down into the stomach.

Dysphagia

Definition and mechanism

The term *dysphagia* means, literally, 'difficulty with swallowing'. The swallowing process involves an intricate coordination of muscle movements and neural messages. It occurs very quickly, and the swallowing reflex itself takes only a second to execute. A malfunction at any stage can disrupt the whole swallowing process and can compromise the person's safety, comfort, and health.

Dysphagia can cause:

- *choking*—obstruction of the airways;
- *laryngeal penetration*—food or drink entering the larynx, but not actually entering the airway, creating a high risk of aspiration; and
- *aspiration*—food or drink entering the airway, creating a risk of chest infections.

The severity of dysphagia is determined by the number of swallowing stages affected, the amount of discomfort to the person, and the level of aspiration risk.

Provided that the person has adequate sensation in the throat and can clear the throat or cough, a small amount of aspiration can be tolerated. However, consistently large amounts of aspiration can cause congestion, infection, and pneumonia.

If dysphagia is severe, and if choking or aspiration pneumonia occur frequently, an alternative means of providing nutrition should be considered. However, gastrostomy feeding does not always prevent aspiration (see 'Contraindications for tube feeding', page 17). A decision to use a gastrostomy tube must always be based on careful consideration of the total context of each individual—including assessment of the environmental, ethical, psychosocial, and medical factors involved.

> *'A decision to use a gastrostomy tube must be based on careful consideration of the total context of each individual … environmental, ethical, psychosocial, and medical.'*

Causes of dysphagia

There are many causes of dysphagia. Table 1.1 (page 5) provides a list of disorders that can be associated with dysphagia—and the mechanisms by which they cause difficulty with swallowing.

Types of dysphagia

As noted on page 2, the normal swallowing process consists of three stages. These stages can be used to describe three types of dysphagia:

Type of disorder	Examples	Mechanism of action
Neurological disorders	cerebral palsy stroke motor neurone disease amyotrophic lateral sclerosis neoplasms (tumours)	decrease strength, range, and coordination of muscle movements
Mechanical disorders	excessive or reduced saliva (secondary to medications or radiation) systemic diseases (e.g. scleroderma)	affect structures in the throat and disrupt movement of bolus
Structural disorders	pharyngeal pouch tumours surgical resections tracheostomy tubes inflammatory conditions	obstructions in gastrointestinal tract from mouth to stomach
Behavioural disorders	depression and anxiety anorexia smoking and alcohol	affect the environment and affect person's desire to eat or drink

Table 1.1 Disorders associated with dysphagia
AUTHORS' CREATION (ADAPTED FROM LOGEMANN 1983; ANDERSON 1991; SONIES 1992)

- dysphagia occurring during the *oral* stage;
- dysphagia occurring during the *velopharyngeal* stage; and
- dysphagia occurring during the *pharyngeal* stage.
  These are discussed below.

Dysphagia occurring during the oral stage

Dysphagia in the oral stage is associated with increased transit time in the mouth. This can be due to a tumour of the tongue or oral cavity (affecting oral movements), decreased or increased saliva (affecting bolus thickness and movement), or muscle weakness.

Examples of muscle weakness include:

- weakened lip muscles—resulting in dribbling and food leakage;
- weakened tongue muscles—affecting bolus formation and movement; and
- reduced tension and/or sensation in the cheek muscles—resulting in food or fluid pooling in the mouth or cheeks.

Dysphagia occurring during the velopharyngeal stage

Decreased muscle strength, poor coordination, or lack of sensation in the velum (soft palate) and pharynx can cause swallowing difficulties in the velopharyngeal stage—which can lead to aspiration or choking.

These swallowing difficulties include nasal regurgitation of the bolus (thus increasing the risk of spillage into the pharynx), slow initiation or absence of a swallowing reflex (thus leaving the airway unprotected), and a tumour or an obstruction (affecting movement of pharyngeal structures).

Dysphagia occurring during the pharyngeal stage

If dysphagia occurs during the pharyngeal stage, food can remain in the pharynx after swallowing has been completed. If the epiglottis does not close off the airway, penetration and/or aspiration of food and fluid can occur.

Dysphagia at this stage can be due to:

- neurological or structural damage to the throat muscles—affecting bolus movement;
- reduced or uncoordinated laryngeal muscle function (affecting movement of the throat, larynx, epiglottis, and vocal cords)—causing incomplete elevation and closure of the larynx;
- an ineffective cough reflex—leaving the larynx unprotected from aspirated food or fluid;
- dysfunction of the cricopharyngeus muscle—resulting in reflux or poor clearing of the bolus; or
- a diverticulum (pouch formation) in the pharyngeal wall.

Dysphagia associated with ageing

Changes in a person's ability to swallow are commonly associated with the ageing process. This can be associated with poor dentition, decreased sensation in the mouth and pharynx, impaired ability to sense the texture of food or fluid, and reduced pharyngeal muscle tone (Sonies 1992). When these changes occur in isolation, they have a negligible effect on swallowing and can be dealt with by various strategies (Sonies 1992).

These strategies include:

- modifying the size or texture of the bolus (for example, by using a teaspoon instead of a dessert spoon); and
- changing eating behaviour (for example, by ensuring that each bolus is swallowed before taking another bite).

A significant swallowing disorder in the elderly is usually due to a combination of ageing and pathology (Sonies 1992; Robbins et al. 1995). For example, a person who has suffered a stroke might also suffer from depression and have a pre-existing pharyngeal pouch. This combination of factors can affect his or her swallowing ability at several different stages in the swallowing process. The swallowing disorder might also exacerbate the person's depression.

Dysphagia in the elderly might also be caused by pathology lower down in the oesophagus. For example, uncoordinated muscle movements in the oesophagus can result in reduced and ineffective peristalsis. This type of swallowing disorder usually requires medical treatment.

Signs and symptoms of dysphagia

Although assessment and management of dysphagia requires referral to a speech pathologist trained in this area, all health professionals should be alert to the signs and symptoms that indicate swallowing problems. Table 1.2 (page 8) summarises the signs and symptoms of dysphagia occurring at various stages in the swallowing process.

These warning signs and symptoms can be used to formulate a checklist proforma for clinical assessment of dysphagia. This is shown in Figure 1.1 (page 10). This checklist suggests some questions to ask a person in whom dysphagia is suspected. The information gained from these questions can help to determine whether the person has dysphagia.

Many warning signs can be observed at mealtimes. These observations should be supported by specific questioning of the person. For example, the person can be asked whether food sticks in the throat or whether he or she is able to cough.

Warning signs and symptoms can occur in isolation or in combination. They can also occur in association with signs and symptoms of co-morbidities that can obscure dysphagia.

Swallowing disorder	Mechanism of action	Signs and symptoms
Oral stage of swallowing		
Weak muscles of the lips	loss of food or drink from the mouth	drooling or dribbling
Weak or uncoordinated movements of the tongue	unable to form a single bolus	lengthy chewing and slow eating or drinking unclear speech
Weak or reduced sensation in cheeks	food remaining in cheek pockets after meal food might fall out of mouth or back into pharynx food might be aspirated	food still in cheeks after meal
Excess or reduced saliva production	dry mouth food not formed into bolus easily lengthy oral stage	person reports dry mouth saliva drools from lips
Velopharyngeal stage of swallowing		
Weak or uncoordinated soft palate and upper pharynx	nasal regurgitation	food or drink regurgitated into nose discomfort runny nose
Delayed or absent swallowing reflex	food or drink pooling in the pharynx potential for aspiration	coughing 'gurgly' or 'wet' voice chest congestion
Pharyngeal stage of swallowing		
Weak or uncoordinated pharyngeal contraction	food or drink remaining in the pharynx after swallowing potential for aspiration	coughing reports of food 'sticking'
Reduced or uncoordinated laryngeal elevation	poorly closed airways food or drink residue in the pharynx potential for aspiration	coughing 'gurgly' voice congestion

Table 1.2 Signs and symptoms of dysphagia

AUTHORS' CREATION

(continued)

Swallowing disorder	Mechanism of action	Signs and symptoms
Pharyngeal stage of swallowing		
Cricopharyngeal dysfunction	food or drink pooling near opening of airways food or drink possibly spilling into airways	'gurgly' voice coughing
Diverticulum (pocket in pharynx)	food or drink pooling in pouch	coughing reports of food 'sticking' in base of throat
At any stage of swallowing		
		subjective complaints of difficulty with swallowing objective observation of signs of dysphagia person avoiding meals or drinks inability to cough or clear airways after penetration or aspiration weight loss dehydration weak or absent cough

Table 1.2 Signs and symptoms of dysphagia *(continued)*

Any person who exhibits signs and symptoms of dysphagia should be referred to a qualified speech pathologist for assessment. This should also be done if there is any significant change in the condition of a person who has already been diagnosed with dysphagia.

Poor oral intake requires referral to a dietitian who will assess the person's nutritional needs and make recommendations.

'Any person who exhibits signs and symptoms of dysphagia should be referred to a qualified speech pathologist for assessment.'

During observation at mealtime, indicate with a tick in the boxes if the answer to the question is 'yes'.

ORAL STAGE:

☐ Does the person drool or dribble?
- ☐ at rest
- ☐ while talking
- ☐ at mealtime
- ☐ while drinking

☐ Does the person take time to chew food?
☐ Does the person take a long time to eat or drink?
☐ Is the person's speech difficult to understand?
☐ Does food remain in the mouth or cheeks long after the swallow or meal?

VELOPHARYNGEAL STAGE:

☐ Is there nasal discharge after swallowing?
- ☐ Is it clear?
- ☐ Does it resemble the fluid being drunk?
- ☐ Does it resemble the food being eaten?

PHARYNGEAL STAGE:

☐ Does the person cough persistently:
- ☐ before swallowing?
- ☐ during swallowing?
- ☐ after swallowing?

☐ Does the person show evidence of distress from coughing?
☐ Is the person able to cough voluntarily or when asked to?
☐ Does the person's voice sound gurgly or wet when speaking:
- ☐ before swallowing?
- ☐ after swallowing?

☐ Does the chest sound congested?
☐ Does the person complain of food sticking in the throat after swallowing?

GENERAL:

☐ Is the person losing weight?
☐ Are there signs of fever or sudden increase in temperature?
☐ Does the person have a past history of dysphagia?

If the person demonstrates more than two of these characteristics consistently, referral to a speech pathologist is indicated.

Figure 1.1 Checklist proforma for dysphagia

AUTHORS' CREATION

Managing dysphagia

Assessment and planning

Dysphagia should be assessed and managed by the whole team involved in the person's care. Having a dedicated and clearly defined team with established guidelines to manage the dysphagia assists the person and his or her family to make decisions about tube feeding.

Ultimately, the person and his or her direct caregivers determine the management goals, and the strategies of management are different for every individual.

'Ultimately, the person and his or her direct caregivers determine the management goals ... the strategies of management are different for every individual.'

The care team must be mindful of the ethical and medical dilemmas involved in management. Typical issues to consider when formulating management goals are:

- the need to prevent choking and aspiration;
- nutrition and hydration requirements;
- the individual's views and preferences; and
- quality of life.

The Box on page 12 provides a list of questions that should be addressed in drawing-up any management plan for dysphagia.

It should be noted that dysphagia following an acute neurological event often resolves (either partially or completely). Resolution depends on the severity of the dysphagia, the cause of the dysphagia and its prognosis, and the management approach implemented.

'Dysphagia following an acute neurological event often resolves ... dysphagia secondary to dementia or a degenerative disease does not usually resolve.'

In contrast, dysphagia secondary to dementia or a degenerative disease does not usually resolve.

Questions to be addressed in a management plan

The following questions should be addressed in drawing-up a management plan for dysphagia.

- What is the effect of dysphagia on the person's quality of life? What are the social implications of dysphagia? How can the social implications be managed while maintaining the person's safety?
- How long is the dysphagia likely to last? Will swallowing function improve or deteriorate with time?
- Is the person able to swallow saliva safely? How often and how much aspiration occurs? What are the effects?
- How much weight is being lost? What are the person's goals for maintaining nutrition and hydration?

Non-invasive management techniques

There are many non-invasive techniques to manage dysphagia. The three main strategies that speech pathologists consider in any management plan are:

- rehabilitation;
- compensation; and
- substitution.

These strategies are discussed below.

Rehabilitation

Rehabilitation strategies need to be regular and consistent to be effective—but they are not necessarily time-intensive. Active therapeutic techniques aim to strengthen the affected structures or muscles. These techniques include:

- brushing and iceing (specific massage to stimulate muscles);
- specific facial exercises that strengthen the muscles of the face (for example, alternating between pouting and smiling); and
- trials of oral intake under direction from a speech pathologist.

Non-invasive management techniques

This part of the chapter discusses non-invasive techniques for managing dysphagia. The three main strategies are:

* rehabilitation;

* compensation; and

* substitution.

It has been suggested that aspects of swallowing can become impaired or lost if they are not practised (Feinberg et al. 1990), and that an 'oral exercise' regimen should be maintained by healthy elderly people (Robbins et al. 1995). A person who receives long-term sustenance via tube feeding only, and who therefore does not practise swallowing, can thus lose the ability to swallow effectively.

Compensation

Compensation constitutes the most common form of management. Strategies are implemented to compensate for changes in swallowing function—often in conjunction with rehabilitative methods to ensure safety. The strategies are also recommended if rehabilitation is not feasible or has been unsuccessful.

Compensation strategies attempt to alter the environment, a person's behaviour, and the texture of the food and fluid.

For example, following stroke or surgery, some people benefit from turning or tilting the head to encourage the food and drink to move down the unaffected side of the pharynx. Other people need to have the texture of their food and drinks modified. Thickened fluids, puréed or vitamised food, and minced meats are the safest for swallowing disorders. For other people, using a teaspoon to control the size of the bolus might be all that is required.

'Compensation strategies attempt to alter the environment, a person's behaviour, and the texture of the food and fluid.'

Substitution

If a person is unable to take oral foods and fluids safely in adequate quantities to sustain nutrition, alternative eating and drinking methods—such as tube feeding—should be considered.

The person's potential for rehabilitation should be assessed before a decision is made to begin tube feeding. This ensures that tube feeding is not seen as a 'quick-fix' alternative to oral intake. However, rehabilitation, compensation, and substitution are not necessarily mutually exclusive options. They can be used in combination—depending on the circumstances, and the objectives of the person and his or her care team. It is important to note that tube feeding can occur even if some food and fluid is being taken orally.

'The status of a person's dysphagia should never be considered static. It should be reviewed regularly and frequently—whether or not tube feeding is taking place.'

The status of a person's dysphagia should never be considered static. It should be reviewed regularly and frequently—whether or not tube feeding is taking place.

Indications for tube feeding

In some cases, the management techniques discussed above do not enable a person to swallow safely and maintain adequate nutrition and hydration. In these circumstances, tube feeding should be considered.

Any person with dysphagia is at risk of nutritional deficiencies and inadequate hydration. Such deficiencies are especially significant in certain people. These include:

- those who are frail and elderly;
- those who are cognitively impaired (for example, those who are suffering from dementia);
- those who have fluctuating consciousness;
- those who have congenital or neurodegenerative disorders; and
- those who have eating disorders.

The risk is increased if the person is ill or exposed to hot weather.

The most common indications for gastrostomy tube feeding are stroke (47%), neurodegenerative disorders (34.7%), and cancer (13.3%) (Callahan, Haag & Weinberger 2000).

A decision to institute tube feeding might be made in the following circumstances (Ciocon 1990; Peck, Cohen & Mulvihill 1990; Kyle 1996; O'Brien, Davis & Erwin-Toth 1999):

'Hospitals and residential-care facilities should devise clear guidelines that outline the alternatives to oral intake and when they should be implemented.'

- for *temporary dysphagia*—in which swallowing function is expected to return;
- for *long-term dysphagia*—in which swallowing function is not expected to improve); and
- for *other disorders*—in which the status of swallowing is unknown or unrelated to oral or pharyngeal dysphagia.

Table 1.3 (page 16) lists some indications for tube feeding under each of these categories and provides a comment on each. Hospitals and residential-care facilities should devise clear guidelines that outline the alternatives to oral intake and when they should be implemented.

Tube feeding in people with dementia is controversial (Fernandez-Viadero et al. 2002; Dharmarajan et al. 2001). When considering tube feeding in a person with dementia, quality of life and the wishes of the person should be foremost in the minds of the decision-makers. In some cases, people with dementia might be able to indicate their wishes, or might have previously indicated their preference.

'When considering tube feeding in a person with dementia, quality of life and the wishes of the person should be foremost.'

As discussed above, tube feeding can complement or supplement oral feeding. A person with dysphagia might be able to tolerate small amounts of food and fluid orally, but not enough to maintain nutritional needs or comfort. In these circumstances, a gastrostomy tube can be

Disorder	Comment
Temporary dysphagia	
Acute neurological disorders (e.g. stroke)	swallowing might improve over time; meanwhile person is unable to obtain adequate nutrition and hydration orally
Acute head injury	swallowing might improve over time; meanwhile person is unable to obtain adequate nutrition and hydration orally
Head and neck cancers	a tumour can obstruct the swallowing structures or disrupt swallowing control in the brain
Long-term dysphagia	
Head and neck cancers	surgery might permanently affect the swallowing structures or nerves
Neurodegenerative disorders (e.g. amytrophic lateral sclerosis)	swallowing and other functions expected to deteriorate
Poor cognition (e.g. dementia)	tube feeding controversial
	in early stages, person might be unable to obtain sufficient hydration or nutrition, but might be able to contribute to decision on tube feeding
Severe oral ulceration or other oral disorder	interferes with structures and mechanics of swallowing
Other disorders	
Problems with consciousness—person unconscious or fluctuating consciousness	person physically unable to take adequate food or drink orally difficult for observer to assess swallowing function
Idiopathic and psychiatric eating disorders	difficult for observer to assess swallowing function due to unreliable responses
Oesophageal obstructions (for example, tumour)	tumour can be in a position that impedes normal digestion and end-processing of oral intake (but not necessarily the placement of the gastrostomy tube)
Upper gastrointestinal tract disorders affecting motility (e.g. tumours, burns, trauma)	food cannot pass into the mid oesophagus (and therefore cannot be digested) tumour can be in a position to minimise reflux
HIV/AIDS	oesophageal involvement can prevent adequate movement of food and drink into (or out of) oesophagus
Persons unable to tolerate nasogastric tubes	PEG alternative might be required

Table 1.3 Indications for tube feeding
AUTHORS' CREATION

inserted to ensure adequate nutrition and hydration while some oral intake is continued under the supervision of the swallowing therapist. This provides taste sensation and some enjoyment for the person, facilitates stimulation of the swallowing mechanism, and enables ongoing monitoring of the person's swallowing function. Combined oral and tube feeding can also be a useful process for gradually increasing oral intake as the person's swallowing function improves. In such cases, eventual removal of the gastrostomy tube should be considered.

Contraindications to tube feeding

As with any procedure, contraindications and ethical dilemmas need to be considered when contemplating tube feeding. The most significant of these is the risk of reflux and aspiration.

Reflux of gastrointestinal and pharyngeal contents places individuals at risk of aspiration—despite the insertion of a gastrostomy tube. Reflux can occur as a result of:

'The risk of aspiration is significant in individuals in the terminal stages of many neurological illnesses.'

- poor cough reflex;
- reduced pharyngeal sensation;
- reduced peristalsis; and
- an inability to modify the person's posture.

The risk of aspiration is significant in individuals in the terminal stages of many neurological illnesses. For these people, tube feeding is contraindicated in certain circumstances (Peck, Cohen & Mulvihill 1980; Groher 1994; Campbell-Taylor & Fisher 1987). These include:

- if the person requires palliative care;
- if the person is unable to sit up for long periods;
- if the person is unable to communicate;
- if there is a known history of aspiration on oral intake;
- if oesophageal function is poor; or
- if there is a history of reflux.

Other contraindications include (Gilbar & Kam 1997):

- persistent vomiting or diarrhoea;
- intestinal obstruction;
- paralytic ileus; and
- gastrointestinal haemorrhage.

In addition to the above contraindications, previous abdominal surgery and obesity can diminish illumination of the gastric wall during an endoscopic procedure. These conditions can therefore be relative contraindications to successful insertion of a gastrostomy tube (Nicholson, Korman & Richardson 2000).

Contraindications to tube feeding

This part of the chapter discusses contraindications to tube feeding. The most important contraindications are:

- palliative care;
- unable to sit up for long periods;
- unable to communicate;
- a history of aspiration on oral intake;
- poor oesophageal function;
- a history of reflux;
- persistent vomiting or diarrhoea;
- intestinal obstruction;
- paralytic ileus; and
- gastrointestinal haemorrhage.

As previously noted, the use of tube feeding in people with dementia is controversial. Tube feeding is often recommended for prevention of malnutrition and weight loss in people with dementia. However, limited mobility in those with severe dementia can increase the risk of aspiration and pneumonia, and this has been shown to be a cause of death in many cases. A link has been found between ' ... easily identified clinical features and death from pneumonia in severely demented, functionally impaired, institutionalized patients ... forced enteral feeding in these patients may be more of an added burden than a benefit' (Chouinard, Lavigne & Villeneuve 1998, p. 155).

The risk of aspiration is therefore a significant concern when contemplating tube feeding. There is no firm proof that tube feeding prevents aspiration (Britton et al. 1997). Nor is there proof that chronic aspiration necessarily leads to pneumonia (Bucholz & Neumann 1998). Therefore, before instituting tube feeding for the management of aspiration, the indications must be strong. In addition, the consequences of this form of management must be fully discussed with the person,

'Before instituting tube feeding for the management of aspiration, the indications must be strong ... the consequences of this form of management must be fully discussed.'

significant family and caregivers, and the team providing care. Regardless of the cause of the dysphagia or eating difficulty, before inserting a gastrostomy tube the following questions must be addressed:

- 'What will the end result of the intervention be?'
- 'Will it ultimately benefit this individual?'

Conclusion

This chapter has explained the swallowing process and has described dysphagia. The chapter has provided options for the management of dysphagia and has discussed the indications for gastrostomy tube feeding. The causes and types of swallowing disorders are complex—as are the management decisions and processes.

There are many ethical issues to be considered when contemplating the insertion of a gastrostomy tube. Individual circumstances need to be carefully considered when making any decisions about tube feeding.

Finally, the status of a person's dysphagia should never be considered static. Dysphagia should therefore be reviewed regularly and frequently—whether or not tube feeding is in place.

Chapter 2

Making Decisions on Tube Feeding

Catherine Barrett and Peteris Darzins

Introduction

In some cases, a decision to use tube feeding is relatively simple—because the benefits for the person are obvious and the potential outcomes welcomed. However, for a significant proportion of people, the outcomes are unclear. In these cases, a decision to use tube feeding is therefore more difficult.

> 'The guiding principle must always be to act in the best interests of the person involved.'

In making these difficult decisions, the guiding principle must always be to act in the best interests of the person involved.

Complexity of decisions

History and profile

In the 1980s, the development of an endoscopic technique for the insertion of gastrostomy tubes simplified the insertion of these tubes and increased the availability of tube feeding. With this development, people who would not previously have been offered tube feeding are now being asked to consider the option of a percutaneous endoscopic gastrostomy (PEG) tube.

Gastrostomy tubes are now inserted to facilitate the transfer of people from the acute sector to aged-care facilities, or to make it possible for people to stay in these facilities (Tealey 1994; Meisel 1995). A significant proportion are cared for in their homes.

Persons receiving tube feeding

An indication of the persons who receive tube feeding is provided by the following statistics for Victoria (Australia) in 1995–96 (DHS 1997).

- 70% of PEG tubes were inserted in people aged between 60 and 89 years.
- The average age of people having a PEG tube inserted was 65.7 years.
- 50% of people were discharged home after PEG insertion.
- 16% of people were admitted to a nursing home after PEG insertion.

Guidelines

Although tube feeding has many advantages, it can be more harmful than beneficial in some older people (Ackerman 1996). Guidelines for tube-feeding decisions can help to identify potential harm. However, few facilities have guidelines to follow when making decisions about tube feeding (Rabeneck McCullough & Wray 1997; Mitchell & Lawson 1999; Cartwright & Steinberg 2000). Consequently, tube-feeding decisions are often not well understood by health professionals (Mitchell & Lawson 1999) and are often inappropriate (Goodhall 1997; Rabeneck, McCullough & Wray 1997).

'Few facilities have guidelines to follow when making decisions about tube feeding.'

A decision as to whether to insert a tube can be complex. The decision might need to be made at a time of crisis—such as after a stroke or accident. Immediately after an acute event it can be difficult to predict the recovery of a person and the appropriateness of tube feeding (Goodhall 1997). Decisions for families are complicated by the stress of their family member's acute illness.

A decision to insert a tube is also complicated by the symbolism attached to food. As discussed in Chapter 5 (page 97), having a tube inserted and being unable to eat or drink can represent significant psychosocial losses for the person and his or her family.

A policy or guide for tube-feeding decisions can help to ensure that the complexities of the decision are adequately addressed, and that any decisions are genuinely person-centred. Furthermore, the provision of a 'decision aid' for family members who are making decisions about long-term tube feeding for cognitively impaired relatives can increase the knowledge of family members about the decision and can decrease decisional conflict (Mitchell et al. 2000).

Key considerations that should be addressed in a policy on tube feeding are shown in the Box on page 24.

Decision-making process

Tube-feeding decisions do not differ conceptually from other treatment decisions. People who have the capacity to make decisions about proposed treatments can make such decisions themselves, and these people can freely give or refuse consent for a procedure after they have received adequate relevant information. People who do not have the capacity to make decisions themselves need others to make decisions for them. As with all treatment options, decisions about tube feeding thus require a clear distinction to be made between those who have the capacity to make decisions and those who lack this capacity. A six-step capacity assessment process to assist in making this decision has been described (Darzins, Molloy & Strang 2000).

'As with all treatment options, decisions about tube feeding require a clear distinction to be made between those who have the capacity to make decisions and those who lack this capacity.'

In clinical practice there can be confusion as to who is ultimately responsible for making tube-feeding decisions. The decision-making flowchart shown in Figure 2.1 (page 25) illustrates a process for involving all relevant people at appropriate stages in such decisions.

Tube-feeding policy issues

The following questions should be addressed when developing a policy on instituting tube feeding.

Who makes tube-feeding decisions?

- How are the views and preferences of the person kept as a central focus in the decision?
- What is the role of surrogate decision-makers?
- What is the role of family members, and how do health professionals ensure that families are acting in the person's best interests?
- Which health professionals are involved, and what are their roles?

How are decisions made?

- Is there a proforma, tool, guideline, or policy to guide tube-feeding decisions?
- Are the views and preferences of the person central to the decision-making process?
- How do health professionals ensure that they separate their professional assessments from their personal views?
- Are benefits and burdens identified? If so, how are these benefits and burdens identified?
- Are the goals of tube feeding identified?
- Has a date been set for a review of tube feeding?
- Under what circumstances can tube feeding be ceased, and who has authority to authorise that it be ceased?
- Has the legal position of the facility been determined?

The views and preferences of the person who is to receive the tube feeding are central to the decision-making process. These preferences might be articulated by the person, or by his or her family members, or by other closely involved parties. If the person's preferences cannot be ascertained, the legal process prescribed in the local jurisdiction for the appointment of substitute decision-makers must be followed. In all cases, healthcare team members have an important role to play in providing information relevant to the decision.

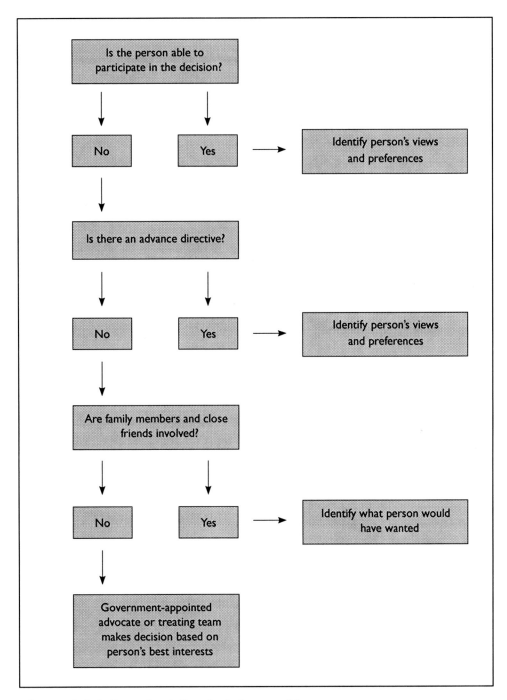

Figure 2.1 A flowchart for decision-making

AUTHORS' CREATION

Person-centred decisions

As noted above, the views and preferences of the person involved are central to tube-feeding decisions. If the person's decision-making capacity is uncertain, it is important to make an assessment of the person's ability to participate in decisions. This is particularly important if the decisions are likely to be contested.

Some people might have documented their preferences in 'living wills', 'advance care directives', or similar documents. In particular, people with progressive diseases (such as dementia or multiple sclerosis) might have articulated or documented their preferences early in the course of their diseases—in anticipation of their being unable to feed safely and being unable to make their wishes known at some point in the future.

However, for many people, tube-feeding decisions are made after a catastrophic acute event—such as a stroke, accident, or head injury. In these circumstances a surrogate decision-maker might be required.

Surrogate decision-makers

Surrogate decision-makers (SDMs) are people who make decisions for others who do not have the capacity to make decisions for themselves. Most legislative jurisdictions now have statutory frameworks that regulate such substitute decision-making processes. Hierarchies of responsibility are described, and mechanisms for making substitute decisions are defined. In most jurisdictions, formal legislative protection is provided to those involved in making decisions on behalf of others.

'SDMs should make decisions for incapable people as though they were making such decisions for themselves ... a "substituted judgment" decision.'

SDMs should, in the first instance, make decisions for incapable people as though they were making such decisions for themselves. When this occurs, a 'substituted judgment' decision is said to have occurred. SDMs following this principle honour the previously expressed wishes or values of the incapable person.

If the SDMs do not know the previously expressed wishes or values of the incapable person, SDMs cannot make such a 'substituted judgment'. The guiding principle then becomes a 'best interests' decision.

'If SDMs do not know the previously expressed wishes or values of the incapable person ... the guiding principle then becomes a "best interests" decision.'

If the person has no known family or close friends, or if there is irreconcilable conflict within families, the SDM might be a government-appointed advocate. More commonly, family members or close friends are asked to describe the person's views and treatment preferences when the person is unable to do so (Tealey 1994).

The ideal situation is one in which incapable persons have previously discussed their views relating to tube feeding with their future SDMs.

The use of SDMs can sometimes complicate tube-feeding decisions. Many SDMs find it difficult to be involved in such decisions (Ackerman 1996; Gillick 2000), and many regret their decisions after they witness the long-term outcomes (Van Rosendaal & Verhoef 1999). In other cases, SDMs do not always act in the genuine best interests of the person (McNabney, Beers & Siebens 1994; Goodhall 1997; Mitchell & Lawson 1999).

'The ideal situation is one in which incapable persons have previously discussed their views relating to tube feeding with their future SDMs.'

There can also be shortcomings in the support provided to SDMs by health professionals. A significant proportion of SDMs report that they need more information on the risks of tube feeding and the alternatives to it (Mitchell & Lawson 1999; Guido et al. 1999). In addition, many SDMs report that their opinions are not sought or not respected (Guido et al. 1999). A significant proportion also report that they were not informed of possible problems—such as the effect on comfort, longevity, suffering, or the possible need for restraints (Callahan et al. 1999).

The involvement of SDMs is thus complex. When involving SDMs in tube-feeding decisions it is important that health professionals carefully consider all the issues involved. The Box on page 28 summarises these.

Involving SDMs in tube-feeding decisions

When involving SDMs in tube-feeding decisions it is important that:

- the opinions of SDMs are identified and respected;
- SDMs articulate what the person's wishes would have been—rather than the SDMs own wishes;
- alternatives to tube feeding are explained;
- limitations (as well as benefits) are identified;
- SDMs understand all information before proceeding; and
- SDMs are offered more information if required.

The role of health professionals

Health professionals have an important role in assisting people and their SDMs to make tube-feeding decisions. However, the exact roles and responsibilities of team members are sometimes unclear, and this can lead to disagreement among team members about who should be involved in the decision-making process and what level of involvement each member should have.

Doctors have a role in assisting patients or SDMs to identify issues involved in tube-feeding decisions (Herrmann & Norris 1998). However, the extent of their role is contentious. Doctors are variously reported as 'dominating' decisions (Goodhall 1997) or, conversely, as providing little more than a 'technical' service (Rabeneck, McCullough & Wray 1997). It has been suggested that speech pathologists, occupational therapists, dietitians, and social workers are better placed to assist in decision-making than physicians (Brockett 1999), and that a minority of SDMs actually speak with a physician regarding the decision (Mitchell & Lawson 1999).

It might be preferable to consult the multidisciplinary team—rather than identify a limited number of individual health professionals within the team for consultation. Consulting the whole team can assist in ensuring that people have all the information they require to make an informed decision.

The development of a proforma for tube-feeding decisions can ensure that all relevant health professionals are involved. Furthermore, a proforma can assist health professionals to understand their various roles in the decision-making process and can ensure that the patient's views and preferences, as best as they can be determined, are central to the decision. The proforma illustrated in Figure 2.2 (page 30) highlights the advisory role of the multidisciplinary team.

In the first section of the proforma, the views and preferences of the person or SDM are identified. If the person has no objection, family members should also be involved. If the person is incapable of giving permission, involving families in the decision-making process helps to ensure family support for the persons' decisions.

The proforma also makes provision for the recording of assessments by relevant health professionals—such as the medical officer, dietitian, speech pathologist, nursing staff, social worker, and psychologist.

The multidisciplinary assessments can then be used to assist the person to identify the benefits and disadvantages of the treatment options. A care plan can then be developed in consultation with the person.

Benefits and burdens ratio

A process of weighing-up the benefits and burdens of tube feeding can assist tube-feeding decisions (Tealey 1994; BMA 1998; Herrmann & Norris 1998). This involves identifying the potential advantages and disadvantages of all treatment options and identifying the 'weight' that the persons involved, and their families, assign to each (Meisel 1995; Ackerman 1996; Kowalski 1996). If the benefits outweigh the burdens, tube feeding is the preferred choice.

'If the benefits outweigh the burdens, tube feeding is the preferred choice.'

For example, a person who considers physical comfort to be important might choose tube feeding if it seems likely to improve that person's comfort through the alleviation of the upper airways irritation and persistent coughing that can accompany oral feeding. Conversely, if a relative has objections to the use of restraints, tube feeding might be

CONSIDERING COMMENCING TUBE FEEDING:	NAME:
	DOB:
	UR:
	BED NO.:

1. Person's views *(person articulates what he or she wants, or content of advance directive)*

Signature: Date:

2. Person's apparent capacity to make this decision *(include basis of capacity assessment, e.g. neuropsych)*

Signature: Date:

3. Views of substitute decision maker
Name: Relationship to person:

Signature: Date:

4. Views of guardian/medical enduring power of attorney

Signature: Date:

5. Views of family members

Signature: Date:

6. Medical assessment

Signature: Date:

Figure 2.2 Proforma before commencing tube feeding
AUTHOR'S CREATION

(continued)

7. Dietitian's assessment

Signature: Date:
_____

8. Speech pathologist's assessment

Signature: Date:
_____

9. Nursing assessment

Signature: Date:
_____

10. Other health professional's assessment

Signature: Date:
_____

11. Potential benefits of tube nutrition for the person *(list of benefits and person's views on each)*

_____

12. Potential burdens of tube feeding for the person

_____

13. Expected duration of tube nutrition

_____

14. Is a trial of nasogastric tube indicated? *(Describe why or why not. Include proposed length of trial, criteria for withdrawal, and hospital legal position.)*

_____

Figure 2.2 Proforma before commencing tube feeding *(continued)*

15. Will restraints be required? *(Describe)*

16. Other considerations or comments

17. Goals of tube feeding *(if commencing)*

18. Action plan

19. Review date *(If commencing tube feeding, also include under what circumstances tube feeding should be reviewed.)*

20. Position of medical officer or facility on tube removal *(outcome of legal consultation if obtained)*

Completed by: Designation:

Date:

Figure 2.2 Proforma before commencing tube feeding *(continued)*

rejected if it seems likely that the person will need to be restrained for tube feeding to be instituted.

Unfortunately, there is little information in the research literature about the benefits and disadvantages of tube feeding (Ackerman 1996). The situation is further complicated by the fact that tube feeding is often used in people who are very unwell. It can be difficult to identify the benefits and disadvantages of tube feeding when many other factors influence a person's physical condition. Studies that identify the potential disadvantages of tube feeding—such as increased mortality—therefore need to be interpreted with caution.

Mortality rates might appear to be higher in those with a gastrostomy tube, but these persons might have cerebrovascular disease or neurological disease (Rabeneck, Wray & Petersen 1996). It is therefore unclear whether the use of the gastrostomy tube introduces significant additional morbidity (Mitchell, Keily & Lipsitz 1998), and whether increased mortality is a result of the gastrostomy tube or the underlying illness (Rabeneck, Wray & Petersen 1996).

'It can be difficult to identify the benefits and disadvantages of tube feeding when many other factors influence a person's physical condition.'

For these reasons, the information provided by health professionals is not based on strong evidence. For example, patients and SDMs are often informed that tube feeding will provide the following benefits:

- increased life expectancy;
- reduced pulmonary aspiration;
- reduced risk of pressure sores;
- improved general physical and psychological function; and
- increased comfort.

However, there are no convincing data to show that tube feeding reduces aspiration, prolongs survival, reduces the risk of pressure sores, improves function, or provides palliation (Finucane, Christmas & Travis 1999).

Similarly, there is insufficient information identifying the disadvantages of tube feeding. Tube feeding is reported to have implications for a person's quality of life (Wilson 1992; Kowalski 1996; Herrmann & Norris 1998), but this area has been poorly researched. Furthermore, the potential disadvantages are less likely to be discussed than the potential benefits. (For more on potential psychosocial complexities of tube feeding, see Chapter 5, page 97.)

In addition to the difficulties of identifying the benefits and disadvantages of tube feeding, there can be difficulty in attributing a weight, or relative importance, to them (Goodhall 1997; Finucane, Christmas & Travis 1999).

Reviewing tube feeding

If a decision has been made to implement tube feeding, the goals should be clarified (Hodges & Tolle 1994; Ackerman 1996; McCann 1999; Van Rosendaal & Verhoef 1999). Tube-feeding goals are particularly useful when reviewing whether to continue tube feeding. Care should be taken to ensure that the identified goals are consistent with the patient's views and preferences (McCann 1999).

'A date for reviewing the outcomes of tube feeding should be made at the time of tube insertion ... or if there is a significant change in the person's condition.'

It is important that a date for reviewing the outcomes of tube feeding be made at the time of tube insertion. In addition, a review should be conducted if there is a significant change in the person's condition.

The review of tube feeding might not be complicated if the person's condition has improved and is capable of an adequate oral intake. However, reviewing tube feeding can be more complex if the person's condition has deteriorated, or if the goals of tube feeding are not being met.

A proforma for reviewing tube feeding outcomes is provided in Figure 2.3 (page 35). This proforma incorporates consideration of a request for the removal of tube feeding.

In the first section of the proforma the actual benefits and burdens of tube feeding are identified and information is provided on whether the goals for tube feeding are being met. The views of the persons involved or their SDMs are also obtained. A care plan is then developed. In the second section of the proforma a request to cease tube feeding is explored.

Request to withdraw tube feeding

A decision to withdraw tube feeding can be controversial. Health professionals and family members can be uncomfortable or distressed by a person's decision to cease tube feeding.

REVIEW OF TUBE FEEDING:	NAME: DOB: UR: BED NO.:

This form could be completed in a meeting with the person, family, and multidisciplinary team

1. When was tube nutrition commenced?

2. Actual benefits of tube feeding

3. Actual burdens of tube feeding

4. Are goals of nutrition being met?

5. Person's views on continuing tube nutrition

6. Views of surrogate decision maker *(if required)*

Relationship to person:

7. Views of family

Relationship to person:

Figure 2.3 A proforma for reviewing tube feeding
AUTHOR'S CREATION

(continued)

8. Action plan

If plan is to continue tube feeding please record date of next review: __/__/__

If plan is to cease tube feeding, please complete the following section

9. Person requesting tube nutrition to be ceased

Name: Designation/relationship:

This person's reasons for request to stop tube nutrition

10. Medical assessment *(include progression of person's condition and implications of ceasing tube nutrition)*

Signature: Date:

11. Speech pathologist's assessment

Signature: Date:

12. Nursing assessment

Signature: Date:

13. Other health professional's assessment

Signature: Date:

14. Position of facility regarding tube removal

Figure 2.3 A proforma for reviewing tube feeding *(continued)*

15. Action plan *(include outcome of family conference/team meeting)*

16. Other considerations/comments

Completed by:

Designation:

Date:

Figure 2.3 A proforma for reviewing tube feeding *(continued)*

For family members, a decision to cease tube feeding can effectively be a decision to let their loved one die (Van Rosendaal & Verhoef 1999). SDMs need assistance and support in coming to understand that it is ethically acceptable to discontinue tube feeding and to allow death to occur (if this is inevitable). Families are often concerned that withholding tube feeding will result in the person suffering from hunger and thirst (Ackerman 1996) and feel that they cannot let the person starve to death (Gillick 2000). Families can also be concerned that the motivation of health professionals is cost reduction—rather than what is best for the person (Van Rosendaal & Verhoef 1999).

Health professionals can find it difficult to separate what they themselves think is best for the person from what the person thinks is appropriate. In some circumstances, health professionals might attempt to convince the person to choose a different option. Nurses often experience a sense of helplessness when a person refuses treatment. For physicians, a fear of litigation might make them reluctant to withdraw tube feeding (Hodges & Tolle 1994).

Quality of life is a key consideration in any decision to withdraw tube feeding (Kowalski 1996). Tube feeding might be removed when goals are not met (Ackerman 1996; McCann 1999; Van Rosendaal & Verhoef 1999), if an adverse event occurs (McCann 1999), or if the person can no longer interact on a cognitive and affective level (Herrmann & Norris 1998; Hodges & Tolle 1994).

A 'trial' of tube feeding might be undertaken to assist the person to make a decision (Hodges & Tolle 1994; Tealey 1994; Herrmann & Norris 1998; Van Rosendaal & Verhoef 1999). A trial usually involves the insertion of a nasogastric tube for a short time to ascertain whether tube-feeding goals can be achieved. If the goals are not achieved, or if tube feeding is too burdensome, it is discontinued.

However, health professionals are sometimes reluctant to withdraw tube feeding if there is no alternative means of ensuring an adequate food and fluid intake. Furthermore, tube removal might not be permitted by the healthcare facility. To ensure that a trial can be stopped if it is unsuccessful, the legal position of the facility should be clarified before making a decision to institute tube feeding (BMA 1998).

Case study

The complexity of the issues discussed in this chapter are highlighted in the case of Mary Smith (Box, below).

Mary Smith

Mary Smith had been admitted to an aged-care facility when her husband, Brian, was no longer able to meet her care needs at home. She had indicated that did not want resuscitation, antibiotics, or pathology tests if she became ill. Mary understood that failure to treat a urinary tract or chest infection could be fatal. Brian had signed a 'Not for Resuscitation Order' on her behalf.

Two years after her admission Mary's swallowing deteriorated significantly. At meal times Mary would often choke, and she took approximately 45 minutes to eat a very small part of her meal.

Mary became increasingly confused and did not recognise her family when they visited. Her poor fluid intake led to dehydration and this,

(continued)

(continued)

in turn, caused urinary tract infections and frequent catheter blockages. Mary often required a catheter change on a daily or second-daily basis, and she also required a change of clothes several times daily.

The option of tube feeding was presented to Mary and Brian as having potential to improve her quality of life by relieving her confusion and reducing the discomfort of catheter and clothing changes. Mary's response to the proposal was that she did not want tube feeding. Many staff members were uncomfortable with her decision, and were unable to comprehend why she would refuse the benefits of tube feeding. Despite Mary's decision being consistent with her previous requests for no active treatment, the conclusion drawn by many staff members was that Mary did not understand the tube-feeding decision.

A neuropsychological assessment was ordered. However, this assessment was inadequate because communication was limited to a 'yes/no' response. These 'yes/no' responses were inconsistent. Staff members continued to ask Mary whether she wanted tube feeding. About a week after her initial refusal Mary indicated she wanted to go ahead with tube feeding. Brian signed the consent form on Mary's behalf.

Twelve months later Brian requested that the tube be removed. Mary's condition had deteriorated; she was now in a vegetative state, and Brian felt sure that Mary would no longer want the tube.

When Brian was informed that the tube could not be removed, he was angry and disappointed. Reflecting on the decision to institute tube feeding made 12 months earlier, Brian said he felt that staff had pressured both him and Mary to accept tube feeding. Brian also felt that staff had pushed the option of tube feeding to make their jobs easier—because Mary then required less time to help with feeding, and because nurses then had fewer wet beds and catheters to change. Brian felt that staff members had repeatedly asked Mary whether she wanted a tube—until she gave the response staff wanted to hear.

The case of Mary Smith is obviously complex, and different people would interpret the issues in various ways. There are no clearcut and obvious answers to the tube-feeding issues raised in this case study. However, the case study does highlight the fact that health professionals must show careful consideration and empathy in taking genuine account of the preferences and desires of the people involved, and their SDMs.

'... careful consideration and empathy in taking genuine account of the preferences and desires of the people involved, and their SDMs.'

Although the case study does not directly address legal issues, health professionals must be aware of the statutory and common law situation in their own jurisdictions. For example, in certain circumstances, legal questions can arise as to whether tube feeding is 'medical treatment' or 'palliative care'. This can have implications as to whether people (or their SDMs) have the legal right to refuse tube feeding (or the continuation of tube feeding). In a significant decision in 2003, the Supreme Court of Victoria (Australia) found that continuing tube feeding represented 'medical treatment', and that a person (or that person's SDM) has a right to refuse such treatment. This decision might not necessarily have direct application in other jurisdictions, but the decision is a significant indication of the legal complexities involved, and all health professionals should ensure that they are aware of the legal situation in their own area of practice.

Conclusion

This chapter has discussed the many complex issues that surround decisions on tube feeding. The specific issues to be considered vary—depending on the views and preferences of individual persons, their prognoses, the policies of healthcare facilities, and the legal situation in the local jurisdiction.

'Health professionals are in a powerful position to advise and support people and families in making tube-feeding decisions.'

Despite the complexities, it is apparent that health professionals are in a powerful position to advise and support people and families in making tube-feeding decisions. Health professionals must ensure that all decisions incorporate the views and preferences of the people involved.

Finally, it is apparent that the development of a written policy or guidelines for tube-feeding decisions is of the greatest importance in assisting health professionals to understand their roles in the decision-making process. Such policies can provide guidance and support to health professionals, and can reduce decisional conflict for all those involved.

Chapter 3
Inserting a Gastrostomy Tube

Michelle Allen and Catherine Barrett

Introduction

Tube feeding has a long history. The ancient Egyptians are known to have used nutrient enemas; and, in the sixteenth century, feeding tubes made from animal bladders were inserted into the oesophagus (Shike 1995). Later developments included the use of nasogastric tubes in the nineteenth century followed by surgical gastrostomies and jejunostomies in the twentieth century (Shike 1995). However, surgical gastrostomies were unpopular because they required laparotomy and general anaesthesia.

'The development of a PEG technique made tube feeding accessible to people who would not previously have been considered.'

In 1979 Gauderer and Ponsky performed the first endoscopic tube insertion (Gauderer, Ponsky & Izant 1998). The development of a percutaneous endoscopic gastrostomy (PEG) technique made tube feeding accessible to people who would not previously have been considered for a gastrostomy tube. For example, in Victoria (Australia), the number of PEG tube insertions increased from 88 in 1990/91 to 691 in 1995/96 (DHS 1997).

Although the insertion of a gastrostomy tube has become a relatively simple day procedure, careful consideration must still be given to the care of the person before and after tube insertion.

This chapter first discusses care needs before the insertion of a gastrostomy tube. The chapter then presents an overview of the procedure for inserting a gastrostomy tube. The chapter concludes with a discussion of care needs after insertion of a tube.

Care before insertion

The gastroenterologist usually prescribes the care required before tube insertion. The prescribed care varies—depending on the type of tube used, the nature of the procedure, the needs of the person, and the preferences of the gastroenterologist.

The matters to be considered include the following:

- informed consent;
- biochemistry and other tests;
- pain management;
- prophylactic antibiotics;
- fasting;
- psychosocial issues; and
- staff preparation.

Each of these is discussed in further detail below. A summary of the issues to be considered before tube insertion is presented in Table 3.1 (page 45).

1. Informed consent

It is important that the person (or his or her surrogate decision-maker) is aware of the benefits and disadvantages of tube feeding, and the alternatives to tube feeding.

Most healthcare facilities require a consent form to be signed by the person (or surrogate decision-maker) and a witness. It is also important that the person is aware that consent can be retracted (if desired).

Issues	Comments
1. Informed consent	Ensure consent form is signed Check that person understands potential benefits and burdens
2. Biochemistry	Is biochemistry required? Are other medical tests required?
3. Pain management	Discuss potential pain or discomfort Consider baseline pain assessment Does person have an analgesia order?
4. Prophylactic antiobiotics	Have prophylactic antibiotics been ordered? Does the person have allergies?
5. Psychosocial issues	Discuss potential effect of tube feeding on lifestyle Show person the tube and tube-feeding equipment Discuss the need to modify clothing to allow easy access for feeding Discuss new feeding regimen Discuss privacy needs Identify flavours and tastes to be provided by tube or orally (if appropriate) Educate family to administer feeds (if appropriate)
6. Fasting	Identify how long the person is required to fast Check whether medications will be missed during fasting
7. Staff preparation	
(i) Post-insertion care plan	Has a post-insertion plan of care been developed? What action needs to be undertaken in preparation for tube feeding?
(ii) Staff education	Is there a need to provide refresher training for staff? Are the unit's policies and guidelines current?
(iii) Care plan before insertion	Consult a proforma for guidance (see Figure 3.1, page 50)

Table 3.1 Issues to be considered before inserting a gastrostomy tube
AUTHORS' CREATION

2. Biochemistry and other tests

Biochemistry tests (such as serum urea, electrolytes, creatinine, albumin, total protein, and glucose) might be performed to identify any abnormalities. A baseline biochemistry screen is also useful for monitoring the effectiveness of subsequent tube feeding.

The gastroenterologist might also order other medical screening procedures—such as X-rays.

3. Pain management

Some people report abdominal pain or discomfort for a day or two after the endoscopic procedure. This pain has been compared to the pain of a pulled muscle (Thompson 1995). Pain and discomfort might also be present as a result of the abdominal incision or from passing the gastroscope.

It is important that people are made aware they might experience pain or discomfort, and that pain relief is available. A pain assessment should be undertaken to establish baseline information—such as current pain and the person's experience of effective pain relief. The person should be reassured that his or her pain will be monitored and that pain relief will be provided.

'The person should be reassured that his or her pain will be monitored and that pain relief will be provided.'

4. Prophylactic antibiotics

The most common complication after placement of a PEG tube is a wound infection. Some gastroenterologists therefore recommend the administration of prophylactic antibiotics before tube insertion (Kulling et al. 2000). Nurses should check whether antibiotics are required and when they should be given. It is also important to note whether the person has any allergies.

5. Fasting

Fasting is usually required to ensure that the person's stomach is empty. The length of the fasting period is determined by the gastroenterologist. It is important to anticipate the effect of the fasting period on the person.

For example, some people might be adversely affected by not taking medications at the usual time.

People with diabetes require careful monitoring of their blood-glucose levels. Two-hourly testing of blood glucose during the fasting period is recommended. An intravenous glucose (dextrose) infusion might be required to prevent hypoglycaemia, particularly if the person has type 1 diabetes. People with type 2 diabetes who take oral hypoglycaemic agents are also at risk of hypoglycaemia, especially when long-acting agents are used. Endoscopic procedures should be performed in the morning to assist these people.

People with diabetes and gastroparesis (as a result of autonomic neuropathy) can have a full stomach despite fasting. It is important to discuss strategies for ensuring that the stomach is empty with the doctor when the procedure is being planned.

6. Psychosocial issues

As discussed in Chapter 5 (page 97), gastrostomy tube insertion can result in significant lifestyle changes for the person and his or her family. After considering the psychosocial implications, health professionals need to identify strategies to prepare the person and family. The Box on page 48 lists some possible strategies.

'Identifying psychosocial issues before the tube is inserted can assist the person to adjust to having a tube. Involving family members can reduce their anxieties.'

Identifying the psychosocial issues before the tube is inserted can assist the person to adjust to having a tube. Involving family members can reduce their anxieties about tube feeding and can help the family to feel involved in the decision-making and care plan.

7. Staff preparation

Before the tube is inserted, it is important to ensure that all staff members are adequately prepared to provide appropriate care to the person after the procedure.

Strategies for psychosocial issues

Gastrostomy tube insertion can result in significant lifestyle changes for the person and his or her family. The following strategies should be considered:

- discussion with the person and family about how tube feeding will affect their lifestyles;
- talking to the person about how he or she feels about having the tube;
- showing the person and family a tube, and encouraging them to touch it;
- showing the person and family the tube-feeding equipment (for example, giving set, flask, and formulae);
- discussing the fact that it might be necessary to modify clothing;
- discussing the new feeding regimen;
- determining whether the person would like to have privacy during tube feeding;
- discussing strategies to manage the person's comfort when others are eating;
- discussing which flavours the person enjoys, and discussing the possibility of adding these to the flask or allowing the person to taste the flavours in very small amounts; and
- instructing the family in the administration of the feeds.

Anticipating care plan after insertion

Before a gastrostomy tube has been inserted, it is important to anticipate the changes that will be required in the person's care plan. For example, it is important to identify the feeding regimen that will be required after the tube has been inserted. The appropriate formulae and equipment should be ordered to ensure that they are ready for the person's return.

If the gastrostomy tube is to be used to administer medication, arrangements should be made with the doctor to change the medication chart to ensure that medications are prescribed in liquid or crushable form. Arrangements should also be made with the pharmacist to ensure that these medications can be made available in the appropriate form.

Educating health professionals

Some health professionals care for a person with a gastrostomy tube infrequently, and some are not familiar with particular types of gastrostomy tubes (such as a low-profile device). It is important to establish whether any of the health professionals in the unit require a continuing education program in gastrostomy care. Members of the care team who are more experienced in these matters (such as the gastroenterologist or the dietitian) might be able to provide such training.

'It is important to establish whether any of the health professionals in the unit require a continuing education program in gastrostomy care.'

In addition, many companies that supply tube-feeding products have educational material or consultants who are available to train staff.

The facility's policy or guidelines for tube feeding should also be reviewed—and updated if necessary. These documents are particularly relevant if some staff members are unable to attend training sessions, or if casual staff are involved in care.

Care plan before tube insertion

In developing an anticipated care plan before insertion of a tube, a proforma can be useful. Such a proforma can help to ensure that the required care is anticipated and provided. A sample proforma is provided in Figure 3.1 (page 50).

Inserting the first tube

A person's first tube is usually inserted using an endoscopic procedure, and is therefore referred to as a 'percutaneous endoscopic gastrostomy tube' (or 'PEG tube'). Subsequent tubes, which are usually inserted without an endoscopy, are referred to simply as 'gastrostomy tubes'.

PEG tubes can be inserted using a 'push' technique or a 'pull' technique. The choice of technique is unlikely to have clinical implications. However, different techniques involve the use of different tubes. In turn, this implies different removal methods.

PRE-INSERTION CARE PLAN	NAME:
	DATE:

Date of tube insertion:

Time of tube insertion:

Name of gastroenterologist:

Hospital where tube will be inserted:

Tube (type, brand, size):

Transport required: Escort required:

Consent form signed: ☐ Yes   ☐ No

Medical screen
Biochemistry required:
Other:

Pain assessment and management
Pain assessment conducted:
Pain relief ordered:

Antibiotics
Prophylactic antibiotics required:
Allergies:

Medication
Time when last dose of medications to be given:
Time when medications will be recommenced:
Pharmacist notified of change to medication route:

Fasting
Date and time when fasting commences:
Special considerations:

Figure 3.1 Proforma of care plan developed before tube insertion
AUTHORS' CREATION

(continued)

Additional instructions (include instructions from gastroenterologist)

Instructions provided by:

Psychosocial issues

Issues identified by person and family:

Has a post-procedure care plan been developed?

Completed by: Designation:

Date:

Figure 3.1 Proforma of care plan developed before tube insertion
(continued)

It is important to identify and record the type, brand, and size of the tube that is inserted (see also Chapter 11, page 197). The insertion of a gastrostomy tube is normally performed by a gastroenterologist and usually requires admission to a day-procedure unit. The person is usually given light sedation to allow insertion of the endoscope. The technique for inserting the tube varies—depending on the gastroenterologist and the needs of the person.

The eight steps that are usually undertaken by the gastroenterologist to insert a tube using an endoscopic technique are described below.

- *Step 1*: the insertion site is selected and prepared.
- *Step 2*: an incision is made, the needle is inserted, the inner stylet is removed, and the endoscopy snare is looped over the end of the cannula.

- *Step 3*: the guidewire is inserted and grasped with the snare, the endoscope removed, and the guidewire brought out though the person's mouth.
- *Step 4*: the feeding tube is fed over the guidewire into the oropharynx and out through the abdominal cannula, which is pushed aside.
- *Step 5*: the internal bumper is moved through the oropharynx into the stomach.
- *Step 6*: the tube bumper is moved up against the gastric mucosa and the guidewire removed.
- *Step 7*: an external skin disc is placed over the external portion of the tube and secured close to the skin. The excess tube is removed. The position of the internal bumper is confirmed with the endoscope.
- *Step 8*: a Y-port adaptor is attached to end of the tube.

The technique for using a Flexi-Flo® Over-the-Guidewire Gastrostomy Kit PEG is illustrated in Figure 3.2 (page 53).

Care after the tube is inserted

After the tube has been inserted, an individualised care plan requires communication among the multidisciplinary team, the person, and the family.

'An individualised care plan requires communication among the multidisciplinary team, the person, and the family.'

The physical and psychological needs of the person largely determine the care. For example, a diabetic who has fasted should be carefully monitored to assess the person's response to the procedure, the response to fasting, and the response to the new feeding regimen.

In general, care needs include:

- vital signs and potential complications;
- tube length;

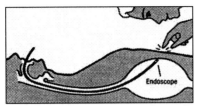

1. Use accepted procedure to select and prepare insertion site.

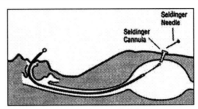

2. Make incision. Insert Seldinger needle. Remove inner stylet, leaving outer cannula in place. Loop endoscopic snare over end of cannula.

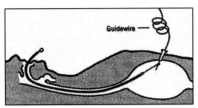

3. Insert guidewire and grasp it with snare. Remove endoscope to bring guidewire out through mouth.

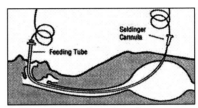

4. Thread tapered portion of feeding tube over guidewire, pass into oropharynx, then out through abdominal wall, pushing cannula out.

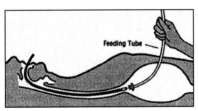

5. As tapered end of feeding tube emerges through abdominal wall, bumper is delivered through oropharynx by endoscopist.

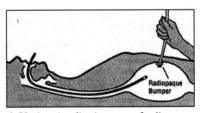

6. Under visualisation, snug feeding-tube bumper gently up against gastric mucosa. Remove guidewire through abdominal site.

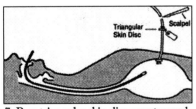

7. Pass triangular skin disc over tapered end of feeding tube and secure close to skin. Cut off tapered dilator portion of the tube and confirm bumper position by endoscopy.

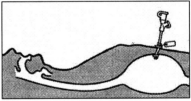

8. Insert adaptor into tube and close caps.

Figure 3.2 Insertion of a gastrostomy tube using a Flexi-Flo® Over-the-Guidewire Gastrostomy Kit PEG

- stoma;
- commencing tube feeding;
- residual volume;
- pain management;
- bowel motions;
- mouth care;
- psychosocial considerations; and
- development of an individualised care plan.

Each of these is discussed in further detail below. A summary of the issues to be considered after tube insertion is presented in Table 3.2 (page 55).

1. Vital signs and potential complications

It is important to monitor the person's vital signs (temperature, pulse, respiration) and the person's blood pressure and conscious state for any change that could indicate potential complications. The frequency of checking the vital signs is determined by the care facility. Monitoring is usually continued for a period of several weeks.

Potential complications include (Fawcett 1995):

- peritonitis;
- pulmonary aspiration;
- wound infection;
- gastrocolic fistula; and
- haemorrhage.

See Table 3.3 (page 56) for a summary of potential complications.

2. Tube length

The skin disc is initially kept tight against the abdomen to ensure that the stoma develops. The recommended length of time before the skin disc can be released varies. This should be checked with the gastroenterologist.

It is important to monitor for possible tube migration. This is done by measuring the length of the tube. The length of the tube protruding

Issues	Comments
1.Vital signs	Identify frequency for checking vital signs Identify how long vital signs need to be checked
2.Tube length	Measure and mark the external tube length Monitor to identify any migration Secure the skin disc to allow the stoma to form
3. Stoma	Observe for exudate Determine whether a dressing will be used (and, if so, what type) Determine when the person is allowed to bathe
4. Commencing tube feeding	Identify the fasting period Check for any contraindications to commencing tube feeding Develop a plan for recommencing medications Develop a plan for commencing tube feeding
5. Residual volume	Identify whether gastric residual volumes need to be measured Identify the expected range of residual volumes Identify how often (and when) residual volumes need to be checked Identify the actions to take if residual volumes are excessive
6. Pain management	Check for any pain regularly and frequently Provide pain relief as needed Check whether pain relief is effective
7. Bowel motions	Report changes in frequency and consistency of bowel motions
8. Mouth care	Identify how often mouth care is required Identify what mouth care is required Identify equipment required
9. Psychosocial considerations	Show the person his or her tube Encourage the person to feel the tube Check how person is feeling about tube and not eating Involve the family in the discussion (if the person agrees)
10. Care plan after insertion	Consult a proforma for guidance (see Figure 3.3, page 60)

Table 3.2 Issues to be considered after inserting a gastrostomy tube
AUTHORS' CREATION

Potential complication	Comment
Peritonitis	Accidental removal of the PEG before the stoma is well developed can lead to peritonitis. Observe the person for abdominal pain, nausea, vomiting, pyrexia, and reduced bowel sounds.
Stoma infection	Observe for inflammation at the stoma site, pyrexia, and changes in vital signs.
Pulmonary aspiration	Observe for change in vital signs, pyrexia, respiratory symptoms, and leukocytosis.
Gastrocolic fistula	Inadvertent puncture of the colon during PEG insertion can lead to formation of a fistula. Observe for pyrexia, changes in vital signs, and discharge.
Haemorrhage	Haematemesis or melaena can occur from erosion of the gastric mucosa due to excess pressure from the internal disc.

Table 3.3 Potential complications after insertion of a PEG tube
AUTHORS' CREATION (ADAPTED FROM VARGO & PONSKY 2000)

externally should be measured, and the tube should be marked at the point closest to the skin. This should be done with a permanent marker pen. The position of the skin disc and the tube should then be checked and documented regularly and frequently.

3. Stoma

Recommendations for the care of the stoma in the immediate period after the tube is inserted vary considerably. Although most experts agree there is a need to keep the stoma dry, there is often disagreement as to how long the patient should wait before recommencing showering or bathing. In addition, controversy surrounds the procedures for dressing and washing the stoma. However, the aims of stomal care in the period immediately after insertion are to prevent infection in the new incision site and to promote formation of a healthy stoma.

'The aims of stomal care in the period immediately after insertion are to prevent infection in the new incision site and to promote formation of a healthy stoma.'

It is important to check with the gastroenterologist as to the stomal care requirements for individual patients. Stomal care is discussed further in Chapter 7 (page 133).

4. Commencing tube feeding

The person usually continues to fast for a short time after the tube has been inserted. The gastroenterologist or dietitian usually recommends a feeding regimen that gradually introduces tube feeds.

The person's condition should be assessed before tube feeding is commenced—especially if there are indications that the person is unwell or if there are signs of a bowel obstruction.

5. Residual volume

Checking residual volume involves aspirating and measuring the contents of the person's stomach after tube feeding to check that the stomach is emptying. Residual volumes can be measured post-operatively to check for bowel obstruction or to determine if the person is receiving the correct amount of formula.

'There is no consensus on what constitutes a "normal" residual volume.'

There is no consensus on what constitutes a 'normal' residual volume. This is not surprising—given the normal variation that exists among people, and given the effects of certain conditions (such as diabetes) on gastric emptying.

A plan for checking residual volume is usually developed by the doctor and the dietitian. It should include instructions regarding:

- how long after a feed the volume should be checked;
- the expected amount of the residual volume;
- for how long residual volumes should be checked; and
- action to be taken if residuals exceed expected volume.

6. Pain management

Because some people (especially older people) might be reluctant to report pain, it is important to undertake pain assessments regularly and frequently. Pain relief should be provided, and the effect of the pain relief should be evaluated. The effectiveness of all pain-management strategies should be documented.

Patients should be encouraged to report any pain that they experience. Verbal reports of pain should be recorded. In addition, non-verbal signs of pain should be documented. Indications that a person might be experiencing pain include:

- elevated blood pressure;
- increased pulse rate;
- rapid breathing;
- agitation; and
- guarding (particularly when the tube or stoma is touched).

If the person is experiencing pain, it might be necessary to administer regular analgesia—rather than wait for the person to report the pain. Regular analgesia is particularly important for people who are unable to communicate their pain verbally.

'Regular analgesia is particularly important for people who are unable to communicate their pain verbally.'

7. Bowel motions

Changes in the consistency and frequency of bowel motions can occur as a result of the tube-feeding formulae. Changes should be discussed with the dietitian and doctor to determine the cause.

8. Mouth care

The person might experience a dry mouth as a result of fasting and oral intake being reduced or ceased. Diligent mouth care is important for health, comfort, and self-esteem. This is described in greater detail in Chapter 9 (page 159).

9. Psychosocial considerations

The person might have difficulty adjusting to the presence of the tube and the new feeding regimen. Particular difficulty might be experienced if the tube represents deterioration in a chronic progressive illness. It is important to understand that some people might be grieving their loss in function.

In the period immediately after the tube is inserted, the person should be given an opportunity to discuss how he or she feels about the tube. Strategies should be developed to minimise any difficulties that become apparent. (For more on strategies to manage psychosocial issues, see Chapter 5, page 97.)

10. Care plan after tube insertion

In developing a care plan after insertion of a tube, a proforma can be useful. Such a proforma can help to ensure that the required care is anticipated and provided. A sample proforma is provided in Figure 3.3 (page 60).

Conclusion

Careful planning for the insertion of a gastrostomy tube is important for the person, his or her family, and the healthcare team. Planning can help the person to understand the potential effects of a gastrostomy tube on his or her lifestyle and body image. Adjusting to having a tube can be easier if the person is encouraged to discuss these concerns.

'Careful planning can help to ensure that the care that is provided is always person-centred and evidence-based.'

For families, planning might involve becoming familiar with the tube-feeding equipment and regimen. This can help to reduce anxieties about tube feeding and can provide families with confidence to continue their involvement with the person's care.

For the healthcare team, planning can help to ensure that the necessary equipment and supplies are available when required. Most importantly, careful planning can ensure that adequate staff training and policy development are in place.

Finally, careful planning can help to ensure that the care that is provided is always person-centred and evidence-based.

| POST-INSERTION CARE PLAN | NAME: |
| | DATE: |

Tube insertion

Date of insertion:

Tube (type, brand, and size):

Post-insertion instructions:

Instructions provided by:

| CARE PLAN |

Vital Signs

Frequency:

Duration:

Tube position

Tube length:

Tube marked:

Stoma site (instructions for care of stoma, include dressings and bathing):

Regimen (for commencing tube feeding):

Residual volumes

Measurement frequency:

Times:

Report to dietitian/medical officer if greater than:

Pain

Frequency of pain assessment:

Pain management strategies:

Psychosocial issues

Issues identified by person and family:

Mouth care:

Completed by: Designation:

Date:

Figure 3.3 Proforma of care plan after tube insertion
AUTHORS' CREATION

Chapter 4

Nutritional Assessment and Tube Feeding

Jacqui Bailey

Introduction

The aim of feeding via a gastrostomy tube is to administer a liquid formula containing sufficient macronutrients and micronutrients to meet a person's needs. Assessment of the person's needs by a dietitian is important to determine which formula to use and how much of the formula is needed each day to meet the person's nutritional needs.

> *'The aim of feeding via a gastrostomy tube is to administer a liquid formula containing sufficient macronutrients and micronutrients to meet a person's needs.'*

This chapter gives an overview of:

- nutritional assessment;
- selection of formulae;
- the equipment and methods used for tube feeding;
- feeding regimens;
- pumps;

- administration of feeds;
- storage of formulae;
- timing of feeds; and
- care and maintenance of equipment.

1. Nutritional assessment

Issues to be assessed

A dietitian usually undertakes the nutritional assessment. This includes consideration of:

- the person's medical and surgical history;
- the person's dietary history;
- current health issues that influence the person's nutritional intake and requirements;
- pathology results (if relevant and available);
- anthropometry—weight, weight history, height, and physical assessments of the person's fat stores and muscle; and
- the person's risk of developing 'refeeding syndrome'.

The term 'refeeding syndrome' refers to a range of metabolic complications that can arise from refeeding a malnourished person. The syndrome occurs as a result of the body's adaptation to prolonged fasting or chronic underfeeding. The syndrome involves severe electrolyte and fluid shifts, and is associated with significant morbidity and mortality. The metabolic irregularities of refeeding syndrome can cause cardiac arrhythmias, cardiac failure, neuromuscular dysfunction, and respiratory failure (Crook, Hally & Panteli 2001).

'Refeeding syndrome involves severe electrolyte and fluid shifts, and is associated with significant morbidity and mortality.'

People who are at risk of developing refeeding syndrome should be closely monitored with regular and frequent checks of their serum potassium, phosphate, and magnesium levels. Prompt supplementation should be provided if needed. Feeding is usually introduced slowly and cautiously in such people.

Nutritional assessment and tube feeding

This chapter gives an overview of nutritional assessment and tube feeding under the following headings:

- nutritional assessment (beginning this page);
- selection of formulae (page 68);
- the equipment and methods used for tube feeding (page 75);
- feeding regimens (page 77);
- pumps (page 79);
- administration of feeds (page 80);
- storage of formulae (page 81);
- timing of feeds (page 82); and
- care and maintenance of equipment (page 83).

Nutritional requirements

In assessing nutritional requirements, dietitians estimate an individual's needs in terms of:

- energy requirements;
- macronutrient requirements (carbohydrate, protein, and fats);
- micronutrient requirements (vitamins, minerals, and trace elements); and
- fluid requirements.

Each of these is considered below.

Energy

Energy is required to support normal metabolic functions, tissue growth and repair, and physical activity. About two-thirds of the energy spent each day by the average person supports the body's basic functions—such as the production of blood cells, maintaining the heart beat, and breathing.

The energy used by a person over a 24-hour period is largely determined by that person's basal metabolic rate (BMR). The BMR is

Nutritional requirements

This portion of the text discusses assessment of nutritional requirements. In judging these requirements, dietitians estimate an individual's needs in terms of:

- energy requirements;
- macronutrient requirements (carbohydrate, protein, and fats);
- micronutrient requirements (vitamins, minerals, and trace elements); and
- fluid requirements.

Each of these is considered in this part of the chapter.

the energy expenditure of a person lying at physical and mental rest in a comfortably warm environment at least 12 hours after the last meal (McNeill 2000). Dietitians use one of several available equations to calculate a person's BMR. To determine the person's overall energy requirements, dietitians then take into account the person's activity level and any catabolic processes.

An example of such a calculation is as follows:

Estimated energy requirement = BMR X activity factors X stress factors

Different estimation equations take into account different parameters—depending on the individual involved. Complex equations take into account such measurements as arterial blood oxygen saturation or the carbon dioxide concentration of expired air. These might be used in intensive-care units or for research purposes. More commonly, equations rely on practical clinical parameters—such as age, sex, height, actual body weight, and ideal body weight.

The standard international unit of energy is the joule. However, because one joule is a very small unit of energy, the kilojoule (kJ) is more commonly used in nutritional contexts. Many people continue to express energy in kilocalories (kcal or Cal). One Calorie (1 kcal) is equal to 4.184 kJ.

After determining the basal metabolic requirements for energy using such an equation, a dietitian must also take into account other factors that influence an individual's energy requirements. These factors include:

- activity level;
- body composition;
- hormonal state;
- climate;
- psychological state;
- pharmacological agents; and
- metabolic stresses and disease states (such as fever, wounds, surgery, fractures, burns, infection, inflammation, cirrhosis, tachycardia, and respiratory distress).

Some conditions can reduce a person's metabolic requirements. For example, mechanical ventilation can result in a decreased BMR because it reduces the work of breathing (although it should be noted that many ventilated people have other physiological stresses that can result in an overall increase in energy needs). Other examples of conditions that decrease BMR include paralysis or other severe incapacity. Paralysed or severely incapacitated people can have a lower energy requirement than a person with a very sedentary lifestyle. Chapter 14 (page 262) discusses how energy requirements are monitored.

Macronutrients

Protein

Protein requirements are determined by taking into account the recommended daily amounts, any increased requirements, any increased losses, and any disease-specific needs.

Some of the factors that influence protein needs are:

- age;
- fistula losses;

- wounds (including surgical wounds, traumatic wounds, and pressure wounds);
- infection;
- fractures;
- burns;
- liver disease;
- renal impairment; and
- dialysis.

Carbohydrate

Because most commercial formulae contain a suitable proportion of energy from carbohydrate, dietitians do not routinely calculate carbohydrate requirements. Specific carbohydrate targets are usually reserved for individuals with a metabolic disorder—such as impaired glucose tolerance. In these cases, a review of carbohydrate requirements and the amount of carbohydrate provided might be necessary.

> *'Most commercial formulae contain a suitable proportion of energy from carbohydrate ... Specific carbohydrate targets are usually reserved for individuals with a metabolic disorder.'*

Another instance in which the carbohydrate content of a formula might be manipulated is for people with chronic obstructive airways disease. Carbohydrate metabolism results in the production of carbon dioxide (CO_2). This is expelled in expired air via the lungs. Some people with compromised respiratory function are unable to expel enough CO_2. In this situation, it might be appropriate to use a lower carbohydrate formula to reduce CO_2 production—thereby reducing the person's respiratory effort.

Fats

Most commercial preparations contain an appropriate proportion of fat (and a suitable ratio of saturated to unsaturated fats) for most people. In determining an enteral formula, the amount of fat is therefore not usually an issue. In most cases, dietitians consider a specific fat requirement only if there is a specific metabolic abnormality or clinical requirement. An example of such a situation is the presence of steatorrhea (fat malabsorption). In this case, medium-chain triglycerides might be required, and a specialised formula has been developed for the purpose.

Micronutrients

The provision of micronutrients (vitamins, minerals, and trace elements) needs to be taken into account when long-term tube feeding is required. International bodies have developed guidelines for the levels of micronutrient intake that are scientifically judged to meet the nutritional needs of most healthy people. However, individuals vary in their nutritional needs, and these reference values are only guides in assessing the adequacy of a diet. For example, the iron requirements of a well-nourished person are quite different from those of a person who has depleted body stores of iron (and who therefore requires additional iron to correct for the deficiency).

'The provision of micronutrients needs to be taken into account when long-term tube feeding is required ... individuals vary in their nutritional needs.'

Some medical conditions produce an increased need for certain nutrients. For example, a person experiencing prolonged diarrhoea might need additional potassium and magnesium to make up for the loss of these nutrients.

Medications can also affect nutritional requirements. Some drugs are known to affect uptake, absorption, or utilisation of certain nutrients.

Fluids

Some conditions increase fluid requirements, whereas others lead to decreased requirements. The Box on page 68 provides examples of these.

If any of these factors arise (or change) after initial assessment by a dietitian, nutrition and hydration needs should be reassessed. Feeding regimens might need to be adjusted accordingly.

Conditions affecting fluid requirements

Increased fluid needs

Causes of increased fluid needs include the following:

- high-output intestinal fistulae (for example, colostomies and ileostomies);
- fever;
- excessive sweating;
- hot dry weather;
- vomiting (or high nasogastric aspirates);
- diarrhoea;
- high urine losses (for example, diabetes insipidus); and
- tracheostomy.

Reduced fluid needs

Causes of reduced needs include the following:

- oedema;
- cardiac failure;
- renal failure (oliguria);
- hepatic failure;
- cerebral oedema; and
- administration of other infusions.

2. Selection of formulae

Once the nutritional requirements have been determined, the dietitian selects a formula that best suits an individual's nutrient needs and absorptive capacity.

Volume of formula

If a person with a gastrostomy tube is able to take some nourishment by mouth, the nutrient content of this oral intake should be taken into account when determining how much formula is needed. The required intake via the gastrostomy tube is calculated by subtracting the oral intake from the total required intake.

Types of formula

Enteral formulae are readily available in both liquid and powder forms. Most formulae provide all the essential nutrients and are described as 'nutritionally complete'. They contain protein, carbohydrate, fat, vitamins, minerals, and trace elements. However, different formulae contain different ratios of energy to protein, and carbohydrate to fat. They also contain various levels of micronutrients. Commercially available formulae are typically free of lactose and gluten.

'Most formulae provide all the essential nutrients and are described as "nutritionally complete".'

If there are several formulae available that meet the nutritional and gastrointestinal needs of a person, factors such as cost and local availability can be taken into account in determining which formula is most appropriate.

Although there are many different formulae on the market, they can be classified into one or more of the following categories:

- standard;
- hypercaloric;
- fibre-enriched;
- specialty;
- elemental (or semi-elemental); and
- modular.

These categories are discussed in further detail below.

Standard formulae

Standard formulae usually contain 4.2 kJ/mL (1 kcal/mL). These formulations are iso-osmolar (or isotonic). This means that they have roughly the same osmolarity as other body fluids and are less likely to cause gastrointestinal upset.

Types of formula

There are many different formulae on the market. They can be classified into the following categories:

- standard;
- hypercaloric;
- fibre-enriched;
- specialty;
- elemental (or semi-elemental); and
- modular.

These categories are discussed in this part of the chapter.

People who require more concentrated formulae are often commenced on a standard formula before progressing to the 'target' formula.

Hypercaloric formulae

Hypercaloric formulae contain 5–8.4 kJ/mL (1.2–2 kcal/mL). They are also known as 'nutrient-dense' formulae—because they have more energy per litre (and often a larger proportion of protein) than standard preparations. These formulations are hyper-osmolar (or hypertonic). This means that they have a greater osmolarity than body fluids.

These formulae are useful for providing nutrition to people on fluid restrictions. They are also useful for supplementary feeding when some nourishment can be taken orally. Hypercaloric formulae are also helpful in meeting very high nutritional needs in people who would otherwise need very large volumes of a formula.

Hypercaloric formulae are often of thicker consistency than standard formulae. This can influence the choice of administration method.

Fibre-enriched formulae

Most tube formulae are low in residue. In contrast, fibre-enriched formulae have added soy or oat polysaccharides.

Fibre formulae can be useful for people with constipation. Unless contraindicated, they are commonly used to provide the benefits of dietary fibre. Examples include the normalising of stool consistency, the lowering of cholesterol levels, and the prevention of some cancers. These factors are especially important if tube feeds are the sole source of fibre for a person.

Fibre-enriched formulae are available in both isocaloric and hypercaloric forms. They are generally thicker than their low-residue counterparts.

As with the introduction of dietary fibre in orally fed persons, it might be necessary to introduce fibre-enriched tube formulae gradually to tube-fed people. This helps to avoid bloating or distension in people not accustomed to fibre.

Apart from using fibre-enriched formulae, additional fibre can be supplied by adding a soluble fibre supplement to any liquid formula. Alternatively, a soluble fibre supplement can be administered as a bolus.

Specialty formulae

Specialty formulae are designed for specific medical conditions, organ dysfunction, or metabolic stress. Examples include formulae for renal disease, hepatic disease, pulmonary disease, glucose intolerance, compromised immune systems, wound healing, or the cachexia of cancer.

Elemental (or semi-elemental) formulae

These formulae are partially or fully hydrolysed using enzymes that break macronutrients into smaller components.

In an *elemental* formula, complex protein structures are reduced to individual amino acids. In a *semi-elemental* preparation, complex protein structures are reduced to small peptides. In both cases, these smaller nutrients are more easily digested and absorbed by people with digestive or absorptive problems—such as pancreatic insufficiency or severe gut impairment (for example, short bowel syndrome).

Caution is needed with these formulae because they are of a high osmolarity—largely because of their free amino acid content.

Modular formulae

Modular formulae contain only single nutrients—such as carbohydrate, protein, or fat. They are usually added to a formula to tailor it to individual nutritional needs. In rare cases, such as metabolic disorders, commercial enteral formulae are not available to meet nutritional needs. In these cases, a mixture of modular formulae and micronutrient supplementation might be required.

Figure 4.1 (page 73) is an example of a decision-making flowchart that can be used to decide which type of formula to use.

Availability and preparation of stock

Some institutions need enteral formulae infrequently, and this can cause difficulties. If product is kept in stock 'just in case it is needed', it might well be wasted. In contrast, if no stock is kept on hand, institutions can experience difficulty in procuring formulae at short notice.

If a person is transferred from another institution (or from home), the person's previously prescribed formula might not be available. The dietitian should be consulted to determine if there is a comparable formula already in stock. If a comparable formula is not available, it might be possible to add nutrients by using a modular formula to make an existing product more suitable for the person.

It can be useful to keep products with multiple uses for unforeseen circumstances. One option is to use formulae designed for oral consumption that are also suitable for use as tube feeds. This allows the formula to be used for patients on oral supplements as well as for those who require tube feeding. However, the extra labour costs of preparation and the risk of microbial contamination of the formulae are important considerations when deciding whether to use pre-prepared or powdered formula. Extra care needs to be taken to maintain adequate hygiene when preparing powdered formulae. All bench surfaces, spoons, whisks, bowls, jugs, and hands need to be thoroughly clean and dry before mixing formulae.

'Extra care needs to be taken to maintain adequate hygiene when preparing powdered feeds.'

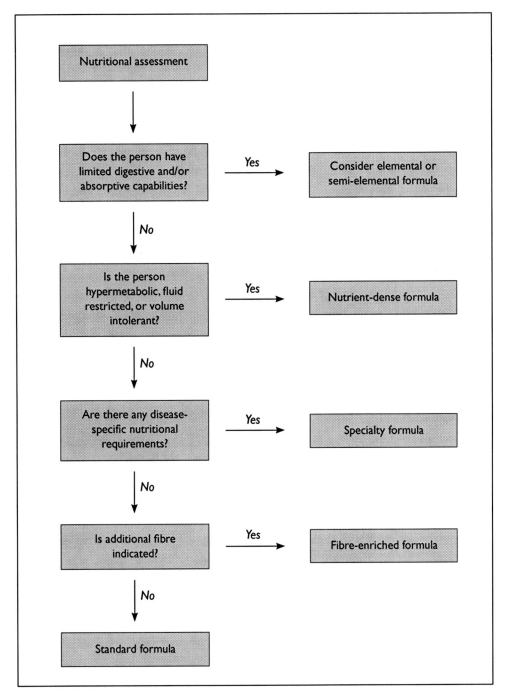

Figure 4.1 Flowchart for deciding type of tube-feeding formula
AUTHOR'S CREATION

When preparing formula from powder, care should be taken to add the powder to the liquid—not the other way around. Pouring liquid over dry powder can cause lumps to form in the formula. These can be difficult to remove by whisking or blending.

Powdered formulae can be made up to a standard or nutrient-dense concentration—which gives a facility more flexibility in terms of having to stock only one product for a range of patient needs. A dietitian can advise whether the appropriate concentration of formula is different from the standard preparation indicated by the instructions on the product packaging.

Many formulae have similar commercial names. To avoid error, the names of the formulae to be used should be carefully checked. For example, two commonly used formulae in Australia are 'Osmolite' and 'Osmolite HN'. In this case, the letters 'HN' stand for 'high nitrogen'. It is important to check that the person receives the formula prescribed by the dietitian. A slight difference in a formula name can mean a significant difference in the composition of the formula, and this can affect nutritional and medical well-being.

Unexpected shortages of formula

If appropriate planning procedures are followed, sufficient formula for each person should always be available. However, shortages can sometimes occur if there is an ordering oversight by a carer or health provider, an unexpected admission of a person with a gastrostomy tube, or other unforeseen circumstances. Should such a situation arise, every attempt should be made to procure the prescribed formula. Local pharmacies, other healthcare facilities, and the company producing the formula can be contacted to see if stock can be provided. Most nutritional companies will arrange for urgent supplies to be sent by courier.

'If it is impossible to obtain replacement stock for the prescribed formula, the person's dietitian should be consulted as soon as possible.'

If it is impossible to obtain replacement stock for the prescribed formula, the person's dietitian should be consulted as soon as possible.

Until dietetic advice is available, water should be substituted for the prescribed formula—using the same volume and administration method as the feeding regimen. Depending on the person's metabolic condition, a doctor might prefer to administer dextrose or saline.

In cases in which a person normally receives elemental, semi-elemental, or specialty formula, the substitution of water or a glucose/ saline solution is the safest option. In cases in which a person normally receives a hypercaloric or fibre-enriched formula, the substitution of a standard formula will not cause any short-term harm.

It should also be noted that most retail pharmacies stock a powdered formula that can be prepared as a standard or hypercaloric formula.

3. Equipment and methods

Equipment

The equipment used for administering formula depends on the prescribed regimen. The most commonly used pieces of equipment are listed in Table 4.1 (page 76).

Containers

Feeding containers are usually plastic containers of 500 mL or 1000 mL that connect to a giving set by means of a screw cap or a spike. Some containers are made of sturdy plastic; these hold their shape. Others are made of collapsible vinyl or foil pouches.

Some containers on the market have pre-attached giving sets. These are sold as a single unit.

Closed systems

Closed systems consist of a container designed to be pierced by a spiked giving set. The spike is kept capped until the user is ready to spike the bag or bottle. There is minimal contact between the formula and the environment outside the bag.

Closed systems minimise the risk of contamination by air, handling, or contaminated equipment. Disadvantages of closed systems are that they

Table 4.1 Equipment used for enteral feeding

AUTHOR'S CREATION

Equipment	Function and description
Container/bottle/bag	reservoir to hold formula during administration
Giving set	tubing to connect the container to the gastrostomy tube often has a 'drip chamber' to allow drips per minute to be counted or detected by a pump
Extension tube	an intermediate piece of tubing between the gastrostomy and the giving set syringe used for low-profile gastrostomy devices
Pump	electronic device that regulates the rate at which the formula is administered via peristaltic or bellows action some can also be set to administer set doses
Hanging device	often an IV pole or hook used to hang the container above the person's head height for gravity or pump feeds
Syringe or funnel	syringes can be used: (i) without the plunger (as a funnel) to administer feeds; and/or (ii) with a plunger to flush the gastrostomy tube with water if a carer has difficulty pouring formula into a small syringe opening (for example, due to shaky hands or poor eyesight), a funnel might be more practical

are often more expensive than other systems and that containers can be used only once.

Decanting

Decanting involves pouring a certain volume of liquid formula from a bottle, tin, sachet, or jug into a container. The container is then attached to a giving set and administered to the person.

The containers and sets can be washed out and reused several times. However, there is a risk of microbial contamination. The used equipment must be thoroughly washed, and the person who decants the formula must use hygienic techniques in handling and storing open bottles and cans of formula.

All containers should be marked with the person's name and the date on which the formula was decanted or prepared. Labelling with the person's name is especially important in healthcare facilities or shared households in which more than one person has enteral feeds. Dating the formula ensures that it is discarded 24 hours after being opened or prepared—thus minimising the risk of harmful microbial colonisation.

4. Feeding regimens

People with a gastrostomy tube come from all walks of life. They have different time constraints, family obligations, and social commitments. These differences must be taken into account in determining the most suitable administration method for each individual. Careful planning is required to suit the requirements and preferences of the person and his or her carers.

The three main regimens for administering formula are:
- continuous feeding;
- intermittent feeding; and
- bolus feeding.

These are discussed in further detail below.

Continuous feeding

Continuous feeding involves the use of a gravity drip or pump to administer feeds constantly throughout the day and/or night (see Figures 4.2 and 4.3, page 78).

Continuous feeding is often used when the person is first introduced to enteral feeds—especially if he or she is likely to experience tolerance problems. Continuous feeding might also be required in the longer term if a person is unable to tolerate an increase to a faster rate—as is needed if the person is to be transferred to intermittent feeding.

Intermittent feeding

Intermittent feeding involves using a pump or gravity drip to administer feeds over shorter periods of time.

Regimens for administering formula

The three main regimens for administering formula are:

- continuous feeding;
- intermittent feeding; and
- bolus feeding.

These are discussed in this part of the chapter.

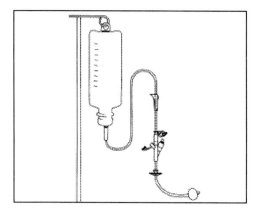

Figure 4.2 Gravity feeding
REPRODUCED WITH PERMISSION OF ABBOTT AUSTRALASIA PTY LTD

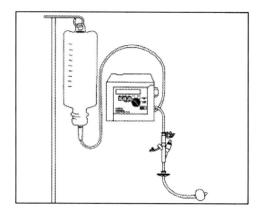

Figure 4.3 Pump Feeding
REPRODUCED WITH PERMISSION OF ABBOTT AUSTRALASIA PTY LTD

Bolus feeding

Bolus feeding involves giving larger volumes of formula (200–500 mL) at regular times over the day (for example, every three hours during the day). Each feed can be administered using a pump, gravity drip, or syringe. Bolus feeding is possible only when feeding into the stomach, rather than into the bowel. Bolus feeds are therefore appropriate for gastrostomies, but not for gastro-jejunostomies.

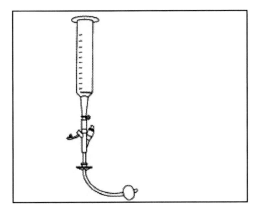

Figure 4.4 Bolus or syringe feeding
REPRODUCED WITH PERMISSION OF ABBOTT AUSTRALASIA PTY LTD

Syringes (with the plunger removed) or funnels can be used to administer bolus feeds. A set volume of formula is measured out and then poured into an open syringe (or funnel) to drain into the gastrostomy tube.

Because intermittent and bolus feeds require larger volumes over a shorter time, the regimen usually involves a gradual increase in delivery rate over a few days to a week to ensure tolerance. Individual tolerance varies, and this ultimately determines the type and timing of feeds.

'Individual tolerance varies, and this ultimately determines the type and timing of feeds.'

5. Pumps

Pumps have various functions and features. They come in different shapes, sizes, and weights. Other differences include the size and colour of print on the digital displays, and features such as volume control, memory, and the ability to set rates, doses, and times for feeding. The various pumps have different instruction manuals, and most company representatives are willing to educate nurses, carers, and patients about the features of their products.

Small, portable feeding pumps are now available. These can be clipped onto a belt or worn in a backpack or satchel to allow less-conspicuous feeding and increased freedom of movement.

Individual needs, financial circumstances, and local availability usually determine the most appropriate pump to use.

Figure 4.5 Portable Pump
REPRODUCED WITH PERMISSION OF ABBOTT AUSTRALASIA PTY LTD

6. Administration of feeds

Positioning for tube feeding

Gastrostomy tube feeds can be administered while the person is:

- seated upright;
- standing; or
- in bed (with the upper body raised to a minimum of a 30-degree angle from the horizontal).

An upright posture helps to prevent reflux and thereby minimises the risk of the person aspirating the feed into the lungs. If gastroparesis is a known problem, an upright posture should be maintained throughout feeds and for at least one hour afterwards.

For continuous feeding regimens the person's position needs to be checked overnight or during sleep. It is often easier to raise the head of the bed to create a 30-degree angle.

Steps in administering feeds

The administration of different types of tube feeds is described and illustrated in Appendix 4.1 (page 85). The appendix describes the steps involved in:

- gravity feeds;
- pump feeds; and
- syringe/funnel bolus feeds.

Documentation of feeding regimen

It is important to document the feeding regimen accurately and clearly. Appendix 4.2 (page 95) illustrates an example of how a feeding regimen can be documented.

7. Storage of formulae

Enteral formula should be stored in a cool, dry place out of direct sunlight. A pantry or cupboard is ideal. Once opened or mixed, the formula should be covered, refrigerated below 4 degrees Celsius, and used within 24 hours.

'Once opened or mixed, formula should be covered, refrigerated below 4 degrees Celsius, and used within 24 hours.'

If formulae are too cold when administered, they can cause gastric upset. Formulae should therefore be removed from refrigeration 15–30 minutes before they are administered, and then brought up to room temperature before administration.

Because enteral formulae are rich in nutrients and energy, they are a perfect medium for microbial growth. The time that a formula can be safely kept at room temperature varies—depending on the manufacturing method and administration techniques. Manufacturers usually have their own recommendation for the safe 'hang-time' of their products. The manufacturer's instructions should be followed. However, these instructions do assume that correct handling and storage techniques are followed.

Commercially prepared 'closed systems' decrease the opportunity for microbial contamination. They can therefore be hung at room temperature for longer than can decanted formulae before harmful numbers of bacteria proliferate. Some companies add anti-microbial agents to their formulae to extend the hang-time.

Careful planning by the healthcare team can minimise wastage by ensuring that formulae are not opened unnecessarily. Once opened, tins or sachets should be used within a safe period of time.

8. Timing of feeds

It is important to ensure that tube-feeding times suit the needs of the person and his or her family. However, each facility has different staff resources, shift times, and work patterns—just as different families have various lifestyles. If the feeding times do not suit the person or if staff members have difficulty preparing and administering feeds at particular times, the dietitian should be consulted so that these issues can be taken into account when planning the feeding regimen.

'It is important to ensure that tube-feeding times suit the needs of the person and his or her family.'

Before changing the feeding times, the dietitian should be consulted to ensure that such changes are appropriate. Some common obstacles to changing feeding times include:

- the safe hang-time of the feed;
- incompatible drug administration times;
- intolerance at faster rates of administration; and
- metabolic considerations (such as glucose intolerance).

Sometimes timing issues are unavoidable. However, in most cases, these problems can be overcome.

Overnight feeds should allow uninterrupted sleep for the person and members of the family or household. If pumps beep in the night, or if sets are being connected and disconnected to the gastrostomy tube, sleep will be disrupted. It is usually possible to administer overnight feeds at a rate that allows the feed to finish at the time that the person normally wakes.

'Overnight feeds should allow uninterrupted sleep for the person and members of the family or household.'

9. Care and maintenance of equipment

If containers are cared for properly and cleaned thoroughly, some can be reused—but they should not be shared among people. After use, the container should be washed with warm soapy water and rinsed well. Excess water should be shaken from the container and the container stored upturned in a refrigerator in a sealed bag. Care should be taken to clean around the neck of the bottle, especially any grooves that might harbour residue and bacteria. Pipe cleaners and brushes designed for cleaning bottles can be useful.

Gravity drip and pump sets are more difficult to clean. They usually need to be replaced more often than containers. After use, warm soapy water should be flushed through the tubing. People who have pumps can utilise them to clean sets by hanging some warm soapy water in a clean feeding container, and then running this (at a high rate) into a sink. After cleaning, the giving set should be rinsed with clean water, and then stored in a refrigerator with the container.

If a container or set cannot be cleaned immediately, it should be submerged in water to prevent the formula drying in the bottle or set (which makes it difficult to clean later). Many people have a sink or tub at home for the purpose of washing all equipment on a daily basis.

Feeding pumps should be cleaned regularly and frequently with a clean damp cloth. The manufacturer usually provides recommendations for pump maintenance and cleaning. If nutritional formula is spilled on a pump it is always best to clean it before it dries—because it can be quite difficult to remove once it sets. Dried formula residue can affect pump function if it drips into moving parts.

Pumps cannot be submerged in water. To prevent electrocution or damage to the pump, electrical equipment should never be stored or left near water (such as baths or sinks), and the pump should always be disconnected from the power source before cleaning.

Appendix 4.1

This appendix describes and illustrates the administration of different types of tube feeds. The appendix describes the steps involved in:

- gravity feeds;
- pump feeds; and
- syringe/funnel bolus feeds.

Steps in administering gravity feeds

The steps to take in administering gravity feeds are described below.

Step 1

Ensure that the person is in an upright position (see Figure 4.6, right).

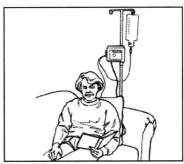

Figure 4.6 Sitting upright
REPRODUCED WITH PERMISSION OF ABBOTT
AUSTRALASIA PTY LTD

Step 2

Wash hands thoroughly (see Figure 4.7, right).

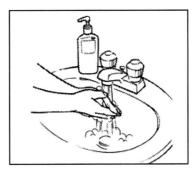

Figure 4.7 Washing hands
REPRODUCED WITH PERMISSION OF ABBOTT
AUSTRALASIA PTY LTD

Step 3

Close the roller clamp
on the gravity drip set
(see Figure 4.8, right).

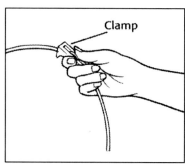

Figure 4.8 Closing the clamp
REPRODUCED WITH PERMISSION OF ABBOTT
AUSTRALASIA PTY LTD

Step 4

Attach the giving set to
the feeding container
(see Figure 4.9, right).

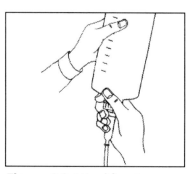

**Figure 4.9 Attaching to
container**
REPRODUCED WITH PERMISSION OF ABBOTT
AUSTRALASIA PTY LTD

Step 5

Hang the feeding
container from a height
above the person's head
(see Figure 4.10, right).

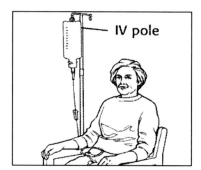

**Figure 4.10 Hanging
container above head height**
REPRODUCED WITH PERMISSION OF ABBOTT
AUSTRALASIA PTY LTD

Step 6

Squeeze the drip
chamber until it is one-
half to one-quarter full
(see Figure 4.11, right).

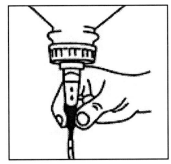

**Figure 4.11 Squeezing the
drip chamber**
REPRODUCED WITH PERMISSION OF ABBOTT
AUSTRALASIA PTY LTD

Step 7

Remove the protective
cap from the end of the
gravity drip set (see
Figure 4.12, right).

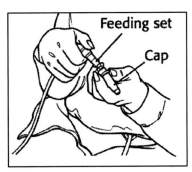

**Figure 4.12 Removing the
cap**
REPRODUCED WITH PERMISSION OF ABBOTT
AUSTRALASIA PTY LTD

Step 8

Slowly open the roller clamp and allow the line to fill with formula, then
close clamp.

Step 9

Clamp off the gastrostomy tube or extension line before opening the
feeding port.

Step 10

Insert the tip of the feeding set into the gastrostomy tube (see Figure 4.13, right).

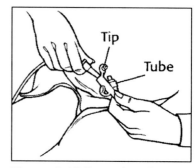

Figure 4.13 Inserting tip
REPRODUCED WITH PERMISSION OF ABBOTT
AUSTRALASIA PTY LTD

Step 11

Secure the giving set to the gastrostomy tube (if a connection is available on the tube).

Step 12

Open the clamp on the gastrostomy tube or extension line.

Step 13

Slowly open the clamp on the gravity-drip set and use the clamp to adjust the flow rate (opening the clamp for a faster rate, or closing it for a slower rate).

Step 14

Clamp the gastrostomy tube and withdraw the giving set when the feed is complete.

Step 15

Draw up at least 20 mL of warm water into a catheter-tip syringe, unclamp the gastrostomy tube or extension tube, and flush well with the water (see Figures 4.14 and 4.15, page 89).

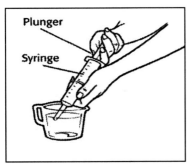

Figure 4.14 Drawing up fluid
REPRODUCED WITH PERMISSION OF ABBOTT
AUSTRALASIA PTY LTD

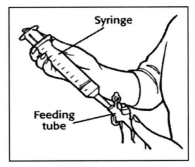

Figure 4.15 Inserting fluid
REPRODUCED WITH PERMISSION OF ABBOTT
AUSTRALASIA PTY LTD

Step 16
Clamp the gastrostomy tube (or extension tube) while withdrawing the syringe.

Step 17
Close the gastrostomy tube until the next feed or flush.

Steps in administering pump feeds
The steps to take in administering pump feeds are described below.

Step 1
Ensure that the person is in an upright position (see Figure 4.6, page 85).

Step 2
Wash hands thoroughly.

Step 3
Close the roller clamp on the giving set (see Figure 4.8, page 86).

Step 4
Attach the giving set to the feeding container (see Figure 4.9, page 86).

Step 5

Hang the feeding container from a height above the pump.

Step 6

If the pump requires a set level of formula within the drip chamber, prime the line according to company directions. Otherwise, simply open the roller clamp to allow formula to fill the tubing before closing roller clamp.

While priming the line, care should be taken not to overfill the drip chamber. The drip chamber should be kept vertical. Because pumps detect the drip of formula through this chamber, any occlusion of the clear plastic by formula on the inside can prevent a drip being read by the electronic 'eye' of the pump.

Step 7

Wind the giving set tubing through the pump rollers (or clip in) as directed.

Step 8

Remove the protective cap from the end of the giving set (see Figure 4.12, page 87).

Step 9

Clamp off the gastrostomy tube or extension line.

Step 10

Insert the tip of the feeding set into the gastrostomy tube (see Figure 4.13, page 88).

Step 11

Set the pump to desired feed rate.

Step 12

Unclamp both the set and the gastrostomy tube (or extension tube).

Step 13

Select 'run' on the pump.

Step 14

When the feed is complete, clamp the gastrostomy tube and withdraw the giving set.

Step 15

Draw up at least 20 mL of warm water into a catheter-tip syringe, unclamp the gastrostomy tube (or extension tube), and flush well with the water (see Figures 4.14 and 4.15, page 89).

Step 16

Clamp the gastrostomy tube (or extension tube) while withdrawing the syringe.

Step 17

Close the gastrostomy tube until the next feed or flush.

Steps in administering syringe/funnel bolus feeds

The steps to take in administering syringe/funnel bolus feeds are described below.

Step 1

Ensure that the person is in an upright position (see Figure 4.6, page 85).

Step 2

Wash hands thoroughly.

Step 3

Measure the desired volume of formula for the bolus feed.

Step 4

Clamp off the gastrostomy tube or extension line.

Step 5

If using a syringe, remove the plunger (see Figure 4.16, right).

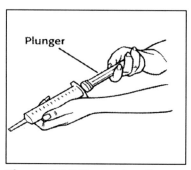

Figure 4.16 Removing the plunger
REPRODUCED WITH PERMISSION OF ABBOTT AUSTRALASIA PTY LTD

Step 6

Insert the tip of the funnel or open-ended syringe into the gastrostomy tube (see Figure 4.17, right).

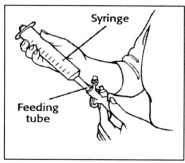

Figure 4.17 Inserting the syringe
REPRODUCED WITH PERMISSION OF ABBOTT AUSTRALASIA PTY LTD

Step 7

Ensure that the opening of the funnel is above the level of the person's stomach.

Step 8

Unclamp the gastrostomy tube.

Step 9

Pour the formula into the funnel and top up as the formula runs through (see Figure 4.18, right).

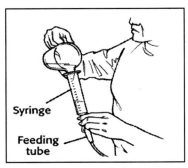

Figure 4.18 Pouring the formula into the funnel
Reproduced with permission of Abbott Australasia Pty Ltd

Step 10

When the feed is complete, clamp the gastrostomy tube and withdraw the funnel.

Step 11

Draw up at least 20 mL of warm water into a catheter-tip syringe, unclamp the gastrostomy tube (or extension tube), and flush well with the water (see Figures 4.14 and 4.15, page 89).

Step 12

Clamp the gastrostomy tube (or extension tube) while withdrawing the syringe.

Step 13

Close the gastrostomy tube until the next feed or flush.

Appendix 4.2

It is important to document the feeding regimen accurately and clearly. This appendix illustrates how a feeding regimen can be documented.

Name: _____   Formula prescribed: _____

Date of Birth: _____   Total daily formula: _____ mL

ID number: _____   Total daily water: _____ mL

Total daily fluid: _____ mL

Pump or gravity feeds

Rate: _____ mL/hr or _____ drips/min

Time(s): _____

Bolus feeds

Times	Volume of formula	Volume of water flush

Further comments: _____

_____

Dietitian's signature: _____

Printed name: _____

Contact number: _____

Date: _____

Figure 4.19 Example of documentation of a feeding regimen

AUTHOR'S CREATION

Chapter 5
Living with a Gastrostomy Tube
Clare Hetzel

Introduction

Living with a gastrostomy tube presents many challenges for the people involved, their families, and the health professionals who care for them. The insertion of a gastrostomy tube can influence a person's perception of autonomy, sense of well-being, body image, sexual expression, and interaction with the world.

> *'For some people, the introduction of tube feeding can prove to be life-enhancing ... for others, the losses and necessary adjustments can be devastating.'*

For some people, the introduction of tube feeding can prove to be life-enhancing, and can have positive outcomes that assist psychosocial adjustment. However, for many people, the losses and necessary adjustments can be devastating.

For some people, the consumption of food has little significance. For these people it is little more than a perfunctory process of providing the body with fuel. For other people, the consumption of food has wider psychosocial functions. It consolidates relationships (Quandt et al. 2001), elicits memories, reinforces family and cultural traditions (Ruark 1999), and provides the foundations for nurturing.

This chapter describes some of the psychosocial responses to tube feeding. A process for assessing psychosocial challenges is outlined to help health professionals understand and facilitate the person's adjustment to tube feeding. In addition, some of the key psychosocial issues and management strategies are discussed. Chapter 6 (page 119) explores in more detail the important role that food plays in society.

Factors affecting adjustment

Many factors influence a person's adjustment to gastrostomy tube feeding. An especially significant factor is the person's level of involvement in the decision-making process. Other factors that can affect adjustment include:

- the medical indications for tube feeding;
- the ability of the person (and family) to understand the swallowing problem;
- the amount of information provided to the person;
- the accuracy of information provided to the person;
- the person's perceived losses and gains; and
- the opportunities to discuss how tube feeding will affect the person's life.

Some people and their families find it difficult to understand the need for tube feeding—especially if the person does not become immediately unwell when he or she eats. Some people benefit from viewing video fluoroscopy of their swallowing process. This enables them to visualise the swallowing problem, and thus gain a better understanding of it.

'People and families adjust to living with tube feeding more readily if they are involved in the decision to initiate the feeding.'

People and families adjust to living with tube feeding more readily if they are involved in the decision to initiate the feeding and are provided with sufficient accurate information. However, they might not comprehend or understand the treatment options (and potential consequences) if the decision is made at a time when the person is unwell and emotions are running high. The family might be in shock or adjusting to potentially life-changing events. To facilitate understanding, it might be necessary to present information several times in different ways—for example, verbal, diagrammatic, and written.

The following information is helpful:

- what the tube looks like;
- what tube-feeding equipment looks like;
- whether any oral intake is possible;
- the expected duration of tube feeding;
- the potential physical consequences;
- the potential psychosocial consequences; and
- the tube-feeding regimen.

It is important to conduct an assessment of the potential psychosocial issues before the tube is inserted.

Psychosocial assessment

Each person is unique, and each family brings a vast array of life experiences to the healing process. An assessment can help to identify the unique needs of each person and his or her family. Proactive management of the issues identified in such an assessment can empower the person and family, and can assist them to adjust to life with tube feeding.

'Proactive management can empower the person and family ... and can assist them to adjust to life with tube feeding.'

If possible, an assessment of the person's psychosocial needs relating to tube feeding should be undertaken before the gastrostomy tube is inserted. However, this might not be possible if the tube is inserted at a time of emotional distress or acute illness.

The assessment involves an exploration of how the person and his or her family understand the consequences of tube feeding. This includes their understanding of such fundamental questions as:

- where the tube will be positioned;
- how long the tube will be in place;

- the side-effects that are expected;
- the hygiene that will be required;
- how often the tube will be changed;
- whether the person will be able to take any food or fluid orally, and how the person feels about reduced (or nil) oral intake;
- how the tube will affect the person's body image; and
- how the tube will affect the person's intimate relationships.

After the tube has been inserted, it is important to give the person (and his or her family) time to adjust to life with the tube. An assessment might require meeting with the person and his or her family over several sessions to explore issues and facilitate adjustment.

'The involvement of patients and families can be empowering ... and assists in ensuring that care strategies are appropriate.'

Some people are readily able to articulate how they feel about the tube and how it has affected their lives. For others, it might be necessary to have some structured questions prepared to explore these issues. Examples of such questions might be:

- How do you feel about the tube?
- How has the tube affected your life?
- What benefits has the tube brought?
- What burdens has the tube brought?
- How do you feel about not being able to eat or drink?
- Are there any aspects of eating that you miss?
- Is it difficult to watch other people eating?
- How do you feel about your body now?

Once the assessment is complete, the person and his or her family can assist in the development of a care plan. The involvement of patients and families can be empowering for those involved and assists in ensuring that care strategies are appropriate.

Because psychosocial adjustment is not static, the care plan needs to be updated regularly and frequently. The assessment might also highlight the need for referral for counselling.

Figure 5.1 (below) shows an example of a psychosocial assessment tool and care plan.

PSYCHOSOCIAL ASSESSMENT FOR TUBE FEEDING	NAME:

Date tube inserted: Date of interview:

Interview with person or carer (if carer, state relationship to person):

How do you feel about the tube?

How has the tube affected your life?

What benefits has the tube brought?

What burdens has the tube brought?

How do you feel about not being able to eat or drink?

Are there aspects of eating that you miss?

Is it difficult to watch other people eating?

Figure 5.1 Psychosocial assessment tool and care plan
AUTHOR'S CREATION

(continued)

How do you feel about your body, now that you have the tube?

What would you like to see changed about tube feeding?

CARE PLAN	
Issue	**Action**
Body image	
Altered lifestyle	
Choice and decision-making	
Privacy and dignity	
Hypersalivation	
Disease progression	
Other	

Completed by:

Designation:

Figure 5.1 Psychosocial assessment tool and care plan *(continued)*

Challenges for the person

The most frequently reported challenges for people after insertion of a gastrostomy tube include:

- coping with an altered body image;
- lifestyle changes;
- autonomy;
- sexual and sensual health;
- privacy and dignity;
- hypersalivation; and
- challenges for families.

Each of these challenges is discussed in further detail below.

1. Body image

Challenges

When people experience an illness or trauma that results in visible physical changes, they are doubly challenged. In addition to dealing with the demands of physical and lifestyle changes, people face the emotional challenges of adjusting to how their bodies have changed and how other people perceive them.

For some people, a gastrostomy tube can significantly alter body image. Many tubes are bulky and protrude from the person's clothing. Other problems include leakage, stains, and the general appearance of the equipment required for feeding. Hypergranulation tissue around the stoma can cause people distress. Others can feel that the presence of the feeding flask gives the impression that they are disabled.

Management

Management includes the provision of counselling to discuss body image and positive reinforcement about the way the person looks. The Box on page 104 lists some management strategies for dealing with problems of body image.

Management strategies for challenges with body image

General strategies

The overall strategy for assisting people who have problems with body image involves:

- the provision of counselling to discuss body image; and
- positive reinforcement about the way the person looks.

Specific strategies

In addition, to these general approaches, the following specific strategies can be used:

- use a low-profile gastrostomy tube whenever possible;
- ensure that the tube does not protrude from the person's clothing;
- change distorted and unsightly tubes;
- remove hypergranulation tissue;
- prevent leakage;
- change stained clothing; and
- pay particular attention to grooming.

2. Lifestyle changes

Challenges

The repercussions of illness and disability can be far-reaching, and it can be very difficult for people to accept their transformation from being able-bodied and independent to being recipients of care who are dependent on others. The transition often involves initial disbelief and denial, followed by anger and unhappiness. Finally, in most cases, acceptance and adjustment can emerge.

> *'It can be very difficult for people to accept their transformation from being able-bodied and independent to being recipients of care who are dependent on others.'*

However, for some people, this adjustment can be very difficult. This is especially likely to be the case if family tension existed previously, or if the need for a gastrostomy tube is taken as a signal of a more global deterioration in a chronic progressive illness. There might be grief that aspects of the person's life have been lost. This grief might occur immediately or later— and it can also be revisited at significant anniversaries or events.

'For people who are unable to eat, social isolation from food-centred activities is a major lifestyle change.'

For people who are unable to eat, social isolation from food-centred activities is a major lifestyle change. Many social activities centre on food. People who are unable to eat might not wish to participate in food-centred activities because they feel uncomfortable watching others eat. Indeed, people with a gastrostomy tube might not be invited to food-centred activities because family and friends might feel uncomfortable eating in the presence of a person who cannot partake.

Those who previously had dysphagia, and who therefore required extensive mealtime support from a carer, can feel the loss of human contact after the insertion of a gastrostomy tube. Some patients with dysphagia require up to 45 minutes of assistance per meal. During this time they have the undivided attention of carers and they engage in (or listen to) stimulating conversation. The introduction of tube feeding can mean that human contact during the provision of a meal is reduced to less than a minute (the time taken to connect the feed to the tube).

People react to these stresses in various ways. Some might become depressed and withdrawn. Others might signal their distress by shouting out or acting in a physically or verbally aggressive manner during mealtimes.

Management

The overall management strategy for lifestyle changes involves discussion with the person about how tube feeding has affected his or her life. This includes identification of ways in which previous lifestyle options can be modified and incorporated into the person's current lifestyle. The Box on page 106 lists some management strategies for dealing with problems of lifestyle change.

Management strategies for challenges with lifestyle

General strategies

The overall strategy for assisting people who have problems with lifestyle changes involves:

- discussion with the person about how tube feeding has affected his or her life; and
- identification of ways in which previous lifestyle options can be modified and incorporated into the person's current lifestyle.

Specific strategies

In addition, to these general approaches, the following specific strategies can be used:

- considering the use of bolus or intermittent feeds (which can be less restrictive than a pump);
- using a portable pump wherever possible;
- using a low-profile device;
- educating family and friends about how to administer tube feeding;
- assisting the person to cope with watching other people eat;
- encouraging family and friends to continue to include the person in social events;
- providing quality contact at mealtimes;
- identifying triggers to behavioural disturbance; and
- providing regular opportunities for the person to disclose and work through his or her feelings of loss and acceptance.

3. Autonomy

Challenges

For many tube-fed people, the biggest challenge is the loss of autonomy—the freedom to exercise choice and self-determination about the way in which they live. Carers can unwittingly add to the person's distress by making important life decisions on his or her behalf. By doing so, carers reduce the person's autonomy—which can have profound effects on the person's sense of purpose, self-esteem, and psychological well-being.

To assist people to maintain their autonomy, it is important to engage them in a respectful and equal partnership. They need to be empowered to make choices about their well-being and lifestyle. Empowering people helps them to recognise that they can adjust to illness or disability.

For some people, the tube itself might represent a sense of powerlessness. This is particularly so if the person was not involved in the decision to initiate tube feeding.

'The decision to start tube feeding must reflect the person's views and preferences.'

Some people (and their partners) have commented that the decision to insert a tube shifts their relationship from equal adult life partners to that of adult and child.

Whether family members or health professionals make the decision to start tube feeding, the decision must reflect the person's views and preferences. People are likely to feel disempowered if the decision does not reflect their views and preferences, or if they were not assisted to understand the burdens of tube feeding. Consequently, the person might become depressed and withdrawn. Some might resist or sabotage tube feeding.

Management
Management of problems with loss of autonomy involves the maximisation of opportunities for meaningful choices in the person's daily life. The Box on page 108 lists some specific strategies.

4. Sexual and sensual health
Challenges
The term 'sexuality' is usually associated with physical activity such as sexual intercourse. However, in its widest sense, 'sexuality' is a broader concept that encompasses body image, self-perception, self-esteem, romance, intimacy, and feeling desirable.

Sexuality is an important part of who people are and how they see themselves. People express their sexuality in how they dress and how they present themselves to the world.

Management strategies for challenges with autonomy

General strategies

The overall strategy involves the maximisation of opportunities for meaningful choices in the person's daily life.

Specific strategies

In addition, to this general approach, the following specific strategies can be used:

- asking the person how he or she feels about the decision to start tube feeding;
- discussing potential benefits and burdens before the tube is inserted;
- ensuring that the person's views and preferences regarding tube feeding are respected;
- offering family counselling (if required to restore greater equality);
- providing a range of choices in relation to flavours (see Chapter 6, page 129);
- involving the person in all decisions affecting his or her care whenever possible; and
- using language that is respectful and engages the person.

If 'sexuality' is understood in this wider sense, it is apparent that having a gastrostomy tube can adversely affect a person's sexuality. In particular, tube feeding can affect:

- body image, sense of self, and sense of personal body space;
- perceptions of physical attractiveness and feelings of sexual desirability;
- libido and desire for sexual intimacy;
- partner's comfort; and
- opportunities for using food as part of 'the love dialogue'.

Management

Management strategies for sexuality and sensuality include offering counselling to the person (and his or her partner if necessary), and encouraging people to discuss their feelings with their partners. The Box below lists some specific strategies.

Management strategies for challenges with sexuality

General strategies

The overall strategy involves the offering of counselling and encouraging people to discuss their feelings with their partners.

Specific strategies

In addition, to this general approach, the following specific strategies can be used:

- asking the person and his or her partner how the tube has affected their relationship;
- suggesting sensual alternatives to meals to lessen the potential sensual losses (for example, a video);
- using a low-profile device;
- encouraging the person to look at the tube, touch it, and to talk about how it makes him or her feel;
- providing tube-fed patients with individualised attention before mealtimes;
- identifying relaxation strategies to minimise frustration or grief at the losses experienced; and
- giving positive feedback to the person and reinforcing the fact that adjustment can fluctuate.

5. Privacy and dignity

Challenges

Most people consider some parts of the body as being 'private', whereas others are considered 'public'. What is considered to be 'public' and 'private' varies—depending on individual and cultural beliefs. In Western society for example, the parts of the body that are generally considered 'public' include the face, arms, neck, legs, hands, and feet. Other parts of the body—such as the genitals, buttocks, lower abdomen, and female breasts—are generally considered to be 'private' parts of the body. In contrast, in some Muslim societies for example, *all* parts of the female body are considered 'private', and are covered.

Regardless of individual or cultural beliefs, the private parts of the body are not usually touched without permission. However, when a gastrostomy tube is inserted, parts of the body that are usually private are exposed or touched by others. In particular, the person's abdomen, which is normally covered by clothing, must be accessed to connect tube feeds. Many people feel vulnerable and anxious when their abdomens are exposed or touched. When health professionals access gastrostomy tubes, some people perceive this to be an 'undignified' invasion of personal body space.

Privacy and dignity can be compromised in tube feeding when:

- clothing is lifted to administer feeds;
- health professionals put their hands down the front of a person's clothing to find the tube;
- the person is rushed and not given adequate explanations;
- the person's clothes gape open while feeds are administered;
- the person's abdomen is exposed in front of other people;
- the person's tube is accessed without permission;
- the person is unable to wear his or her own clothing due to difficulty accessing the tube;
- a bulky extension tube is used;
- tubes are positioned to protrude from the top of clothes to allow easier access; and
- the person perceives that the presence of the flask of feed publicly signals their inability to eat.

People with cognitive impairment can respond to their privacy and dignity being compromised by using verbal or physical aggression.

Others might misinterpret their clothing being adjusted and their private parts touched as a sexual invitation, and can respond with sexual behaviour or language. It is important that health professionals understand the person's perspective. Although health professionals might perceive their actions as routine care, the person might perceive the actions as an invasion of privacy.

Management

In preserving privacy, the overall management principle is to be aware that accessing a person's gastrostomy tube in an insensitive manner can erode the person's dignity. The Box below lists some specific strategies.

Management strategies for challenges with privacy and dignity

General strategies

The overall management principle is to be aware that accessing a person's gastrostomy tube in an insensitive manner can erode the person's dignity.

Specific strategies

In addition, to this general approach, the following specific strategies can be used:

- always asking permission before checking or touching the person's tube;
- never rushing the person;
- securing and maintaining privacy when checking or touching the tube;
- checking the person's preferences for tube feeding;
- avoiding leaving the tube protruding from clothing;
- offering the person the option of having the feed administered in his or her room;
- attempting to modify clothing to allow access while preserving privacy (rather than changing unsuitable clothing);
- using language, tone, and non-verbal communication that signals respect;
- considering covering the flask of feed during feeding; and
- explaining all procedures to the person.

Challenges

The most frequently reported challenges for people after insertion of a gastrostomy tube include:

- coping with an altered body image;
- lifestyle changes;
- autonomy;
- sexual and sensual health;
- privacy and dignity;
- hypersalivation; and
- challenges for families.

A full discussion of these challenges, and their management, forms the overall framework for this chapter.

6. Hypersalivation

Challenges

People who have a significant swallowing problem can also have difficulty swallowing their saliva. Swallowing might be so impaired by brain injury or neurological illness—such that the person drools continuously, independently of food arousal. Drooling saliva can also be a sign of mouth ulcers or poor positioning of the person's head (GISS 1992).

Drooling can embarrass the person, decrease body image, diminish self-esteem, and be a barrier to intimacy. It can be perceived by other people as an indication that the person has a significant level of cognitive impairment.

As well as embarrassing the person, family and friends can also feel embarrassed. Drooling can thus produce social isolation.

Drooling can cause excoriation around the mouth, chin, and neck, and can necessitate frequent clothing changes.

Management

Management strategies aim to minimise the negative effects on the person, rather than reducing the amount of saliva produced. Specific strategies are listed in the Box on page 113.

Management strategies for challenges with hypersalivation

General strategies

The overall management principle is to minimise the negative effects on the person, rather than reducing the amount of saliva produced.

Specific strategies

In addition, to this general approach, the following specific strategies can be used:

- positioning the person's head so that drooling is minimised;
- treating mouth ulcers (if present);
- assessing the appropriateness and effectiveness of medications used to reduce hypersalivation;
- identifying an effective way for the person to clean up his or her saliva;
- protecting clothing in a dignified manner, rather than using bibs;
- checking and cleaning the person's clothing and face regularly; and
- protecting the skin around the mouth with barrier cream.

7. Challenges for families

Challenges

Having a gastrostomy tube inserted presents challenges for the person's family. These include the loss of food-centred activities, fear of the tube, and fear of poor outcomes for the person.

'Food-centred activities make a substantial contribution to a family's shared history ... this has implications for the quality of life of all members of the family.'

As noted above, food has significant social symbolism, and food-centred activities make a substantial contribution to a family's shared history. If one family member loses the ability to eat and drink, this has implications for the quality of life of all members of the family.

If a member of the family requires tube feeding, traditions of food and celebratory feasting can change. Some family members feel guilty that they can eat while their relative cannot, and this can diminish the family's enjoyment of food in the presence of this family member.

Family members who previously used food to nurture the person might not know how they can now express their nurturing role. Involving family members in tube feeding can be a useful way of providing them with an opportunity to use food-centred activities in nurturing the person. However, families can be reluctant to touch the tube for fear of hurting the person. Educating family members is helpful in allaying anxiety and increasing confidence with tube feeding.

'Family members who previously used food to nurture the person might not know how they can now express their nurturing role.'

As described in Chapter 2 (page 22), tube-feeding decisions are often made at a time of crisis (Goodhall 1997), and many families regret their decisions after they have witnessed the long-term outcomes (Van Rosendaal & Verhoef 1999). People who have made a recovery sometimes blame their families for the decision that was made. These sorts of problems create extra challenges for family members who made tube-feeding decisions on the person's behalf. Family mediation might be required if there is evidence of anger or guilt in the person or family members.

Management

The overall management strategy is to ascertain how the tube has affected relationships among family members, and to offer family counselling and support as required. Specific strategies are listed in the Box on page 115.

Management strategies for family challenges

General strategies

The overall management strategy is to ascertain how the tube has affected relationships among family members, and to offer family counselling and support as required.

Specific strategies

In addition, to this general approach, the following specific strategies can be used:

- asking family members how tube feeding has affected their lives;
- asking family members how they feel about the tube;
- invite the family to participate in tube-feeding education programs;
- inviting the family to assist in developing the tube-feeding regimen;
- asking surrogate decision-makers how they feel about the decision they made;
- identifying strategies to involve the person in food-centred activities; and
- helping the family to identify new ways of nurturing the person without food.

Case study

Some of the issues discussed in this chapter are highlighted in the case study presented in the Box on page 116.

Allan Jones

Allan Jones was a 32-year-old engineer admitted for rehabilitation after a stroke. Allan was wheelchair-dependent, had difficulty communicating, and required a gastrostomy tube. Allan was expected to make a partial recovery with therapy, but was likely to remain wheelchair-dependent and unable to swallow safely.

Allan was extremely frustrated by the profound effects of the tube on his life. Before suffering from the stroke Allan had been a healthy engineer who enjoyed an active social life with his fiancée, Debbie. Food had featured prominently in the social events that Allan attended. Every Friday night he had shared a few beers with work friends, on Saturdays he had enjoyed long lunches at his favourite café after bicycle rides, and he had spent Sunday nights at the cinema or at a special dinner with family or friends.

The greatest frustration for Allan was his gastrostomy tube. The long lunches with friends and family had been replaced with long feeds. These were administered over an hour to reduce his nausea and vomiting. Allan struggled with depression, a major loss of self-esteem, and bouts of frustration and aggression. Allan felt that his life had changed dramatically and that he 'was going nowhere fast'.

In the weeks immediately after the stroke, Allan's friends used to visit the hospital and take him into town in his chair. However, most of his friends were uncomfortable when Allan insisted on food or drink. On one outing Allan had convinced his friends to buy him a beer. He had choked so badly that an ambulance had to be called. Unable to cope with the pressure from Allan, and uncomfortable with his level of disability, his friends had stopped visiting.

Debbie began to shows signs that she was not coping and that the relationship was unstable. She did not say overtly that she had difficulties adjusting to the changes. However, Allan was aware that she did not touch him as she had done previously, and that the gaps between her visits were becoming longer.

(continued)

(continued)

Counselling was provided to assist Allan to understand and adjust to the tube. Part of the counselling process involved identifying how he felt about the tube. A time was organised for him to view a fluoroscopy video of his swallowing.

A low-profile gastrostomy tube was inserted, and Allan helped in the development of a program of interesting meal choices to be administered through his tube. 'Couple counselling' was also provided to Allan and Debbie to discuss their relationship and grief issues. Debbie was also educated about how to administer tube feeds and how to select pleasing flavours that could be administered by the tube when she and Allan went out.

Allan began to feel he had more control over his life and began to reapply himself to his rehabilitation program. The difference was noted by several therapists who reported that he was more focused and more interested in his recovery.

Conclusion

There is very little published research about the psychosocial effects of tube feeding. Patients, families, and health professionals often have difficulty knowing what to expect from tube feeding. Despite the paucity of published research, health professionals must take steps to understand these psychosocial effects and must attempt to minimise the burdens of tube feeding on the person and his or her family.

'Health professionals who acknowledge potential psychosocial challenges ... are ideally placed to assist people to adjust to life with a gastrostomy tube.'

Health professionals who acknowledge the potential psychosocial challenges, costs, and benefits are ideally placed to assist the person and his or her family to adjust to life with a gastrostomy tube.

Chapter 6

Reintroducing Meal Choices

Clare Hetzel, Catherine Barrett, and Sally Bowen

Introduction

Tube feeding provides an opportunity to replace oral food and fluid intake with nutritionally complete tube-feeding formulae. Regular biochemistry tests can be performed to check that the person is receiving all nutritional and hydration needs, and to guide any adjustment that might be required to the feeding formula.

'Food has great symbolism and meaning in people's lives.'

However, the importance of food is not limited to its nutritional value and importance in maintaining hydration. It is a mistake to believe that food does nothing more than provide sustenance, and such a view underestimates the role that food plays in people's lives. Food has great symbolism and meaning in people's lives.

Many aspects of daily living are structured around food, and people with a gastrostomy tube—who do not have an oral intake—can have difficulty adjusting to a lifestyle that lacks food-centred activities. In their attempts to improve the quality of life for these people, health professionals need to be aware of the significance of food.

This chapter explores the symbolism of food, and the losses experienced by people who can no longer take food orally.

Meanings of food

Historians, anthropologists, social scientists, artists, and food experts have long recognised the powerful role that food plays in the nutritional, physiological, psychosocial, and spiritual fabric of life (Lupton 1994; Barkan 1999). The Box below lists some of the many ways in which the consumption of food holds significance beyond the nutritional benefits of eating. The extent of the list reflects the wide-ranging role of food in life. It is quite apparent from this list that a tube-feeding formula might replace the nutritional value of oral intake, but it can never replace all aspects of oral intake in a person's life.

'A tube-feeding formula might replace the nutritional value of oral intake, but it can never replace all aspects of oral intake in a person's life.'

Meanings of food

The consumption of food holds significance beyond the nutritional benefits of eating. Food can be:

- an expression of cultural identity, ritual, and behaviours (Ruark 1999);
- an expression of solidarity or an expression of conflict (Kaplan 2000);
- a means of binding relationships (Quandt et al. 2001);
- an important aspect of family, religious, and societal traditions;
- a celebration of the changing seasons;
- an expression of welcome, friendship, love, caring, empathy, forgiveness, or bereavement;
- a stimulus for the senses; an artistic expression; an aphrodisiac; a trigger for memories;
- an opportunity to nurture; and
- an opportunity to manipulate and control people we cook for or those who cook for us.

From infancy, sustenance is intertwined with security, comfort, and nurturing, and food is the centre of many important celebrations, rites of passage, and rituals. Examples include birthday parties, birth celebrations, weddings, afternoon teas, picnics, and religious celebrations. All of these occasions would be very different without food. People expect to eat at such social functions. For people with a gastrostomy tube, these functions can thus present a social challenge. They might *choose* not to attend because they cannot eat. In some cases, they might not even be *invited* to attend because they cannot eat. Either way, a person with a gastrostomy tube can experience a sense of social isolation from important celebrations, rites of passage, and rituals.

'A person with a gastrostomy tube can experience a sense of social isolation from important food-centred celebrations, rites of passage, and rituals.'

In addition to its social and cultural implications, food is also an important aspect of sensory and sensual stimulation. People with a gastrostomy tube who have no oral intake often grieve the loss of important aspects of their sensual engagement with the world through food—not only the loss of the taste of food but also the loss of seductive aromas. The human nervous system is very sensitive to small changes in the environment. If the surrounding stimuli become predictable, people become bored and 'tune out'. Too much predicability can be just as stressful as too much stimulation, and people who are bored are thus motivated to seek novel stimuli. It is therefore important to ensure that people with a gastrostomy tube are offered a range of stimuli that arouse interest and provide motivation. If people have previously enjoyed a variety of alternatives in their eating habits, the provision of monotonous tube-feeding formula alone does not acknowledge the physiological importance of varied gustatory stimuli.

'It is important that people with a gastrostomy tube are offered a range of stimuli that arouse interest and provide motivation.'

Personal experience and learning underpins how different people register hunger or satiation. Depending on personal experience, the smell of garlic pizza can 'kick start' the salivary glands, the sound of a coffee espresso machine might elicit thirst, the smell of baking bread might arouse hunger, and the appearance of Brussels sprouts might quell the appetite. It is important to acknowledge that people are motivated to seek out foods that are emotionally and culturally satisfying and to avoid foods that they find abhorrent.

In summary, it is important for health professionals to reflect on the full significance of food in human life. When people lose the ability to eat, they face wider potential losses than mere nutritional intake. Health professionals need to understand these wider losses— social, cultural, and sensory—if they are to assist such people to adjust to this significant life change.

> '*When people lose the ability to eat, they face wider potential losses than mere nutritional intake.*'

Losses associated with not eating

To understand the losses associated with not eating, health professionals should ask themselves how they would feel if they were never able to eat again. They should reflect upon the pleasures they derived from a recent enjoyable meal:

- what the food looked like;
- the aroma of the food;
- the texture and taste of the food;
- the satisfying sensation as the food passed through the mouth;
- how the food felt in the stomach; and
- the sense of satiation and nurturing.

Having reflected upon these things, health professionals should then ask themselves how they would feel if that was their last oral meal. If illness or trauma meant that they were required to have a gastrostomy tube, all future food and drink would be given to them via a gastrostomy tube. How would they feel? What would they miss most?

A person who has become ill and needs tube feeding (especially those who can no longer take any food or fluid orally) can experience

Losses associated with not eating

People who are unable to take oral food and fluid suffer many losses other than a potential loss of nutrition. They also face:

- loss of involvement in nurturing activities;
- marginalisation from other people;
- reduced involvement in a variety of food-centred activities;
- loss of eating and tasting food;
- social isolation during mealtimes;
- alienation from 'food dialogue' (talk associated with food);
- not being involved in food preparation;
- no anticipation of enjoying a meal;
- loss of a sense of satiety; and
- loss of the cultural expression conveyed by food.

This section of the text discusses these issues—and the importance of health professionals being aware of the significance of these potential losses.

many losses. Familiar nurturing routines within the family might be changed or abandoned. Family members can be confused about how they can care for the person if they can no longer use food as part of the nurturing exchange. In many cases, the person can be unwittingly marginalised at the very time that he or she is experiencing the greatest need for engagement and inclusion with other people. The person and his or her family can both experience the loss of the social and nurturing anchors that food can represent.

'A person can be unwittingly marginalised at the very time that he or she is experiencing the greatest need for engagement and inclusion with other people.'

Other losses for a person who is no longer able to eat and drink might include:

- reduced involvement in food-centred activities;
- loss of eating and tasting food;

- social isolation during mealtimes;
- alienation from 'food dialogue' (talk associated with food);
- not being involved in food preparation;
- no anticipation of enjoying a meal;
- loss of a sense of satiety; and
- loss of the cultural expression conveyed by food.

As discussed in Chapter 5 (page 97) people who are unprepared for the lifestyle changes associated with not being able to eat or drink can find it very difficult to adjust. Discussing the potential lifestyle changes with the person and family before the tube is inserted is an important aspect of facilitating this process of adjustment.

Guidelines and education

Most people desire and expect a variety of food in which their individual choices are accommodated. In Australia, guidelines for residential aged care state that all people have a right to access nutrition and hydration that (DHFS 1998):

- is varied;
- takes into account individual preferences; and
- accommodates dietary customs.

Several other countries have guidelines that embody similar principles. These principles are usually applied to people who have an oral intake. The challenge for health professionals is to rethink the way in which these guidelines can be applied to the care of people who are fed via a tube. Continuing to enjoy food is still an option for people with a gastrostomy tube. Some people are be able to tolerate small tastes of food or fluid, and many others are able to have a range of foods through a gastrostomy tube.

'Continuing to enjoy food is still an option for people with a gastrostomy tube.'

Adding flavours is an effective way of reintroducing the person to the pleasures of a mealtime by providing stimulation of the senses and engagement with society. Adding flavours also provides the person with choices and increased control.

Education for family members can also help them to participate in the reintroduction of meal alternatives, if appropriate. This can give family members an opportunity to nurture the person through food and to re-engage the person in food-centred social events.

Assessing oral intake

Unfortunately, not all people who are tube-fed can tolerate food orally. It is essential that the person be assessed by a qualified speech pathologist before a menu for oral intake is developed. The speech pathologist will determine whether the person can tolerate *any* oral food or fluid. If so, the speech pathologist will advise on:

- the *amount* of oral food or fluid that the person can tolerate;
- the *consistency* of oral food or fluid that the person can tolerate; and
- the *frequency* of oral food or fluid that the person can tolerate.

A person might be capable of taking some food or fluid orally, but this intake might have to be restricted to very small amounts of thickened or semi-thickened food.

The person might need to be assessed over a period of time to identify whether his or her swallowing ability fluctuates over the course of the day. Special precautions might also be needed after the person drinks alcohol because coordination of the muscles involved in swallowing might be affected—thus placing the person at greater risk of aspiration. Similarly, a person might not be able to swallow as well after having alcohol via his or her tube.

Suitability of tubes

Providing a range of foods via a tube is easiest through a large-bore tube. With finer-bore tubes—such as nasogastric or duodenal tubes—there is an increased risk of the tube becoming blocked.

Assessing oral intake

The speech pathologist will advise on:

- the *amount* of oral food or fluid that the person can tolerate;
- the *consistency* of oral food or fluid that the person can tolerate; and
- the *frequency* of oral food or fluid that the person can tolerate.

Tubes might have to be changed more frequently if the person is offered a range of foods other than standard tube-feeding formulae. To minimise the risk of tube blockages it is important to ensure that food is well puréed and that the tube is thoroughly flushed afterwards. Flushing with cola beverages can also help to clear the tube of food debris.

Although it is important to take into account the greater potential for tube blockages if a range of foods is introduced, health professionals should also assess the many benefits that the person will receive from having a choice of meals.

Frequency of meal choices

When the present authors first started experimenting with a range of meal alternatives for people with a gastrostomy tube, we offered meal choices as a special treat for patients when staff had time. Each person had two separate care plans relating to his or her tube feeding. One care plan referred to the person's formulae and the other referred to his or her special meal choices.

After a short time it became apparent that offering meal choices had a profound positive effect on people and some families. Staff in the unit then decided that every person—whether or not that person had a gastrostomy tube—had a right to choose from meal alternatives at every mealtime.

Consequently, meal choices were incorporated into the daily formula regimen of every person.

Team involvement

The person's tube-feeding care plan should be developed in conjunction with the person, his or her family, and the multidisciplinary team. A range of skills and input is required.

The role of the *speech pathologist* has already been discussed (see 'Assessing oral intake', this chapter, page 125).

A *dietitian's* assessment is required to determine the type of food and fluid that can be offered via a person's gastrostomy tube. These meal alternatives are then added to the person's tube-feeding care plan. The dietitian assists in the development of the care plan to ensure that:

- the total hydration and nutritional needs of the person are achieved;
- the person's regimen compensates for the diuretic effects of some beverages; and
- fluids that curdle with formulae are administered separately.

The *pharmacist* might also provide recommendations about potential adverse interactions between certain foods and medications.

The *social worker*, *cultural officer*, *nurse*, or *psychologist* might need to liaise with the family, the dietitian, and the speech pathologist to identify how cultural and social food rituals can be incorporated into the person's feeding regimen without putting the person at risk.

'A tube-feeding care plan should be developed in conjunction with the person, the family, and the multidisciplinary team. A range of skills and input is required.'

It is important to discuss all aspects of the proposed meal choices with the person's *medical officer*.

Following input from all members of the team, a care plan for meal choices should be drawn up. Figure 6.1 (page 128) shows an example of such a plan.

Beginning the process

In reintroducing food choices, the individual capacities and wishes of each person should be carefully assessed in consultation with the speech pathologist and dietitian.

| INTAKE CARE PLAN: PERSON WITH GASTROSTOMY TUBE | NAME: ID: BED NO: |

Medical officer recommendations:

Signature:

Speech pathologist recommendations:

Signature:

Dietitian recommendations:

Signature:

| Time | Enteral intake | | | | | Oral intake | | Special instructions Other activities with meals |
	Formula or fluid type	Volume	Delivery rate	Water flush volume	Additives to flask	Type	Amount	
Breakfast (8 am)								
Morning tea (10:30 am)								
Lunch (12:30 pm)								
Afternoon tea (3 pm)								
Dinner (6 pm)								
Supper (8:30 pm)								

Completed by:

Date:

This menu highlights options for reintroducing meal choices and should not be used without a medical, dietetics, and speech pathology assessment.

Figure 6.1 Proforma of a care plan for introducing meal choices

AUTHORS' PRESENTATION

Some people might be unable to tolerate fluid orally but might be able to tolerate small quantities of a flavour of their choice introduced on a swab stick. The tongue, lips, and side of the mouth can be gently swabbed, thus stimulating the taste buds. Some people have reported delight when small tastes prompt memories. Increased alertness, dialogue, and social engagement are often observed in people after taste choices are reintroduced.

If a person can tolerate slightly greater amounts of liquid or food, food tastes can be introduced via a teaspoon or the person's finger. If appropriate, the person can be assisted to place

'Increased alertness, dialogue, and social engagement are often observed in people after taste choices are reintroduced.'

the correct amount of food on a spoon and use the spoon independently. Alternatively, encouraging the person to use his or her own finger (dipped into the flavour) has the advantage of stimulating culturally accepted behaviour—such as washing the hands and being involved in traditional preparations for eating.

Providing a combination of formulae and food tastes has an important therapeutic function. It compensates for reduced food variety and stimulates other senses.

Educating carers

Educating health professionals, family, and friends is an important part of reintroducing meal choices. Health professionals and family members who provide oral food to people need to understand the principles of dysphagia management. The speech pathologist might be able to provide such education.

It is vitally important to educate family and friends about acceptable types and quantities of food. If families are not fully aware of the need to restrict the food that is offered orally, they might offer inappropriate foods and inadvertently compromise the person's physical health.

It is important for carers to be given opportunities to consider other ways in which they can sensually nurture the person. Conversations should be held with the family and person to identify which aspects of familiar (pre-tube) meal interactions can be accommodated now that the person has a tube. Activities might include:

- listening to the evening news;
- having a pre-dinner taste of gin and tonic (and giving the remainder via the tube); or
- offering a hot scented facecloth before or after the meal.

For many people, food-centred activities and eating help to relieve stress. With creativity, it is possible to re-create some aspects of these familiar relaxation activities. Cognitive, sensual, and social engagements can be provided for the person—all of which are significant components of the healing process.

Case study

The case study in the Box below highlights some of the issues discussed in this chapter.

Mrs Tuscano

Mrs Tuscano, who had suffered a stroke and who had required a gastrostomy tube, was becoming increasingly depressed. Her family reported that she had been the centre of the family's social life before her illness. Her house had always been bustling with family and friends who dropped in to sample her culinary delights. The family had found solace and emotional nurturing over a bowl of minestrone or a snack of almond bread. Troubled teenagers had been heartily fed, and then commandeered into drying dishes—during which time Mrs Tuscano's life wisdom had fallen on receptive ears. Food preparation for weddings, births, and wakes had been negotiated over the old oak table in the centre of the kitchen. Marital crises, career plans, and holidays had been discussed over strong coffee or homemade wine.

After the stroke, family members had found it difficult to visit the hospital and rehabilitation centre. It was challenging to see their relative so frail and dependent—especially as she had previously commanded

(continued)

(continued)

such respect for her strength of personality. It was especially distressing for relatives to observe how Mrs Tuscano's nurturing, food-centred role within the family had been taken from her (and from them).

In an attempt to facilitate Mrs Tuscano's recovery, the family tried to feed her orally with mashed vegetables, minestrone broth, and crumbled almond bread. A few days later, Mrs Tuscano developed a chest infection. Most of the food had been aspirated as a result of Mrs Tuscano's poor swallowing function.

The situation was discussed at a meeting involving Mrs Tuscano, her close relatives, the dietitian, the speech pathologist, the unit manager, and the psychologist. After consultation with Mrs Tuscano, the family was invited to watch video fluoroscopy of Mrs Tuscano's swallowing function. This clearly revealed the extent of her swallowing difficulties.

Family members were assisted to grieve the loss of food-centred activities as they had known them in the past. They were encouraged to develop different ways of incorporating Mrs Tuscano's rich knowledge and care into the family's social fabric. This was done by:

- establishing a timetable to reintroduce appropriate food tastes in collaboration with the healthcare team;
- setting a date to review Mrs Tuscano's swallowing function, and involving the family in documenting her progress;
- encouraging Mrs Tuscano to pass on some of her 'trade secret' recipes to allow the family food history to continue;
- enabling Mrs Tuscano to supervise some of the celebratory preparations of her special recipes; and
- involving Mrs Tuscano in some of the food preparation—for example, by placing an appropriate swab of tomato sauce on her tongue, so that she could give feedback to the cooks as to what ingredients were required.

All of these management strategies recognised Mrs Tuscano's role as oral historian and family educator. Taken together, the strategies aimed to compensate Mrs Tuscano and her family for the very real losses they had suffered. As a result of these interventions, Mrs Tuscano's personal dignity was restored and her depression was alleviated.

Conclusion

In the management of a person with a gastrostomy tube, the social functions and symbolic meanings associated with food and eating are often overlooked. It is important for caring health professionals to reflect on the symbolism of food in their lives. Health professionals who do this become much more aware of the losses that a gastrostomy tube represents for a person who can no longer eat normally. Once they are aware of the reality of these losses, health professionals are well placed to minimise the multitude of losses suffered by these people and their families.

'It is important for caring health professionals to reflect on the symbolism of food in their lives.'

Chapter 7

Stomal Care

Julie Garreffa

Introduction

Alterations to the integrity of a gastrostomy stoma can cause pain to the person and can cause difficulties for health professionals in delivering tube feeding. Furthermore, some stomal problems can negatively affect the person's body image and reduce his or her self-esteem.

To care for a stoma, health professionals need to be aware of the normal appearance of a stoma, how to care for it, and what action to take if problems occur. An important aspect of stomal care is education of the person and family members. Involving the person and his or her carers in stomal management can facilitate the early detection of problems and can help to reduce anxiety (Taylor, Lillis & Lemone 1997; Bowers 2000).

> *'Health professionals need to be aware of the normal appearance of a stoma, how to care for it, and what action to take if problems occur.'*

This chapter outlines the fundamental principles of care required to maintain a healthy gastrostomy stoma, and discusses how to identify and treat some of the problems that are commonly associated with stomas.

Principles of care

In general, maintaining a healthy stoma involves:

- the provision of good daily routine care; and
- recognising, understanding, and managing problems if they occur.

Stomal care should be incorporated into the person's daily routine. Some of the key features of routine care are outlined in this chapter. However, it should also be noted that special considerations are required in the period immediately after the tube has been inserted (see Chapter 3, page 52).

Routine care

The stoma should be monitored and cleaned at least daily. For people who are at risk of skin breakdown or infection, it might be necessary to check the stoma and provide care more frequently. For example, the stoma should be cleaned twice a day if it is exudating (O'Brien, Davis & Erwin-Toth 1999).

The exact nature of the care to be provided depends on the needs of the person. However, in general, routine daily care might include the interventions described in the Box on page 135.

The position of the skin disc should not be adjusted in the period immediately after tube insertion (see Chapter 3, page 54). Showering is an ideal opportunity to provide stomal care. The shower water can be used to wash away crusted exudate, and bathing provides health professionals with an opportunity to examine the stoma and surrounding area on a regular basis to ensure early detection of problems.

Managing problems

Health professionals should be aware of potential problems and the appropriate preventive care. This allows early detection of problems and enables a quick response to resolve any problems that might arise. Prevention and early detection can minimise inconvenience and discomfort for the person, and can eliminate the need for expensive treatments (Bowers 2000).

Routine care

In general, routine daily care might include the following interventions:

- observing the stoma for signs of inflammation (such as redness, swelling, or tenderness);
- lifting the skin disc to check the skin beneath;
- cleaning under the skin disc with a cotton bud;
- ensuring that the skin disc is positioned 1–2 mm from the skin (Arrowsmith 1996);
- washing the stoma and surrounding skin with warm soapy water;
- ensuring that soap residue is rinsed away;
- drying the area thoroughly after cleaning;
- removing exudate and fluid that leaks from the tube (Arrowsmith 1996; Bowers 2000);
- rotating the tube 360 degrees each day to reduce skin irritation and ulceration, and to prevent the tube adhering to the stoma; and
- checking that low-profile devices are not too tight or loose.

Health professionals should be aware of the following potential problems:

- fluid leakage and skin excoriation;
- cellulitis;
- dermatitis;
- ulceration;
- bleeding; and
- hypergranulation.

Each of these is discussed in greater detail in the rest of this chapter. In addition to the discussion in the text, Table 7.1 (page 136) provides a convenient 'quick guide' to the causes and management of these problems.

Table 7.1 Causes and management of stoma problems

AUTHOR'S CREATION

Problem	Causes	Interventions
Fluid leakage and skin excoriation	Poorly positioned skin disc and tube migration Tube size no longer appropriate Failed anti-reflux valve Skin disc too tight Inadequate cleaning and drying of the stoma and surrounding skin	Ensure that the skin disc is 1–2 mm from the skin Discuss the need to change tube size with the gastroenterologist Change the tube if the skin disc is fixed and weight gain has occurred Clean at least daily Ensure soap residue is rinsed away Dry thoroughly
Cellulitis (including folliculitis)	Infection by microorganisms from the gastrostomy tube Trauma during removal of tape used to secure tubes or dressings (causing folliculitis) Inadequate hand-washing	Medical advice Swabs for culture and sensitivity Antibiotics Topical antibiotics and antifungal preparations Monitor use of standard precautions Eliminate need for tapes Shave and seal skin before applying the tape Use adhesive remover to remove the tape
Dermatitis	Leaking of gastric contents Skin sensitivity to products (toiletries, tubing, dressings)	Identify cause of leakage Identify allergens and chemical irritants Use a barrier cream
Ulceration	Pressure from skin disc	Ensure that the skin disc is 1–2 mm from the skin
Bleeding	Mechanical trauma	Identify and treat cause Ensure tubing is secure Seek medical advice if bleeding is prolonged or if large amounts of blood are lost
Hypergranulation	Excessive moisture Altered skin integrity Poorly fitting tube	Cauterisation using silver nitrate pencil

Fluid leakage and skin excoriation

The acidic gastric contents can leak from the stoma and cause excoriation of the person's abdomen. The following factors can cause leakage of gastric contents:

- loose skin disc allowing the tube to migrate;
- incorrect tube size; and
- dysfunctional anti-reflux valve on a low-profile device.

The skin disc should be secured 1–2 mm from the skin (Arrowsmith 1996) so that there is only slight movement of the tube in and out of the stoma. If the tube is leaking, a review by a gastroenterologist might be warranted to determine whether the person needs a larger tube.

Given the excoriating effects of leaked fluid, it might be necessary to use a barrier cream around the stoma to protect the person's skin. However, the type of barrier cream used should be carefully selected because greasy creams allow the skin disc to slip and thus cause the tube to migrate (Arrowsmith 1996). It is not usually advisable to apply a dressing to the stoma because dressings become wet and cause further skin damage (Liddle 1995). If a dressing is necessary, it should be kept dry and changed frequently.

If the skin around the stoma does become reddened it is important to determine the cause and manage any symptoms appropriately.

Causes of excoriation include:

- a tight skin disc; and
- a build-up of moisture.

Tight skin disc

To avoid the disc being too tight, it is important to ensure that the skin disc is positioned 1–2 mm from the skin (Arrowsmith 1996). If the person gains weight and the skin disc is fixed (such as in a low-profile device) the skin disc can cause pressure.

Moisture build up

A build-up of moisture usually results from inadequate cleaning or incomplete drying. Management strategies include increasing the frequency

Problems with stomas

Health professionals should be aware of the following potential problems with gastrostomy stomas:

- fluid leakage and skin excoriation;
- cellulitis;
- dermatitis;
- ulceration;
- bleeding; and
- hypergranulation.

A discussion of each of these problems forms the framework for the text of this chapter.

A 'quick guide' to these problems can be found in Table 7.1 (page 136).

of stomal washes and ensuring that the stoma is thoroughly dried. It is important to note that placing gauze under the skin disc can lead to erosion and ulceration of the abdominal skin (O'Brien, Davis & Erwin-Toth 1999).

Cellulitis

Cellulitis results from an infection of the skin and subcutaneous tissues. The gastrostomy tube can provide an entry point for microorganisms—thus leading to infection.

The signs and symptoms of cellulitis are pain and tenderness, erythema (redness), and fever. If these signs and symptoms are identified, medical advice should be sought. If cellulitis is diagnosed, the person should receive antibiotic therapy and appropriate wound care.

The following specific cellulitis infections can occur in people with a gastrostomy stoma:

- bacterial infection;
- candidiasis; and
- folliculitis.

Bacterial infection

Bacterial infection can occur as a consequence of contamination by a variety of pathogenic microorganisms. To avoid this, standard precautions should be used when attending to the stoma. Hand-washing is an important basic strategy to prevent the spread of infection. Health professionals should wash their hands before and after attending to the person's gastrostomy tube or stoma.

'Hand-washing is an important basic strategy to prevent the spread of infection.'

If infection is present, management usually involves the taking of swabs for culture and sensitivity. Appropriate antibiotic therapy is then prescribed.

A review of practice should be undertaken to identify ways of improving the standard precautions that are being followed (Duszak 2002).

Candidiasis

Candidiasis is an infection caused by *Candida albicans*—a yeast-like fungus. The infection is characterised by patches of red macropapules and outlying 'satellite' lesions. Leakage from the stoma can result in the growth of *Candida* (O'Brien, Davis & Erwin-Toth 1999).

Treatment involves antifungal preparations and strategies to address the leakage from the tube (Lee & Bishop 1999).

Folliculitis

Folliculitis (infected hair follicles) can occur as a result of inappropriate removal of the tape that is used to anchor the gastrostomy tube or to secure dressings around the stoma (O'Brien, Davis & Erwin-Toth 1999). Localised folliculitis can develop into more widespread cellulitis of the surrounding skin.

Treatment of the immediate infection might require topical antimicrobial powder. It might also be necessary to consider longer-term strategies to reduce the need for tapes around the stoma. Most gastrostomy tubes come with a skin disc that anchors the tube externally. If taping is required to prevent the person pulling at the tube, it might be more effective to consider using a low-profile device. If tape is used to secure a dressing over the stoma, the need for the dressing needs to be reviewed.

Dermatitis

Dermatitis is inflammation of the skin. The signs and symptoms of dermatitis include pain, itching, redness, and blistering. Dermatitis associated with gastrostomy stomas is usually due to:

- chemical irritation; or
- allergy.

Chemical dermatitis

Chemical dermatitis usually occurs as a result of the acidic gastric contents leaking onto the skin around the stoma. The skin becomes swollen, reddened, moist, and painful.

The primary management strategy is to identify the cause of the leakage to prevent recurrence. Treatment might also involve applying a barrier cream to protect the skin. Some clinicians have recommended protecting the area around the stoma by applying a thin smear of liquid antacid to reduce the excoriating effects of the acidic gastric contents (O'Brien, Davis & Erwin-Toth 1999).

Allergic dermatitis

Allergic dermatitis can develop if the person's skin is sensitive to the tubing, dressings, creams, or soap. The area appears red and swollen, and can bleed or weep.

To help to identify the cause of the allergy, a careful history should be taken of any previous allergic reactions. Soaps, creams, and tapes should be changed in an attempt to find non-allergenic alternatives.

Ulceration

Pressure ulcers can form at the stoma site as a result of unrelieved pressure on the stoma and surrounding area. A tight or poorly positioned skin disc is the most likely cause of pressure. Pressure can also be caused if a person with a fixed skin disc (such as a low-profile device) gains weight. Monitoring the stoma every day, and rotating the tube, are essential preventative measures (Hess 1999).

The most important aspect of management is relief of pressure. The skin disc should be checked to ascertain whether it is incorrectly positioned, and the position adjusted if necessary.

The treatment for ulcers is dependent on their depth, grading, and location.

'The most important aspect of management is relief of pressure.'

Bleeding

Bleeding at the stoma site is usually associated with trauma. Trauma to the stoma can occur if the person or a health professional inadvertently pulls at the tube. The tube can get caught when the person's position is changed or if his or her clothing is removed.

Some health professionals prefer to tape tubes to the person's abdomen to reduce the risk of trauma, bleeding, or accidental removal. However, it can be more effective to locate the position of the tube routinely before each intervention to ensure that it is not being pulled.

'The person might be experiencing difficulties adjusting to the presence of the tube and might require support and counselling.'

Some people deliberately pull at their tubes, thus causing trauma and bleeding. It is important to attempt to ascertain why the person is pulling at the tube. Possible causes include the following:

- the person wants to remove the tube;
- the person does not understand why he or she has a tube; and
- the tube is causing local irritation or pain.

In attempting to understand why the person is trying to remove the tube, it is important to appreciate that the person might be experiencing difficulties adjusting to the presence of the tube and might require support and counselling (see Chapter 5, page 97). If the tube is causing pain or irritation, a medical review is required.

In some cases a decision might have to be made to remove the tube and cease tube feeding. The process for ceasing tube feeding is discussed in Chapter 2 (page 34). If the tube feeding is to continue, the use of a low-profile device can sometimes prevent the person from pulling at the tube.

Hypergranulation

The formation of granulation tissue is a normal response to a wound. However, in some cases, hypergranulation (the formation of excess granulation tissue) occurs. The risk of developing excess granulation tissue is increased if there is excess moisture around the stoma, altered skin integrity, or a poorly fitting tube.

'It is important to assess the effect of hypergranulation on the individual person—and treat the problem accordingly.'

Because granulation tissue is considered to be harmless, excess tissue is sometimes not removed. However, in some cases, hypergranulation can be associated with:

- distress of the person (or his or her carer);
- serous exudate;
- increased risk of infection; and
- bleeding.

It is important to assess the effect of hypergranulation on the individual person—and treat the problem accordingly.

If indicated, cauterisation can be undertaken using a silver nitrate pencil. The frequency and duration of cauterisation varies according to the amount of granulation tissue formed and the effectiveness of the treatment. When using a silver nitrate pencil, it is important to be aware that the moistened stick is very caustic. Staff should ensure that there is no contact with surrounding skin or the gastrostomy tube.

Case study

The case history in the Box on page 143 outlines some of the issues discussed in this chapter.

Roslyn

Roslyn was a 75-year-old woman with a past history of stroke which had necessitated the insertion of a PEG tube. Roslyn was admitted from home for assessment and treatment of an infected stoma.

Roslyn had a fixed skin disc that had become tighter as she gained weight. Roslyn's husband, Bill, had assisted her in the shower each morning, but he had not cleaned under the skin disc. On admission, Roslyn's stoma was ulcerated under the skin disc, and the ulcer was discharging thick, green exudate. The stoma was very tender to touch, and Roslyn was uncomfortable when tube feeds were connected and disconnected.

Swabs were taken for culture and sensitivity, and intravenous antibiotics were commenced. After a course of antibiotics, the skin around the stoma healed and a new tube with an adjustable skin disc was inserted.

As part of Roslyn's discharge plan, Bill assisted in the development of a stomal care plan. Bill had been unaware that he needed to clean under the skin disc. He was worried about touching that part of the tube in case he hurt Roslyn. With education, support, and encouragement Bill became comfortable and adept at providing appropriate stomal care.

This case study highlights the importance of educating the person and carers about how to care for the stoma. Education at the time of initial discharge and revision of the information when they had settled at home might have prevented this adverse event.

Conclusion

Health professionals should be aware that gastrostomy stomas require particular care. An understanding of the principles of good stomal care enables health professionals to maintain a healthy stoma and to be aware of the problems that can occur. Early intervention can be instituted as required.

Proper stomal care has many potential benefits. It can promote health, assist in the maintenance of a positive body image, promote self-esteem, provide comfort, and facilitate convenience.

Health professionals caring for a person with a gastrostomy stoma must ensure that they never lose sight of the *person* who has the stoma.

Chapter 8

Care of the Gastrostomy Tube

Catherine Edgar

Introduction

Most problems encountered with gastrostomy tubes can be prevented if attention is paid to the proper care and maintenance of the tube. This chapter discusses the common problems encountered when managing gastrostomy tubes and the likely causes of these problems. The chapter also offers suggestions to reduce (or prevent) their occurrence.

> *'Most problems encountered with gastrostomy tubes can be prevented if attention is paid to the proper care and maintenance of the tube.'*

Geometry of a tube

As discussed in Chapter 11 (page 193), there is a wide range of tube types. Although each type of tube is different, they all have certain shared features. Most tubes have the following three components:

- an *internal bumper or retention device*—a balloon, a mushroom-tip bumper, a crossbar, or a disc that holds the tube in place internally;
- a *skin disc*—a bumper, disc, or flange at the external point of the tube designed to hold the tube in place externally; and

- a *Y-port connector*—a two-way port to connect the tube to the giving set that allows medications to be administered (tubes with balloons have an additional side port to inflate the balloon).

Figure 8.1 (below) illustrates these features.

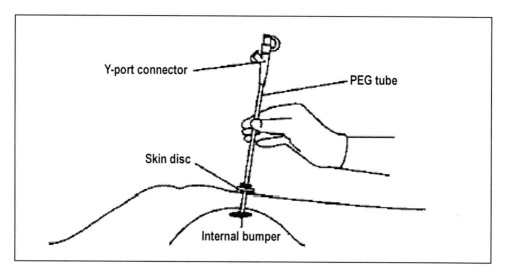

Figure 8.1 Components of a typical gastrostomy tube as illustrated in an Abbott Durapeg® tube

REPRODUCED WITH PERMISSION OF ABBOTT AUSTRALASIA PTY LTD

Commonly encountered problems

The most common management problems encountered with gastrostomy tubes include:

- tube blockage;
- tube displacement;
- 'buried bumper' syndrome;
- spontaneous balloon deflation;
- build-up of gas; and
- damage to the tube.

These are discussed in further detail below.

Commonly encountered problems

The most common management problems encountered with gastrostomy tubes include:

- tube blockage;
- tube displacement;
- 'buried bumper' syndrome;
- spontaneous balloon deflation;
- build-up of gas; and
- damage to the tube.

A discussion of these problems forms the framework for this chapter.

1. Tube blockage

Causes of a blocked tube

A gastrostomy tube can become blocked as a result of:

- the tube kinking;
- using high-caloric, viscous feeding formulae;
- inadequate flushing with water after feeding; and
- gastric reflux.

Kinked tube

Over time gastrostomy tubes can become soft and less elastic—which predisposes them to kinking. A kinked tube occludes the flow of formula. In these circumstances, the feeding formula can coagulate in the tube and cause a blockage.

'Kinking can be avoided by correct placement of the person, the gastrostomy tube, and the tubing.'

Kinking can be avoided by correct placement of the person, the gastrostomy tube, and the tubing connected to the enteral feeding container. This should ensure that the flow of feeding formula into the stomach is not interrupted (Broscious 1995).

Causes of a blocked tube

A gastrostomy tube can become blocked as a result of:

- the tube kinking;
- using high-caloric, viscous feeding formulae;
- inadequate flushing with water after feeding; and
- gastric reflux.

These problems are discussed in this portion of the text.

Thick formulae

The risk of tube blockage is increased if a thick formula is being administered—particularly if a small-bore tube (such as a duodenal tube) is used.

If the can of formula is shaken well before use, blockages are less likely to occur. If the tube blocks repeatedly, it might be necessary to consult with a dietitian about the possibility of changing the formula to a less viscous consistency.

Inadequate flushing

Flushing the gastrostomy tube with water is one of the most effective means of ensuring that the tube remains patent—thus preventing blockages. Regardless of the method used to deliver the feed, a regular flushing regimen should always be incorporated into the person's plan of care.

Gastrostomy tubes should be flushed with water:

- after confirming that the tube is correctly placed;
- before and after administering medications; and
- after tube feeds.

Some authorities recommend that the tube should be flushed at least every four hours. This maintains tube patency and reduces possible bacterial growth (Smeltzer & Bare 1992).

Many health professionals use 50 mL of water to flush a tube, but opinion varies on the ideal volume to use.

The use of a feed pump with an automatic flush feature has been shown to reduce the number of tube blockages (Guenter & Silkroski 2001). One study found that tube blockage occurred in 75% of tubes that were manually flushed, in comparison with only 5% of tubes using a feed pump with an automatic flush feature (Krupp 1998). It is essential that a flushing regimen be developed for every person.

'It is essential that a flushing regimen be developed for every person.'

Gastric reflux

Reflux of gastric contents into the tube predisposes the tube to blockages. The interaction of gastric contents and formula causes the formula to coagulate and block the tube (Guenter 1989; Eisenberg 1994; Ricciardi & Brown 1994; Klang 1996). Measures that can be effective in preventing and reducing the incidence of gastric reflux include:

- ensuring that the person is placed in an upright position during and after feeding;
- using a pump-assisted device (if appropriate);
- checking gastric residuals to ensure that the stomach is emptying adequately;
- slowing the rate of delivery; and
- using medication to increase the speed of stomach emptying.

Clearing a blocked tube

Various methods have been suggested for clearing a blocked tube. Table 8.1 (page 150) outlines these strategies and the issues to consider when attempting to clear a blocked tube.

The most commonly used method is to flush the tube with water or other fluid. Various agents have been suggested for clearing a blocked gastrostomy tube—including cranberry juice, cola beverages, and enzymatic solutions. However, cranberry juice and cola beverages are acidic in nature and can actually cause formula to coagulate (Krupp 1998; Metheny, Eisenberg & McSweeney 1988).

Table 8.1 Clearing a blocked gastrostomy tube
AUTHOR'S CREATION

Strategy	Techniques and comments
Flush	*water:* flush tube with warm water; common method of clearing blockage
	cola beverages: often used empirically, but little research evidence for effectiveness; might damage tube; might coagulate formula and exacerbate blockage
	cranberry juice: might coagulate formula and exacerbate blockage
	bicarbonate of soda: used empirically, but little research evidence for effectiveness; neutralises gastric contents
	pancreatic enzymes: used empirically, but little research evidence for effectiveness; thought to facilitate breakdown of coagulated mass
Milking or suctioning tube	can damage the gastric mucosa if performed by inexperienced clinicians
	syringes smaller than 50 mL can cause excessive pressure and rupture the tube
	not recommended for general use; only experienced professionals should use milking or suctioning techniques
Mechanical devices	can damage tissues or tube
	not recommended for general use; only experienced professionals familiar with the mechanical device being used should attempt this technique

Some researchers report that tubes can be unblocked by 'milking' or suctioning tubes. However, these techniques can damage the gastric mucosa if they are performed by inexperienced clinicians, and they are therefore not recommended (Guenter & Silkroski 2001).

'Milking or suctioning tubes can damage the gastric mucosa if they are performed by inexperienced clinicians; they are therefore not recommended.'

Specially designed catheters and plastic devices can be inserted into tubes to unblock them mechanically. However, these implements are also associated with some risks and can cause tissue or tube damage (Kohn-Keeth 2000; Guenter & Silkroski

2001). Mechanical clearance of a tube should be undertaken only by an experienced practitioner who is familiar with the device being used.

Ideally, the best form of management for a blocked gastrostomy tube is to replace it.

'The most effective strategy is to prevent tube blockages in the first place.'

The most effective strategy is to prevent tube blockages in the first place. If a tube becomes blocked the causes should be identified and processes established to ensure that it does not recur.

2. Tube displacement

Problems with tube displacement

The gastrostomy tube can be displaced if the tube is not anchored securely at skin level. Unsecured gastrostomy tubes can potentially move in and out of the gastrostomy tract.

If the gastrostomy tube is not securely anchored, the following problems can occur:

- stomach erosion and ulceration of the tract and stoma (Eisenberg 1994);
- stomal infection secondary to ulceration widening the stoma;
- leakage of gastric contents from the widened stoma and consequent burning of skin (Eisenberg 1994);
- development of granulation tissue around the stoma; and
- blockage of the pyloric sphincter resulting in abdominal distension, nausea, and vomiting (McMeekin 2000).

To prevent these problems, the skin disc must be secured at skin level.

Checking for tube displacement

The tube length should be checked to ensure that the tube has not migrated inwards. Most manufacturers provide external markings on the gastrostomy tube to indicate its position. However, the markings on some tubes can wear off over time.

The Box below describes the steps that should be taken to measure the length of the tube.

Measuring the length of a tube

The following steps should be taken to measure the length of a gastrostomy tube.

- *Step 1:* Hold the tube with one hand at the level of its exit site from the stomach.
- *Step 2:* Slide the skin disc away from the exit site along the tube.
- *Step 3:* Gently rotate the tube between the index finger and thumb.
- *Step 4:* Gently pull the gastrostomy tube away from the abdomen until slight resistance is felt.
- *Step 5:* Slide the skin disc back down to a position 1–2 mm from the abdomen.
- *Step 6:* Mark the tube at its exit site using an indelible pen.
- *Step 7:* Measure the tube from its exit site on the abdomen to its external tip or end.
- *Step 8:* Record the length in the person's care plan.
- *Step 9:* Check that the marking is visible on a daily basis.

Difficulty in moving the tube might indicate that the tube has migrated further into the stomach and is trapped in the pyloric sphincter or gastric wall. The person's doctor should be notified. An abdominal X-ray might be indicated to see if the gastrostomy tube is correctly positioned in the stomach (Broscious 1995).

Preventing tube displacement

The simplest method to prevent migration of a gastrostomy tube is to ensure that the skin disc is positioned 1–2 mm from the abdominal wall (Arrowsmith 1996). Care should be taken to ensure that the skin disc is maintained in (or restored to) its correct position after providing hygiene, administering medications, or delivering enteral feeds.

There should be no traction on the tube and the tube should be positioned to prevent pulling on the tube. The tubing or giving set attached to the container used to deliver the enteral feed should also be positioned so that it is always visible—thereby reducing the possibility of pulling or excessive traction being applied to the tube.

3. 'Buried bumper' syndrome

The term 'buried bumper' refers to the development of pressure necrosis and ulceration—either externally at the gastrostomy tube exit site or internally at the mucosal layer of the stomach wall (Eisenberg 1994). 'Buried bumper' syndrome is a potentially serious complication because it can mean that the tube has to be removed and replaced at another site.

'Buried bumper' syndrome usually occurs when excessive pressure has been maintained between the internal bumper and the skin disc. Excessive traction and tension on the tube can also occur if bulky dressing materials are placed under the external retention bumper.

Signs that indicate the development of 'buried bumper' syndrome include (Eisenberg 1994; Ricciardi & Brown 1994):

- bleeding at the stomal site;
- leaking of feeding formula or gastric contents; and
- sudden intolerance to enteral feeding.

To prevent 'buried bumper' syndrome, it is important to ensure that there is no excessive tension exerted between the skin disc and internal bumper. The skin disc should be positioned 1–2 mm from the abdominal wall (Arrowsmith 1996). No bulky dressing materials should be applied under the external retention bumper (Eisenberg 1994).

4. Spontaneous balloon deflation

Mechanism of spontaneous deflation

The internal bumper on some gastrostomy tubes is a balloon inflated with water. These tubes have a double lumen with two ports—one port is used to administer the enteral feed and the second port is used to inflate the balloon. The balloon port has a tip designed to take a Luer-lock syringe and often has the amount of water required to inflate the balloon printed on the rim of the port.

Over time, small amounts of water can leak from the balloon. If there is insufficient water in the balloon there is a risk that the tube can become displaced or accidentally removed. It is important to monitor the volume of water in the balloon on a regular basis to ensure that the gastrostomy tube is maintained in the correct position in the stomach.

'It is important to monitor the volume of water in the balloon on a regular basis.'

Monitoring balloon function

To check the balloon volume, a Luer-lock syringe should be inserted into the tip of the balloon port of the gastrostomy tube. Some pressure might be required to ensure that an adequate seal is achieved. The plunger of the syringe is then withdrawn, thus removing the water from the balloon. The volume of water that is withdrawn should be compared with the original amount instilled. This should correspond with the manufacturer's instructions (as marked on the rim of the balloon port).

If the volume of water that is withdrawn is less than the volume originally instilled, the recommended volume required to keep the balloon adequately inflated should be instilled. The amount of water withdrawn from the balloon and the amount of water reinstilled should be documented.

Inability to aspirate water from the balloon can indicate that:

- the balloon has ruptured;
- the one-way valve in the balloon side port is malfunctioning;
- the inner lumen is blocked; or
- the inner lumen of the balloon port is damaged.

To determine if a balloon has ruptured, the tube should be gently pulled. If it moves freely and can be pulled out further than the original site markings without resistance at the stomach wall, it can be assumed that the balloon has ruptured. Regardless of the cause, the tube will need to be replaced.

5. Build-up of gas

Some people receiving enteral feeding develop abdominal distension as a result of a build-up of gas in the stomach. Abdominal distension is uncomfortable for the person, and the increased pressure in the stomach can be transmitted up the tube. This can cause the gastric contents to leak or it can cause the protective cap (or feeding set) to disconnect.

An effective method to remove excess air and gases is to vent the tube, as described in the Box below.

Venting a gastrostomy tube

The following steps should be followed to vent a gastrostomy tube.

- **Step 1:** Hold the tube upright.
- **Step 2:** Protect eyes and clothing (both person and healthcare professional) from potential spray of gastric contents.
- **Step 3:** Uncap the tube and allow the air to escape.
- **Step 4:** Replace the cap.

Because low-profile gastrostomy tubes have a one-way valve to prevent gastric contents leaking, it is necessary to attach the specific decompression tubing supplied with the tube (Guenter & Silkroski 2001). Venting the tube can be done before each feed or on a regular predetermined basis—depending on the individual needs of the person.

6. Damage to the tube

Over time, as a result of exposure to gastric contents and medications, the gastrostomy tube can show signs of deterioration. Signs of deterioration

'A deteriorated tube can rupture and should be replaced as soon as practicable.'

include a blistered appearance on the tube with small aneurysms along the walls of the tube. In some cases there can be visible cracks.

A deteriorated tube can rupture and should be replaced as soon as practicable.

Gastrostomy tubes deteriorate more quickly if they are not flushed with water on a regular basis (Eisenberg 1994). Gastrostomy tubes should never be occluded or pinched using forceps or any other mechanical device. To close the tube, the cap provided with the tube should be used. Alternatively, to maintain a closed system, a spigot can be inserted into the tube.

> '*Gastrostomy tubes should never be occluded or pinched using forceps or any other mechanical device.*'

Some effective measures to prolong the life of a tube and to reduce tube damage and deterioration include (Metheny, Eisenberg & McSweeney 1988):

- avoiding the use of forceps or any other device to pinch or occlude a tube;
- establishing a regular flushing regimen;
- using an appropriately sized syringe; and
- inspecting the tube daily for signs of deterioration.

Case study

The case study below illustrates some of the issues discussed in this chapter.

David

David was a 27-year-old man who had had a gastrostomy tube in place for more than ten years. He was on a continuous enteral feeding regimen that included 4-hourly water flushes. David also required large doses of medication to control his long-standing epilepsy.

Despite flushing of his tube before and after administering medications, his tube had become distorted and had developed a blistered appearance with small aneurysms along the external shaft of the tube. The tube kinked and blocked frequently, which necessitated repeated tube replacements (approximately every three months).

(continued)

(continued)

A new management plan was devised whereby the tube was flushed every three hours with 50 mL of warm water. The new flushing regimen was successful in prolonging the life of the tube. After the introduction of the new flushing regimen his tube remained functional and in place for longer periods of time. Thereafter, his tube required replacement every twelve months.

Conclusion

Most problems encountered with gastrostomy tubes can be prevented if attention is paid to the proper care and maintenance of the tube. An effective preventive management plan should include regular flushing of the tube with water, securing the tube, and monitoring the integrity of the tube.

'An effective preventive management plan includes regular flushing of the tube with water, securing the tube, and monitoring the integrity of the tube.'

Although the research literature offers a variety of approaches to the care of gastrostomy tubes, there is little consensus on a single best approach. In particular, although a regular flushing regimen is frequently mentioned, there is little research-based evidence to support the methods used to clear a blocked tube. If confronted with a blocked gastrostomy tube that does not unblock with water, a more conservative approach is to replace the tube.

Chapter 9

Mouth Care

Raquel Rogers and Julie Ryan

Introduction

Oral health is compromised in persons with a gastrostomy tube, particularly those who have no oral intake. This is significant because the effects of mouth disorders are not limited to oral health. In addition to affecting the mouth, poor oral hygiene has been linked to (Joshipura et al. 1996):

- pulmonary infections;
- brain abscesses; and
- cardiovascular disease.

Oral health is also important for psychosocial well-being. Concerns about appearance, facial expression, and the freshness of the breath all affect the ways in which people perceive themselves and communicate with others.

> *'The effects of mouth disorders are not limited to oral health.'*

This chapter discusses: (i) assessment of oral health; (ii) identification of risk factors; and (iii) the provision of care to optimise oral health.

Framework of the chapter

This chapter discusses mouth care under the following headings:
- assessment of oral health (page 160);
- identification of risk factors (page 165); and
- provision of care (page 165).

Assessment of oral health

Holistic approach

In addition to assessment of the oral cavity, holistic assessment of oral health should include consideration of the person's general physical health, lifestyle, and preferences on the status of his or her mouth. Holistic mouth assessment thus involves:

- identification of the person's preferences;
- consideration of the person's oral and dental history;
- identification of co-morbidities and factors that place the person at risk of poor oral hygiene or disease; and
- examination of the oral cavity.

Obtaining the person's history will assist in identifying risk factors such as alcohol use, smoking, or a previous history of oral disease. Identification of the person's views and preferences can help carers understand the importance that the person places on mouth care. Some people might never have previously prioritised mouth care. Education might be required to ensure that the person understands the potential consequences and risks associated with inadequate mouth care.

'Education might be required to ensure that the person understands the potential consequences and risks associated with inadequate mouth care.'

Assessment tools

A mouth-care assessment tool can help to ensure that all appropriate assessments are conducted and that all the important factors are considered.

To ensure that it is incorporated into regular practice, any proposed assessment tool should be easy to use and not take too long to complete.

An assessment tool helps to guide health professionals through the process of identifying risk factors, obtaining a dental history, undertaking a physical examination of the person's mouth and surrounding structures, and identifying the person's preferences.

An example of an oral-assessment tool and care plan is shown in Figure 9.1 (see Appendix 9.1, page 173).

Assessment process

Examining the person's mouth is relatively simple if the person is conscious and able to cooperate. However, people who are confused or have altered consciousness might be unable or unwilling to cooperate. These people are particularly at risk of oral disease or trauma and require more frequent and careful examination.

'People who are confused or have altered consciousness might be unable or unwilling to cooperate; these people are particularly at risk.'

It is important to assess whether the person is able to assist during oral assessments and care, because people who clench their jaws place themselves and the health professional at risk of injury. If possible, the person should be given time to open the mouth spontaneously. A pen light can be used to view the oral cavity if the person is unable to open the mouth wide enough.

When conducting an assessment of a person's mouth, it is important to consider the following:

- jaw;
- tongue;
- lips and oral mucosa;
- teeth or dentures; and
- breath.

Each of these is discussed in further detail below.

Jaw

The jaw plays an important role in masticating food. Adequate jaw function is required for people who maintain an oral intake, or for those who are having short-term tube feeding.

The jaw should be examined to ensure that:
- the face shape around the jaw is symmetrical (because an asymmetrical or painful jaw can cause difficulties in speech and in the chewing and swallowing phases of eating);
- the upper and lower teeth are aligned when the jaw is clenched;
- the jaw moves without causing pain; and
- the teeth do not deviate from their normal alignment.

Assessment of the mouth

When conducting an assessment of a person's mouth, it is important to consider the following:
- jaw;
- tongue;
- lips and oral mucosa;
- teeth or dentures; and
- breath.

Each of these is discussed in this portion of the text.

Tongue

The function of the tongue is to assist in masticating food and moving the food bolus through the mouth. Smoking, alcohol, medications, malnutrition, and infection can affect the tongue surface.

When examining the tongue, it is important to check that:
- the surface is pink and moist;
- the tongue is centred (and not deviated to one side);
- there are no cracks or blisters; and
- there are no signs of inflammation or discolouration (for example, white coating).

Any abnormal findings or changes should be reported to the person's medical officer.

Lips and oral mucosa

The lips and oral mucosa (the inside of the cheeks, the roof of mouth, and the gums) maintain oral hydration by acting as a barrier to trauma and infection. The lips, inner surface of the cheeks, roof of the mouth, and gums should be examined. It is important to ensure that:

- the lips are not dry or cracked;
- there is no ulceration on the lips or oral mucosa;
- the lips seal when the mouth is closed;
- the lips and oral mucosa are pink and moist; and
- the gums are not inflamed or bleeding (which can be signs of gingivitis).

Cracking, bleeding, and ulceration of the lips can indicate dehydration. Ulcers of the mouth and lips can be painful and usually require treatment to increase the person's comfort.

'Cracking, bleeding, and ulceration of the lips can indicate dehydration.'

When examining the lips and oral mucosa it is important to inspect the person's saliva. Saliva assists in the digestion of food, cleanses the mouth, and protects against bacteria. When checking the saliva it is important to ensure that the person does not:

- have a dry mouth from insufficient saliva production;
- have pools of saliva in the cheeks;
- dribble saliva from corners of the mouth; or
- have a hoarse, raspy, or gurgly voice.

Most people produce 1500 mL of saliva every 24 hours (Fuller & Shaller-Ayers 1994). If saliva production exceeds this volume or if the person has difficulty swallowing, the person might drool or choke. These conditions can result in increased anxiety, an abnormal voice (gurgly, hoarse, or raspy), and altered body image and self-esteem.

People who do not produce enough saliva often have a dry, painful mouth. Xerostomia (dry mouth) is usually due to a failure of the salivary glands to secrete saliva, but it can also be a consequence of dehydration or oxygen therapy. As well as being painful, xerostomia can contribute to difficulties with speech and physical expression.

If they do not have an appropriate balance of saliva, people are prone to mouth infections or inflammation. Some people benefit from treatment to alter the volume of saliva—medication to reduce the volume of saliva produced or commercially prepared saliva stimulants to lubricate the mouth.

Teeth or dentures

Teeth assist the mechanical digestion of food by cutting, grinding, and mixing it with saliva before it is swallowed. Examining the teeth involves checking to ensure that the teeth are:

- clean and free from debris;
- unbroken and free of sharp edges;
- free from plaque build-up around the base of the teeth;
- not decayed;
- not painful or aching; and
- not discoloured.

It is important to note whether any teeth are missing and to ensure that the person visits the dentist regularly and frequently.

If the person has dentures, it is important to ensure that:

- they fit well (by checking that they do not move in the mouth when the person is speaking); and
- they are not causing pain or ulceration.

Breath

The person's breath should be checked during the examination. The breath should be odourless. Malodorous breath (halitosis) can be caused by dental caries, xerostomia, or infection.

Halitosis can affect the person's self-esteem and intimate relationships. It can lead to social isolation. Halitosis can also be challenging for families and carers.

Identification of risk factors

There are several co-morbidities, medical treatments, and lifestyle choices that can place a person at risk of poor oral health. Because people with gastrostomy tubes often have other health problems, it is important that health professionals are aware of the range of conditions that can adversely affect oral health. Table 9.1 (page 166) outlines some of these risk factors.

Providing mouth care

Planning mouth care

The information obtained from the assessment allows health professionals to prepare a care plan for the person. The care plan should be:

- based on the principles of best practice; and
- developed in association with the person, taking into account his or her views and preferences.

Best practice for mouth care is now well documented in the research literature. However, despite this body of evidence, mouth care is often based on tradition and custom. Mouth care has not always been seen as a priority area for practice change, and healthcare professionals often cite lack of time as the main reason for not attending to proper mouth care. It is important that all healthcare professionals appreciate the importance of mouth care and that they provide appropriate care, according to best practice, as often as it is required.

'Best practice for mouth care is now well documented ... However, despite this body of evidence, mouth care is often based on tradition and custom.'

Frequency of mouth care

The frequency of mouth care is dependent on the needs of the individual person as identified in the assessment. However, the following general

Table 9.1 Risk factors in oral health

AUTHORS' PRESENTATION

Risk factors	Comments
Diabetes	Decreased capillary flow predisposes gums to inflammation and infection (Walton, Miller & Tordecilla 2001)
Anaemia	Might have gingivitis and associated vitamin deficiency (Ebersole & Hess 1994)
Vitamin deficiency	Deficiencies of vitamins B and C can cause cracks in corners of the mouth, painful swollen tongue, mouth ulcers, receding and bleeding gums, loose teeth, and poor tissue healing
Chemotherapy	Increased risk of mouth ulcers and infection Nausea and vomiting
Radiotherapy	Impairs growth of oral mucosa (Miller & Kearney 2001) Hypertrophy of salivary glands (Miller & Kearney 2001)
Medications	Increased incidence of dental caries, oral disease, and infection is associated with morphine, anticholinergics, antidepressants, antispasmodics, barbiturates, bronchodilators, and diuretics (Evans 2001)
Antibiotic therapy	Normal oral bacteria can be altered; increased risk of thrush and herpes simplex infections
Oral endotracheal tube	Can cause stomatitis and tooth damage (Hickey 1997) Can introduce bacteria and increase infection risk
Ageing process	Decreased saliva production; drying of oral mucosa Tooth loss
Alcohol use	Associated with vitamin deficiencies and halitosis
Cigarette smoking	Damage to oral mucosa Increased risk of lip and tongue cancer (Ebersole & Hess 1994)
Self-care deficit	Accumulation of debris and plaque formation Predisposition to infection
Immunosuppression	Optimal oral health important in prevention of oral infection and inflammation

principles apply (Miller and Kearney 2001). Mouth care should be undertaken:

- every 4–6 hours for people at risk of infection;
- every 2 hours for people who are semiconscious or unable to control their oral secretions; and
- every hour for people who are receiving oxygen therapy, those who are unconscious, or those who are suffering from an infected mouth.

Providing mouth care

This section of the text discusses the provision of mouth care under the following headings:

- planning mouth care (page 165);
- frequency of mouth care (page 165);
- equipment for mouth care (page 167);
- cleaning solutions for mouth care (page 169);
- mouth lubricants (page 169); and
- denture care (page 171).

Equipment for mouth care

Brushing the person's teeth and cleaning his or her mouth are important aspects of mouth care. The use of a toothbrush in association with regular, gentle flossing prevents the build-up of plaque (soft non-calcified microbial deposits around the surfaces of the teeth). It is important to minimise the occurrence of plaque because it is the primary cause of dental caries and gingivitis.

A range of mouth-care equipment is available through medical suppliers, supermarkets, and chemists. Table 9.2 (page 168) gives an overview of available mouth-care equipment and its uses.

When using equipment in the mouth, care needs to be taken to avoid trauma to the oral mucosa and gums. Inappropriate technique and overuse can result in damage and bleeding. In addition, the person is at risk of damage to the teeth if he or she bites on equipment during mouth care. When choosing equipment for people who are able to undertake their own

'Care needs to be taken to avoid trauma to the oral mucosa and gums. Inappropriate technique and overuse can result in damage and bleeding.'

Table 9.2 Equipment for mouth care
AUTHORS' PRESENTATION

Equipment	Comments
Soft-tooth brush	Soft outer bristle massages gum line Tapered head increases access
Curved-head toothbrush	Easy to use for person and carer Has a better reach than standard brush
Suction toothbrush	Indicated for those at high risk of aspiration Requires a suction machine Brush handle can damage teeth if it is bitten
Electric toothbrush	Provides gum massage and reduces gum hypertrophy Can damage soft tissue of palate in at-risk people
Mouth swab	Usually a cotton-tipped applicator Useful for moistening the person's mouth Presence of swab in the mouth can promote salivation and improve mouth vascularity through gentle massaging action Not effective in removing plaque from the teeth Not efficient in removing debris from the mouth Usually used in combination with brushing
Finger	Piece of gauze on health professional's finger tip to clean the person's mouth Unpleasant for the person Carer at risk of being bitten Person at-risk of choking and aspiration if the gauze is dislodged
Dental floss	Daily use often recommended Removes plaque A flossing applicator can be useful

mouth care, it is important to ensure that selected equipment is easy to grip and use.

Cleaning solutions for mouth care

As noted above (page 165), although best practice for mouth care is now well documented in the research literature, many practices in mouth care continue to be based on traditional methods. This is especially so in the selection and use of cleaning solutions for oral hygiene. Cleaning solutions are often selected on the basis of custom and convenience. There is now a growing body of evidence to suggest that many of the traditional cleaning solutions are ineffectual or harmful.

'Cleaning solutions are often selected on the basis of custom and convenience ... many of the traditional cleaning solutions are ineffectual or harmful.'

In choosing a cleaning solution, it is important to consider the available evidence and the individual preferences and needs of the person. Some commonly used cleaning solutions and their effects are summarised in Table 9.3 (page 170).

Mouth lubricants

Saliva plays an important role in lubricating the mucous membrane of the mouth and preventing infection. In the absence of saliva, the pH of the mouth becomes more acidic due to bacterial waste—which causes softening of the tooth enamel and increased risk of tooth decay. Saliva substitutes are commercially available and can be used to relieve some of the discomfort of a dry mouth.

'Saliva plays an important role in lubricating the mucous membrane of the mouth and preventing infection.'

Some medications can contribute to dry mouth, These include anticholinergics, antidepressants, antipsychotics, diuretics, antihypertensives, barbiturates, antihistamines, opiates, bronchodilators, and antispasmodics. If possible, these medications should be avoided in persons with mouth problems.

A list of commonly used mouth lubricants is shown in Table 9.4 (page 171).

Table 9.3 Solutions used in mouth care
AUTHORS' PRESENTATION (ADAPTED FROM MILLER & KEARNEY 2001)

Solution	Comments
Mouthwash	Removes food debris and kills bacteria
	Prevents plaque formation and gingivitis
	Moistens the mouth
	Person must be able to rinse, gargle, and spit out mouthwash without aspirating
	Wide range of alternatives available; suitability of ingredients should be checked—for example, some contain sugar (increases risk of tooth decay and unsuitable for diabetics)
Toothpaste	Helps to prevent cavities, plaque, and gum problems
	Might strengthen tooth enamel and protect against bacteria
	Residue from poor rinsing after brushing can dry mouth
	Foaming action can provoke a gag reflex
Hydrogen peroxide	Anti-plaque action
	Can irritate oral mucosa if not adequately diluted
	Can have unpleasant taste; can cause nausea
	Can increase sensation of dry mouth
	Promotes an alkaline environment—thus increasing risk of infection
Sodium bicarbonate	Can decrease thickness of oral mucosa
	Can help to maintain appropriate saliva consistency
	Can cause superficial bleeding
	Can be unpleasant to taste
	Requires rinsing after use
Lemon and glycerine	Stimulates saliva production
	Can exhaust salivary glands resulting in dry mouth
	Can cause decalcification of tooth enamel leading to dental caries and tooth decay
Chlorhexidine	Antifungal and antibacterial properties
	Helps prevent plaque build-up
	Can discolour teeth
	Can cause mucosal damage if not adequately diluted
	Can be unpleasant tasting
Water; normal saline	Useful for moistening oral mucosa
	Does not remove plaque

Table 9.4 Mouth lubricants

AUTHORS' PRESENTATION (ADAPTED FROM MILLER & KEARNEY 2001)

Lubricant	Comments
Artificial saliva	Used to relieve discomfort of dry mouth Does not have anti-bacterial properties of saliva Short-term action; requires regular application Certain products are mucin-based (pig-based) and are unsuitable for some people
Effervescent vitamin C	Saliva stimulant Can cause a burning sensation Can cause teeth demineralisation Risk of aspiration
Chewing gum	Saliva stimulant Unsuitable for people with poor swallowing function (risk of aspiration)
Acupuncture	Saliva stimulant Can increase feelings of well-being Mechanism of action poorly understood

Denture care

Dentures and other dental prostheses need regular care. As with natural teeth, dentures can collect food and microorganisms. Dentures and other dental prostheses should be carefully removed from the mouth and cleaned according to the individual needs of the person.

In caring for dentures it is important to ensure that they are:

- stored in water (if left out overnight);
- cleaned in cool water (because hot water can alter their shape); and
- handled carefully (because they are easily broken or chipped).

Some people use toothpaste to clean their dentures. Others prefer commercially prepared products especially prepared for dentures and dental prostheses.

Conclusion

Health professionals are ideally placed to recognise early changes in the status of the oral cavity and to prevent the development of potentially serious complications. However, a major barrier to best practice is that many health professionals do not appreciate the importance of oral care. Education is required to overcome this problem, and to ensure best practice in choosing the most appropriate equipment and products to use.

> *'Mouth care based on the principles of best practice should support the independence of people by accommodating their individual preferences and needs.'*

Documentation of oral assessment and care planning should be included in existing documentation to ensure that mouth care is incorporated into routine clinical practice. This documentation should include a mouth-care policy, an assessment tool, and a care plan.

Mouth care should always be based on the principles of best practice, and should support the independence of people by accommodating their individual preferences and needs.

Appendix 9.1

This appendix presents a comprehensive assessment tool and care plan for oral health.

ORAL ASSESSMENT AND CARE PLAN	NAME:

Section A: Risk factors

1. General risk factors:

☐ Alcohol use   ☐ Tobacco use
☐ Oxygen therapy   ☐ Radiotherapy
☐ Endotracheal tube   ☐ No oral intake
☐ Altered conscious state   ☐ Vitamin deficiency
☐ Diabetes   ☐ Anaemia
☐ Altered immune system   ☐ Impaired gag reflex

2. Medications:

☐ Barbituarates   ☐ Anticholinergics
☐ Antibiotics   ☐ Antidepressants
☐ Bronchodilators   ☐ Antispasmodics
☐ Diuretics   ☐ Other . . . .

Section B: Relevant history

1. History of:

☐ Mouth ulcers   ☐ Gingivitis
☐ Dental abcess   ☐ Painful mouth
☐ Major dental works   ☐ Antispasmodics
☐ Other . . . .

2. Frequency of dental reviews: . . . .

3. Mouth care routine: . . . .
. . . .

Section C: Examination

1. Jaw:

☐ Malalignment   ☐ Limited movement

2. Amount of salivation:

☐ Dry   ☐ Moist

Figure 9.1 Assessment tool and care plan for oral health
AUTHORS' CREATION   *(continued)*

3. Appearance of tongue:
- ☐ Dry
- ☐ Coated
- ☐ Pink

- ☐ Moist
- ☐ Red
- ☐ Other ....

4. Appearance of gums:
- ☐ Dry
- ☐ Red
- ☐ Other ....

- ☐ Moist
- ☐ Pink

5. Appearance of lips:
- ☐ Dry
- ☐ Cracked
- ☐ Smooth

- ☐ Moist
- ☐ Rough
- ☐ Other ....

6. Breath:
- ☐ Halitosis

- ☐ Odourless

7. Voice quality:
- ☐ Clear, strong
- ☐ Gurgly

- ☐ Raspy

Section D: Teeth

1. Are there natural teeth present?
- ☐ Yes

- ☐ No *(if no, proceed to section E)*

2. Are teeth:
- ☐ Intact?
- ☐ Loose?
- ☐ Stained?

- ☐ Broken or cracked?
- ☐ White?
- ☐ Coated?

3. Does the person require referral to a dentist?
- ☐ Yes

- ☐ No

Section E: Dentures

1. Does the person have dentures?
- ☐ Yes

- ☐ No *(if no, proceed to section F)*

2. Are teeth:
- ☐ Full uppers?
- ☐ Partial uppers?
- ☐ Cracked or broken?
- ☐ Rough dentures?

- ☐ Full lowers?
- ☐ Partial lowers?
- ☐ Smooth dentures?
- ☐ Well fitting?

Figure 9.1 Assessment tool and care plan for oral health *(continued)*

3. Does the person require referral to a dentist or dental technician?

☐ Yes   ☐ No

Section F: Self-care

1. How much assistance does the person require with mouth care?

☐ No assistance, able to self-care   ☐ Supervision

☐ Some assistance   ☐ Full assistance

Section G: Care plan

1. Person's perferences and routines: ....
....
....
....

2. Toothbrush type:

☐ Electric   ☐ Suction

☐ Curved   ☐ Soft

☐ Swab stick

3. Cleansing agent:

Type: ....   Strength: ....

4. Lubrication:

Type: ....   Frequency: ....

5. Frequency of mouth care: ....
....

6. Position of person for mouth care: ....
....

7. Special instructions *(include safety needs for person and staff)*:
....
....
....
....

Completed by: ....

Designation: ....   Date: ....

Figure 9.1 Assessment tool and care plan for oral health *(continued)*

Chapter 10
Troubleshooting

Alison Bowie

Introduction

Gastrostomy feeding is increasingly common, and it should be a simple, manageable means of providing people with their nutritional and hydration needs. However, people often experience complications—and carers and clinical staff can have difficulties in managing these problems.

'Some problems can be improved by adjusting the enteral regimen. However, there are often underlying causes that should be identified and resolved.'

The most common complications in gastrostomy feeding are diarrhoea and constipation, nausea and vomiting, aspiration, tube blockage, abdominal cramps, and dehydration. Some of these problems can be improved by adjusting the enteral regimen. However, there are often underlying causes that should be identified and resolved.

This chapter identifies some common problems and provides guidance in resolving and preventing them.

Some common problems associated with gastrostomy feeding are:

- diarrhoea;
- tube blockage;

- aspiration;
- nausea and vomiting;
- abdominal cramping;
- constipation;
- dehydration;
- leakage from the stoma; and
- diabetes management.

These are discussed in further detail below.

1. Diarrhoea

Diarrhoea is common with tube feeding. Apart from the discomfort that it produces, untreated diarrhoea can lead to malnutrition, dehydration, electrolyte imbalances, and skin breakdown.

Carers are often quick to blame the feed itself, and it is not uncommon for feeds to be reduced, diluted, or even ceased at the first sign of diarrhoea. However, ceasing the feeds puts the person at risk of malnutrition. It has long been thought that diarrhoea is caused by administering hypertonic (concentrated) formula. However, undiluted hypertonic formula does not necessarily increase the incidence of diarrhoea compared with isotonic or diluted formula (Keohane et al. 1984).

'When a person develops diarrhoea, a carer's first actions should be to exclude causes not related to the tube feeds.'

It is also important to note that a 'normal' bowel motion in a tube-fed person is different from a 'normal' bowel motion in an orally fed person. The 'normal' bowel motions of tube-fed people are often described as being of a 'mayonnaise' or 'toothpaste' consistency.

When a person develops diarrhoea, a carer's first actions should be to exclude causes *not* related to the tube feeds. This is especially important when a person who has been tube-fed for a long time develops diarrhoea as a new problem.

Framework of the chapter

Some common problems associated with gastrostomy feeding are:

- diarrhoea;
- tube blockage;
- aspiration;
- nausea and vomiting;
- abdominal cramping;
- constipation;
- dehydration;
- leakage from the stoma; and
- diabetes management.

A discussion of each of these problems forms the framework for this chapter.

In seeking causes of diarrhoea not related to tube-feeding, carers should consider the following possibilities:

- medications;
- hypoalbuminaemia;
- bacterial infection;
- constipation (spurious diarrhoea);
- rapid rate of administration;
- lack of fibre; and
- temperature of formulae.

These are discussed in further detail below.

Medications

Hyperosmolar medications, histamine agonists, antibiotics, and medications containing magnesium and sorbitol are all potential causes of diarrhoea (Edes, Walk & Austin 1990; Burns & Jairath 1994; Bliss & Lehmann 1999).

Causes of diarrhoea

This section of the chapter discusses the following causes of diarrhoea:

- medications;
- hypoalbuminaemia;
- bacterial infection;
- constipation (spurious diarrhoea);
- rapid rate of administration;
- lack of fibre; and
- temperature of formula.

People on tube feeds are often prescribed medications in liquid forms—and liquid forms of medication often contain sorbitol. In large doses, sorbitol can cause abdominal cramps and diarrhoea.

Many antibiotics can also cause diarrhoea. Antibiotic-related diarrhoea can be prevented or decreased by using a formula containing fibre. The fibre can assist the gut in maintaining sufficient normal flora (Bass et al. 1996).

'In many cases, people have been prescribed aperients before tube feeds commence, and these might not be ceased when feeds begin.'

Aperients (laxatives) are a common cause of diarrhoea. In many cases, people have been prescribed aperients before tube feeds commence, and these might not be ceased when feeds begin. If diarrhoea develops, it is important to check for possible overuse of aperients.

If medication is suspected of causing diarrhoea, it is important to have the person's medications reviewed by a doctor or pharmacist. See Chapter 12 (page 217) for more information about the safe use of medications in tube-fed patients.

Hypoalbuminaemia

Albumin is an essential protein in the blood. The level of albumin can be low in people who are malnourished or critically ill, and in those who

Medication causing diarrhoea

Mr Long developed diarrhoea two days after having had a gastrostomy tube inserted. He was receiving a standard isotonic formula via a pump at 100 mL/hr over 24 hours with a 100-mL water flush every four hours.

In seeking potential causes, it was found that Mr Long had been having lactulose twice daily every day for several years. The lactulose was ceased and the diarrhoea then resolved. Mr Long then established a regular pattern of one formed motion each day.

have had recent surgery. Low serum albumin can cause oedema in various part of the body, including the gut. This can lead to poor absorption of nutrients and, possibly, diarrhoea.

Research into hypoalbuminaemia as a cause of diarrhoea in tube-fed people is inconclusive. Some studies suggest that albumin levels below 26 grams per litre are associated with increased diarrhoea, whereas other studies have found no significant difference (Burns & Jairath 1994).

If hypoalbuminaemia *is* suspected of causing diarrhoea, the administration of an elemental formula can aid digestion and decrease diarrhoea. An elemental formula is one in which the nutrients have been broken down into basic elements—such as peptides, sugars, and triglycerides. If an elemental formula fails, it might be necessary to use an anti-diarrhoeal medication (such as loperamide or codeine phosphate). It is important to rule out infection before using these agents.

Bacterial infection

Bacterial infection is a common cause of diarrhoea in tube-fed people. Potential causes of bacterial contamination are poor hygiene practices, long hanging times, and decanting formula into recycled containers.

'It is important to use aseptic techniques at all times.'

It is important to use aseptic techniques at all times, and to follow manufacturers' guidelines with respect to hanging times and reusing equipment. It might be necessary to use ready-to-hang feed systems if problems continue (Bockus 1991).

A range of bacteria can cause diarrhoea. In particular, hospitalised, tube-fed patients are at increased risk of developing diarrhoea from infection with *Clostridium difficile*. The bacteria can be passed from the hands of carers or in formula contaminated by non-septic techniques.

'Tube-fed people with diarrhoea should have their stools tested for Clostridium difficile.'

Lack of fibre in feeds and the use of antibiotics can also cause an overgrowth of *Clostridium difficile* (Bass et al. 1996; Bliss et al. 1998). Tube-fed people with diarrhoea should have their stools tested for *Clostridium difficile*. If the test is positive, they should be referred to medical staff for treatment.

To minimise bacterial contamination, the precautions listed in the Box below should be followed by all health professionals.

Minimising bacterial contamination

To minimise bacterial contamination, the following precautions should be followed.

- Wash hands before and after contact with any individual.
- Change gloves between contacts with different people.
- Wash bottles, bags, and giving sets with warm soapy water between feeds.
- Dry giving sets and bottles between feeds.
- Ensure that the person's gastric syringe is not put directly into the mortar and pestle when administering crushed medications.
- Write the name of the person on a bottle or giving set to ensure that the same equipment is not used for another person.
- Keep unused feed containers covered and refrigerated.
- Change bottles and giving sets regularly and frequently, as per manufacturers' guidelines.

Constipation (spurious diarrhoea)

Diarrhoea can be caused by overflow of fluid as a result of constipation. This is known as 'spurious diarrhoea'.

Rectal examination or abdominal X-ray will enable the diagnosis to be made. If constipation is identified as the problem, it is important to review and modify the feeding regimen.

Rate of administration

Rapid administration of tube feeds can cause diarrhoea. Such rapid administration occurs with intermittent or bolus feeding.

If feeds have been omitted for several days, feeding should be recommenced at a slow rate and increased gradually as tolerated. Administration should begin at a rate of 40 mL/hr, and increased in increments of 20–40 mL/hr.

'If the size of a bolus feed does cause diarrhoea, it might be necessary to give a smaller volume more frequently.'

If the size of a bolus feed does cause diarrhoea, it might be necessary to give a smaller volume more frequently—such that the amount of feed over the day remains unchanged.

Lack of fibre

The use of a formula that contains fibre decreases the incidence of diarrhoea in tube-fed people (Bass et al. 1996).

'Bulking agents must be used with extreme care because they can cause tube blockages if the tube is not flushed adequately after the feed is finished.'

Bulking agents containing psyllium can decrease diarrhoea. However, they must be used with extreme care because they can cause tube blockages if the tube is not flushed adequately after the feed is finished. When using bulking agents such as psyllium, the tube should always be flushed with at least 100 mL of water after administering the agent.

Lack of fibre

Mr Brown had been fed through a gastrostomy tube for three years. He had been maintained on a 1.5 kcal/mL formula five times each day. Each feed consisted of one can of formula (237 mL) and 150 mL of water. Usually his bowels were regular with a semi-formed motion every second day.

When Mr Brown began having large amounts of watery diarrhoea and continuous faecal oozing, various possible causes were investigated.

His medication was reviewed. No aperients were being used. However, Mr Brown had recently commenced a course of antibiotics for a chest infection.

A stool sample was taken and tested for *Clostridium difficile* and other bacteria. These tests were negative.

Codeine phosphate was commenced. This resolved the diarrhoea, but caused significant nausea.

Psyllium was therefore commenced. This was administered twice per day through the PEG tube and flushed with at least 100 mL of water.

As a result of treatment with this bulking agent, Mr Brown's diarrhoea resolved. He had two formed motions each day during the course of the antibiotics.

Temperature of formula

Diarrhoea can occur if the formula is too cold when it is administered—for example, immediately after being removed from the refrigerator. It is therefore important to ensure that formula is at room temperature before administration.

2. Tube blockage

A blocked feeding tube is a common and frustrating problem. The most frequent causes of blocked tubes are: (i) clots in the formula; (ii) inadequate crushing of medications; and (iii) inadequate flushing of the tube after feeds.

A tube is more likely to become blocked if it is of a small diameter (such as those used in nasogastric and jejunostomy feeding) or if the feeds run continuously (DeLegge & Rhodes 1998; Bliss & Lehmann 1999).

To prevent blockages it is important to:

- always flush the tube with at least 30 mL of water before and after administering medications;
- flush the tube every four hours during continuous feeding;
- flush the tube before and after each intermittent feed;
- use liquid medications (or crush medications adequately with 30 mL of water);
- use an intermittent delivery rather than a continuous delivery (if possible); and
- ensure that all staff and carers are aware of strategies to prevent tubes becoming blocked.

Once a tube has become blocked, there are several ways to remove the blockage. These are noted in the Box below.

Strategies to remove blockage

Once a tube has become blocked there are several ways to remove the blockage. These include:

- using a syringe with water to apply gentle pressure (which should unblock most obstructions);
- flushing with a cola-based beverage (although this can damage the tube);
- adding sodium bicarbonate to water (dosage according to doctor's written order), and flushing the solution through the tube; and
- using a pancreatic enzyme solution (dosage and administration according to doctor's written order) to dissolve blockages (Marcuard et al. 1989).

3. Aspiration

Tube feeding is often recommended to prevent aspiration of food and fluids into the person's lungs. However, although a person who commences tube feeding is no longer at risk of aspiration of food and fluids ingested by mouth, there is still a risk of aspirating tube formula and saliva.

The risk of aspiration is increased by: (i) impaired gag or cough reflexes; (ii) advanced age and debilitation; (iii) a history of reflux or aspiration; and (iv) the presence of a tracheostomy or delayed gastric emptying (Bockus 1991).

Aspiration pneumonia can be difficult to detect. Some signs include tachycardia, rapid or difficult breathing, coughing, wheezing, cyanosis, and fever. If aspiration is suspected it is important to stop the feed immediately and seek medical attention. A chest x-ray is usually needed to confirm aspiration pneumonia (Bockus 1991).

Some strategies to decrease the risk of aspiration are noted in the Box below.

Strategies to decrease aspiration risk

Some strategies to decrease the risk of aspiration include:

- keeping the person's head elevated (at least 30 degrees from the horizontal);
- administering feeds into the jejunum (Bliss & Lehmann 1999);
- feeding continuously via a pump;
- using antinausea medication or an agent to speed up gastric emptying in those who have delayed gastric emptying; and
- monitoring gastric residuals to ensure adequate emptying.

4. Nausea and vomiting

Nausea and vomiting caused by tube feeding can usually be prevented. Contributing factors include:

- the rate of administering the feed;
- the temperature of feeds;
- bacterial contamination; and
- delayed gastric emptying.

Causes of delayed gastric emptying include gastric inflammation, abdominal surgery, head trauma, malnutrition, diabetes, Parkinson's disease, or administration of anticholinergic and opiate medications (Drickamer & Cooney 1993).

Some strategies to reduce the risk of nausea and vomiting are noted in the Box below.

Strategies to reduce nausea and vomiting

Some strategies to reduce the risk of nausea and vomiting include:

- beginning or recommencing feeds at a slow rate; then increasing the feeding rate gradually;

- using aseptic techniques to reduce the likelihood of bacterial contamination;

- identifying the appropriate residual volume, and checking when required;

- using antinausea medication (or medication to speed up gastric emptying);

- ensuring that the formula is delivered at the appropriate temperature; and

- checking the delivery rate after commencing the feed to ensure that it is still appropriate.

5. Abdominal cramping

Tube-fed people can experience abdominal cramps if the formula is too cold when it is administered. In addition, abdominal cramps can also be caused by people receiving large volumes of feed intermittently, overuse of aperients, and excessive gas in the stomach.

Apart from these common causes of abdominal pain, the possibility of bowel obstruction should always be kept in mind. A medical opinion should be sought if abdominal pain is severe or persistent—especially in association with vomiting and a lack of bowel actions.

Some strategies to reduce the incidence of abdominal cramps and bloating are shown in the Box on page 188.

Strategies to reduce abdominal cramps

Some strategies to reduce the incidence of abdominal cramps and bloating include:

- ensuring that the formula is administered at room temperature;
- beginning feeding at a slow rate, and then increasing the rate gradually; and
- venting the tube before each feed by opening the feeding port and allowing the air to escape from the stomach.

Abdominal cramps and bloating

Mrs May was receiving a 1.5 kcal/mL formula five times each day. Each feed contained 237 mL and was followed by a 150-mL water flush. Mrs May had complained of bloating and abdominal cramps since commencing tube feeds.

Mrs May's medications were reviewed, and her aperients were ceased. The feeding rate was slowed down and each feed was administered over one hour. The feeding regimen was changed to six feeds per day to decrease the size of each bolus. None of these strategies had any effect.

Finally, stomach gas was vented before each feed. As a result, the abdominal cramping and bloating subsided.

6. Constipation

Constipation in tube-fed patients can be caused by insufficient fluid, poor mobility, and poor fibre intake. Patients with spinal injuries are also at high risk of constipation due to decreased bowel motility. Furthermore, analgesia containing codeine and morphine can also cause constipation.

Some strategies to reduce the risk of constipation are listed in the Box on page 189. If a person has chronic constipation despite these measures, it might be necessary to seek the advice of a continence specialist.

Strategies to reduce constipation

Some strategies to reduce the risk of constipation include:

- ensuring that each person's individual needs are adequately assessed;
- ensuring that the fluid intake is adequate;
- reviewing feed regimens (especially in hot weather) and including more fluid if necessary;
- using a formula that contains fibre; and
- encouraging the person to be as mobile as possible.

7. Dehydration

Most people require approximately 30–40 mL of fluid per kilogram of body weight per day. Health professionals should be aware that only 80% of the fluid from most tube feeds is available for hydration—that is, only 800 mL of 1000 mL of formula is available as water.

Fluids can be lost through urine, stools, tears, saliva, sweat, ulcers, fistula sites, and tracheostomies (Bliss & Lehmann 1999). Extra fluids might be needed in hot weather or when a person is suffering from a fever, diarrhoea, or urinary tract infection.

'An easy way to monitor hydration is by checking and recording the colour of the person's urine.'

People who are being fed formula with a high concentration (1.5–2 kcal/mL) are at greater risk of dehydration. Special care should also be taken with older people who have reduced renal function (Drickamer & Cooney 1993; Bockus 1993).

Tube-fed people who have reduced consciousness might not be able to monitor their own hydration or complain of thirst. These people are at particular risk of dehydration.

An easy way to monitor hydration is by checking and recording the colour of the person's urine. Urine is generally a pale-yellow colour in a well-hydrated person. It is useful to identify the person's normal urine colour so that any changes can be identified.

Some strategies to decrease the risk of dehydration are noted in the Box below.

> ## Strategies to reduce dehydration
>
> Some strategies to reduce the risk of dehydration include:
>
> - measuring fluid input and fluid output, and monitoring the fluid balance;
> - assessing any person who has a rapid weight loss to ensure that he or she is not dehydrated;
> - increasing the water flushes in hot weather, or if the person has a fever or urinary tract infection; and
> - providing extra fluids to patients who develop diarrhoea.

8. Leakage from the stoma

Some discharge from the stoma is normal, and leakage is unavoidable with coughing or turning. However, leakage of formulae or gastric contents from the stoma can cause skin excoriation and discomfort.

'Some discharge from the stoma is normal.'

A stoma might leak large amounts of feed if the stomach is too full. When a person is first commenced on gastrostomy feeds it is important to start slowly and use a pump or a slow drip rate. People with delayed gastric emptying also need to be fed slowly.

If leakage occurs even when feeds are administered slowly, it might be necessary to test gastric residuals. If a large residual volume remains even after decreasing the administration rate, medical review might be indicated. Medication to speed up gastric emptying might also be indicated.

Some strategies to reduce the risk of leakage are noted in the Box on page 191.

Strategies to reduce leakage

Some strategies to reduce the risk of leakage include:

- ensuring that the skin disc is 1–2 mm away from the abdomen;
- beginning new feeds slowly using a pump or slow drip rate;
- measuring gastric residuals and reviewing the volume of formula delivered;
- using an antacid agent to lower the pH of the gut to reduce skin excoriation;
- using antacids to reduce gastric secretions (Drickamer & Cooney 1993); and
- using an agent to speed up gastric emptying.

9. Diabetes management

Diabetes management is likely to require adjustment if a diabetic requires feeding through a gastrostomy tube.

Some feeding formulae are high in glucose—and extra doses of insulin or oral hypoglycaemic agents might therefore be needed to maintain an acceptable blood glucose range (4–8 mmol/L). If possible, formulae with a low glycaemic index should be chosen because they have less adverse effect on the blood glucose level. In addition, feeds with a *high* glycaemic index can predispose the person to osmotic diarrhoea and fluid loss—increasing the risk of hyperosmolar coma. Fluid intake should be adequate to avoid dehydration and hyperosmolar coma, especially in hot weather (Thomas 2001).

'If possible, formulae with a low glycaemic index should be chosen.'

If it is necessary to increase the strength of feeds, these should be increased gradually to avoid a sudden glucose load and consequent hyperglycaemia.

Administration times for insulin and oral hypoglycaemics might have to be altered for tube-fed people. This should be discussed with the person's doctor or diabetes educator. Consideration has to be given to the severity of:

- the person's diabetes;
- the type of feed; and
- the pharmacokinetics of the hypoglycaemic agents being administered.

To reduce the risk of hypoglycaemia, it might be necessary to give insulin and oral hypoglycaemics at a different time from the general drug administration times (Dunning 2003). Those who are malnourished—and therefore have limited glucose reserves in the liver and muscles—are particularly at risk of hypoglycaemia. People who are fasting (for example, before a new tube is inserted) are also at risk.

When gastrostomy feeding is first introduced, blood-glucose levels should be checked before the feed (fasting level) and two hours after the feed. Until the levels are stable, blood glucose should then be checked every four hours. Once blood-glucose levels are stable, testing once a day is usually sufficient. However, the frequency should be increased if:

- the feeding regimen changes in any way;
- the person needs to fast; or
- the person becomes ill.

Diabetic medication doses are adjusted according to the blood-glucose pattern.

Conclusion

Gastrostomy feeding is essential for some people to keep them adequately hydrated and well nourished. However, complications do occur, and they can cause significant discomfort and stress for carers and families.

This chapter has outlined some of the most common complications of gastrostomy feeding, and has provided advice on how to prevent, minimise, or treat them. With good carer training and expert care, most of these complications can be prevented or minimised. However, it is important to have the feeding regimen and progress of each person reviewed regularly and frequently by a doctor and dietitian.

Chapter 11

Changing a Gastrostomy Tube

Catherine Barrett

Introduction

The range of gastrostomy tubes on the market continues to increase. Tubes vary in size, shape, length, outlet, skin disc, internal bumper, life expectancy, and cost.

It is important to be aware of the different types of tube to ensure that tubes are selected to meet individual needs and to ensure that the appropriate method of tube change is used. Using an incorrect technique to remove a gastrostomy tube can mean that the attempt to change the tube fails. It can also cause injury to the person.

Types of tubes

It is important that health professionals understand the differences among various types of gastrostomy tubes. With this information health professionals are enabled to:

- select the most appropriate tube for each person;
- prepare for tube change in an appropriate fashion; and
- maximise the safety of the person.

Framework of the chapter

This chapter is arranged as follows:

As shown in Figure 11.1 (page 195), gastrostomy tubes can be divided into two general categories—long tubes and short tubes. *Long tubes* protrude from the stomach by approximately 20 cm (or more in some cases). *Short tubes*, which are also known as 'low-profile devices', sit flat against the person's abdomen.

Within these two categories, subcategories can be defined according to the style of inner bumper and the procedure for removal.

Subcategories of *long tubes* include endoscopic-removal tubes and nonendoscopic-removal tubes. Nonendoscopic-removal tubes are further categorised according to whether the internal bumper is a balloon or a soft disc (which inverts on traction).

Subcategories of *short tubes* are defined according to whether or not they require an obturator for insertion and removal.

Within each of the categories presented in Figure 11.1, further differences can exist—depending on the brand or the manufacturer.

General principles of tube change

The procedure for a tube change varies according to:

- the type of tube being changed;
- the person's needs; and
- the policy of each facility.

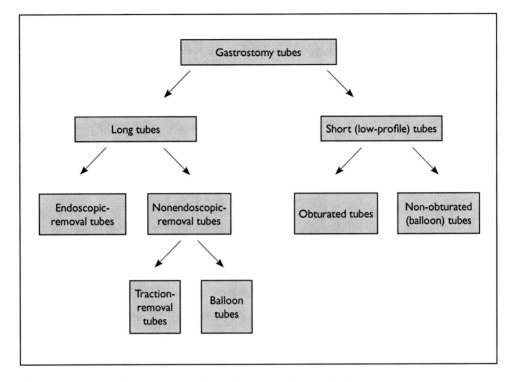

Figure 11.1 Major categories of gastrostomy tubes
AUTHOR'S PRESENTATION

However, even allowing for specific circumstances, there are several general factors to be considered in undertaking tube change. These include:

- the skills required;
- preparation;
- comprehensive records;
- timeliness of tube replacement; and
- gastrostomy tract maturity.

Each of these is discussed below.

Skills required

Some tubes (such as endoscopic-removal tubes) need to be changed by a gastroenterologist. Other tubes (such as long balloon tubes) can be changed by a registered nurse—depending on the nurse's training and skill. However, to ensure patient safety, training must be updated and competencies must be assessed. This is especially important for facilities in which there are limited opportunities to develop practical skills and maintain competency. Many companies that manufacture gastrostomy tubes have staff members who will provide training.

'To ensure patient safety, training must be updated and competencies must be assessed.'

Some residential aged-care facilities do not have staff members with sufficient skills to change gastrostomy tubes. These facilities usually transfer residents to an acute-care hospital to have their tubes changed. Alternatively, some hospitals provide specially trained staff members who visit residential aged-care facilities to change gastrostomy tubes.

Health professionals should not change a gastrostomy tube unless they are qualified and trained to do so. It is important that health professionals make themselves aware of the resources available in their local areas to enable gastrostomy tubes to be changed with minimal inconvenience to a person with a tube.

'Health professionals should not change a gastrostomy tube unless they are qualified and trained to do so.'

General principles of tube change

This portion of the chapter discusses the general principles of tube change. The text discusses the following:

- skills required;
- preparation;
- comprehensive records;
- timeliness of tube replacement; and
- gastrostomy tract maturity.

Preparation

Preparation for a possible tube change should begin as soon as a person with a tube is admitted. It is important to determine who is able to replace a tube, and to provide any training required. It is also important to ensure that a replacement tube is available in case it is required unexpectedly— for example, if a tube is dislodged accidentally.

Before beginning a tube change, the following matters require attention:

- ensuring that the type, brand, and size of the existing tube is known;
- checking that the balloon functions before inserting a balloon tube;
- ensuring that analgesia has been considered;
- ensuring that the tract is mature (see 'Gastrostomy tract maturity', page 200);
- using standard precautions (hand-washing, gloves, safety glasses);
- ensuring that the person has fasted;
- explaining the procedure to the person; and
- inviting the person to have a support person or family member present.

Comprehensive records

It is important to maintain a comprehensive record of gastrostomy tube changes. When a tube is accidentally displaced it can be difficult to identify the tube type, brand, and size. Although many tubes have this information printed on the side of the tube, this wording often wears off—and it can be difficult to search for the information in volumes of personal medical files.

'It is important to maintain a comprehensive record of gastrostomy tube changes.'

To minimise inconvenience, it is helpful to keep this information in a central record. A proforma for recording this information is presented in Figure 11.2 (page 198). Some health professionals also attach a copy of the information from the tube package to this proforma.

| RECORD OF GASTROSTOMY TUBE CHANGE | NAME: |
| | ID: |

Initial tube inserted (record type, brand, size)

Instructions for changing tube

Recommended frequency of change

Details of tube changes

Date	Tube details				Comment	Signature
	Type	Brand	Size	Balloon volume		

Figure 11.2 Record of gastrostomy tube change
AUTHOR'S PRESENTATION

Timeliness of tube replacement

Gastrostomy stomas without a tube remain patent for a variable length of time. This depends on the individual and the maturity of the stoma.

Tubes are often displaced for some time before this is noticed. This can compromise stomal patency quite quickly. In some people, even those with a mature stoma, it can be impossible to reinsert a tube as soon as two hours later. It is therefore important to insert a new tube as quickly as possible. The case study on page 200 highlights the difficulties that can be experienced if a tube is not replaced immediately.

> '*It is important to insert a new tube as quickly as possible.*'

If there is no replacement tube available, a urinary catheter can sometimes be used to maintain stomal patency. However, the use of urinary catheters for tube feeding is contentious. The use of urinary catheters has been associated with:

- tube migration and bowel obstruction (O'Dell, Gordon & Becker 1991; O'Keefe, Dula & Varano 1990; Pereira & Mersich 1991);
- disintegration of latex catheters;
- spilling of gastric contents (due to lack of appropriate external clamp); and
- accidental disconnection of feeding sets (due to poor fit between catheter and feeding set).

However, another study produced more favourable results. The study compared the efficacy and safety of silicone urinary catheters with tubes manufactured specifically for gastrostomy tube feeding (Kadakia, Cassaday & Shaffer 1994). The urinary catheters were fitted with a skin disc and a plastic ring to prevent migration. The study found that there were no significant differences with respect to need for replacement, and that tube migration was not a problem.

The initial outlay for a urinary catheter is minimal. However, despite the more positive study on complications noted above, the cost in terms of potential harm to the person might still be significant. Consequently, the use of a urinary catheter as a replacement for a gastrostomy tube cannot be recommended.

Mary

Mary was a 57-year-old woman with multiple sclerosis who had had a gastrostomy tube inserted to supplement her oral intake. As staff members assisted Mary to her bed for her afternoon nap, they noticed that her 20-Fr. balloon tube had fallen out. The balloon appeared to have spontaneously ruptured. It was impossible to be sure how long the tube had been out, but it might have been several hours.

Immediate attempts to reinsert a 20-Fr. tube were unsuccessful. Mary was in discomfort and was very anxious—especially about the prospect of having another gastroscopy to insert a new tube. Each time that tube insertion was attempted, Mary became very tense and experienced muscle spasms.

After discussion with Mary's doctor, analgesia and a small dose of a muscle relaxant were administered. Thirty minutes later, reinsertion with a smaller (18-Fr.) tube was successful.

Gastrostomy tract maturity

Gastrostomy tract maturity is a very important consideration in tube replacement. During the initial period after tube insertion the anterior part of the stomach is held in position against the anterior abdominal wall by the tension between the internal bumper and the skin disc. This assists the fistula tract to mature as adhesions form between the stomach and abdominal wall.

'No attempt should be made to reinsert a gastrostomy tube in the initial 2–4 weeks after insertion, until the tract has matured.'

Attempts to reinsert a gastrotomy tube before the tract is mature can result in the tube being inadvertently inserted into the peritoneal cavity. The person can then develop peritonitis when tube feeding is commenced. Consequently, no attempt should be made to reinsert a gastrostomy tube in the initial 2–4 weeks after insertion, until the tract has matured.

Recommendations for the management of accidental tube removal in an immature tract include the following (Marshall & Barthel 1994):

- Assume that a minimum of 2–4 weeks (after the initial gastrostomy) is required for fistula integrity to have been established.
- X-ray the person if tube placement is questioned.
- Tube replacement in an immature tract should be performed by a gastroenterologist.
- If a tube is accidentally removed, and a gastroenterologist is not available to attempt replacement, allow 7–10 days for stoma to close, provide nasogastric suction for 48 hours, administer IV antibiotics, and observe vital signs.

Replacement of long tubes

The initial gastrostomy tube is a long tube (see Figure 11.1, page 195). The tube length allows for ease of access by health professionals in connecting tube feeds. Long tubes vary, but they have a similar external appearance. They typically have an internal bumper, an external skin disc, and a long length of tubing. The skin disc is usually adjustable to enable cleaning and alteration as the person gains or loses weight. Figure 11.3 (below) illustrates an example of a long tube.

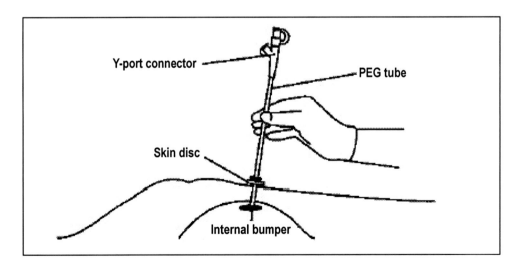

Figure 11.3 Example of a long tube: Abbott Durapeg® tube
REPRODUCED WITH PERMISSION OF ABBOTT AUSTRALASIA PTY LTD

All long tubes have a Y-port connector. In a balloon tube, the Y-port connector is manufactured as part of the tube, and is fixed. In contrast, tubes inserted via endoscopy have their Y-port connector attached after tube insertion (to allow passage of the tube down the endoscope). In these tubes, the Y-port connector is detachable and can be replaced if the seal loosens.

Although long tubes have a fairly similar external appearance, they have different internal bumpers. The differences in internal bumpers correspond with different uses and procedures for tube change. These differences are discussed in more detail below.

Non-endoscopic removal tubes

Balloon gastrostomy tubes

A balloon gastrostomy tube has a balloon inflated with water that acts as an internal bumper. It is usually used as a replacement tube—after the initial PEG tube has been removed. Balloon tubes are usually made from silicone and have an adjustable skin disc.

An example of a balloon gastrostomy tube is shown in Figure 11.4 (page 203). This tube comes in various sizes (16 Fr., 19 Fr., and 20 Fr.), and usually lasts about six months. Other features of this tube include:

- round tip for easier insertion;
- centimetre graduations to monitor tube migration;
- port for balloon inflation (which indicates tube size and balloon volume); and
- separate port for medication administration.

The importance of choosing the correct long tube for a person's needs is illustrated in the case study on page 203.

Changing balloon gastrostomy tubes

Procedures for the removal of a balloon tube vary—depending on the person's needs and the facility's policy. General procedures for removal might include the following.

- Explain the procedure to the person and his or her family.
- Ask person to lie flat on his or her back.

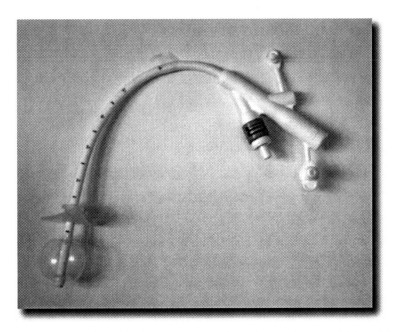

Figure 11.4 Example of a balloon gastrostomy tube: Abbott Flexi-Flo® tube

REPRODUCED WITH PERMISSION OF ABBOTT AUSTRALASIA PTY LTD

Meredith

Meredith was a 42-year-old woman who had had a traction-removal tube inserted after a severe stroke. Two years after the initial tube had been inserted it began to block frequently. It was replaced with a long balloon tube.

Three months later, Meredith had a small 'coffee-grounds' vomit. Although there was no significant blood loss, Meredith and her family consented to a gastroscopy to identify the cause of the bleeding. Identification of the cause was urgent because Meredith was a Jehovah's Witness and did not want to receive a blood transfusion if she had a significant haemorrhage.

The gastroscopy revealed a small area of gastric erosion opposite the tip of the balloon tube. It was concluded that the tip of the tube had irritated her stomach lining, thus causing some bleeding. The tube was replaced with a traction-removal tube. No further bleeding occurred.

- Deflate the gastrostomy tube balloon.
- Use anaesthetic gel around the stoma (if required).
- Rotate tube 360 degrees to ensure that there is no adherence.
- Move tube slightly in and out.
- Gently support abdomen around stoma with a flat hand.
- Gently and slowly remove the tube.
- If resistance is felt, stop the procedure and seek medical advice.
- If the person is experiencing pain, stop the procedure and seek medical advice.

Difficulty in balloon deflation can indicate yeast formation in the balloon lumen (Hall, Brennan & Heximer 1996). If this occurs, it can be helpful to attach a syringe (without the plunger) to the valve outlet. This can be left to drain, or 1 mL of water can be syringed down the balloon lumen to dislodge the blockage (Hall, Brennan & Heximer 1996).

The internal portion of the old tube is often discoloured from gastric secretions. This discolouration, and the normal position of the skin disc, are used to measure the length required when inserting a new tube. After the length has been measured, and the tip of the new catheter has been lubricated, the new tube is inserted.

The procedure for insertion of an Abbott Flexiflo® gastrostomy tube is shown in Figure 11.5 (page 205).

Traction-removal tubes

A traction-removal tube is usually inserted as an initial tube via endoscopy. Its external appearance is often the same as an endoscopic-removal tube, but it has a different internal bumper. Upon traction, the internal bumper on a traction-removal tube inverts, or elongates, to allow for removal. Removal takes some force, but people have been known to remove their own tubes.

An example of a traction-removal tube is shown in Figure 11.6 (page 206). In this photograph, the soft round bumper can be seen. The tube comes in a 20-Fr. size and lasts up to 18 months. It has a Y-port connector and an adjustable, triangular skin disc with air holes.

Step 1: Slide skin disc up towards Y-port connector and gently insert tube through stoma into stomach.

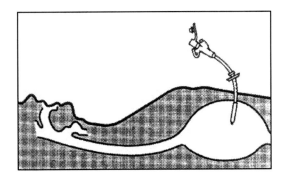

Step 2: Fill balloon with sterile water to volume indicated. Then withdraw tube slightly until balloon is seated gently against gastric mucosa.

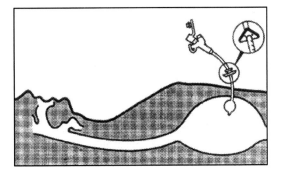

Step 3: Slide skin disc down gently against abdominal wall.

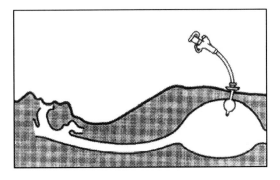

Figure 11.5 Insertion of an Abbott Flexiflo® gastrostomy tube

REPRODUCED WITH PERMISSION OF ABBOTT AUSTRALASIA PTY LTD

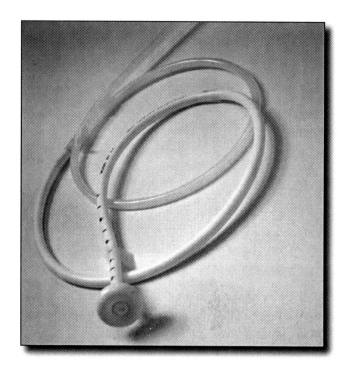

**Figure 11.6 Example of a traction-removal tube: Abbott Flexi-Flo®
Inverta PEG**
REPRODUCED WITH PERMISSION OF ABBOTT AUSTRALASIA PTY LTD

Changing traction-removal tubes

A traction-removal tube is usually changed by a gastroenterologist at the
person's bedside. Alternatively, it can be changed in a day-procedures unit
under light sedation. The person can experience some pain or discomfort,
and analgesia might be required.

The inversion action of a traction-removal tube is shown in Figure
11.7 (page 207).

The change process for a traction-removal tube consists of the
following steps (Abbott 2002).

- Prepare the person.
- Rotate the tube 360 degrees and move in and out slightly. Do not
  remove tube if does not move freely.

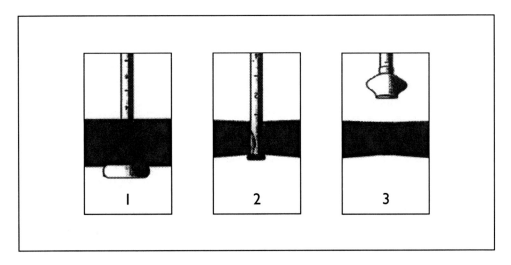

Figure 11.7 Inversion action of a traction-removal tube (Abbott Inverta-PEG® tube)

REPRODUCED WITH PERMISSION OF ABBOTT AUSTRALASIA PTY LTD

- Anaesthetise the stoma (if desired) by applying anaesthetic gel to the base of the tube. Work gel into the stoma by moving the tube slightly.
- Wrap towel around base of tube to absorb any spills.
- Put on gloves. Grasp the tube close to the stoma with one hand. Use other hand against the person's abdomen.
- With tube positioned between thumb and first finger, apply gentle counter-pressure.
- Apply slow, deliberate traction to remove the tube. Avoid sudden pulls.
- If tube cannot be removed, use endoscopy.
- Insert new tube.
- Never cut the tube and allow to pass in the faeces.

Endoscopic-removal tubes

The initial PEG tube is usually an endoscopic-removal tube. It is designed for long-term use, and is inserted and removed via endoscopy.

Such tubes are made from silicone, have an adjustable skin disc, and are fitted with a Y-port connector. An example of an endoscopic removal tube is shown in Figure 11.8 (below). The tube comes in 20 Fr. and has a life-expectancy of up to five years. The rigid, reinforced, webbed internal bumper reduces the risk of accidental removal. This is a consideration for people who are likely to pull at the tube.

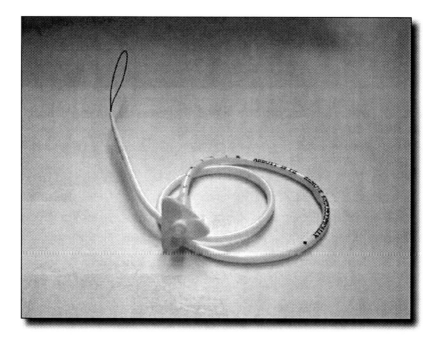

Figure 11.8 Example of an endoscopic-removal tube: Abbott Durapeg® tube
REPRODUCED WITH PERMISSION OF ABBOTT AUSTRALASIA PTY LTD

Changing endoscopic-removal tubes

As the name suggests, endoscopic-removal tubes should always be removed by endoscopy. This would appear to be self-evident, but the case study on page 209 highlights the importance of health professionals' being aware of the appropriate technique for removal of all tubes.

Malcolm

Malcolm had had an endoscopic-removal tube inserted more than two years ago. Malcolm's carers felt the tube now needed to be replaced because it was distorted and blocked frequently.

The tube was changed by cutting the existing tube off at skin level and using the replacement tube to push the remaining portion of the old tube into Malcolm's stomach.

This technique is *not* recommended. It has been known to cause intestinal obstruction as a result of the rigid internal bumper lodging in the intestine.

Malcolm was not adversely affected. However, the incident provided a timely warning to his carers. Training was provided to ensure that every health professional understood the different types of tubes and the appropriate procedure for tube change.

All health professionals have a responsibility to ensure that their own practice is safe. In addition, they must be prepared to act as advocates for those in their care by questioning the practice of others if they are unhappy with any proposed procedure.

Summary of long tubes

Table 11.1 (page 210) presents a summary of the characteristics of long tubes. The table provides a guide to their uses, insertion, and removal.

Replacement of short tubes

Short tubes (see Figure 11.1, page 195) are often referred to as 'low-profile gastrostomy devices' (LPGDs). The first LPGD was developed in the mid 1980s (Kaufman, Faller & Lawrence 1995). LPGDs have a short tube length and a discreet skin disc—which enable the tube to sit discreetly against the person's abdomen, hidden under clothing. Because of their short length, LPGDs come with an anti-reflux valve to prevent leakage. They also have connection tubing (including a right-angled adapter) for venting and feeding.

Table 11.1 Gastrostomy long tubes

AUTHOR'S PRESENTATION

	Balloon tube	Traction-removal tube	Endoscopic-removal tube
Use	replacement tube	initial PEG tube	initial PEG tube (for people likely to try to remove tube)
Insertion	at bedside	endoscopy	endoscopy
Removal	balloon deflation	traction removal	endoscopy
Made from	silicone	silicone	silicone
Skin disc	adjustable	adjustable	adjustable
Internal bumper	balloon	roll-tip bumper	rigid webbed bumper
Approx. life-expectancy	6 months	18 months	5 years
Port	fixed Y-port connector	detachable Y-port connector	detachable Y-port connector
Size	16, 18 and 20 Fr.	20 Fr.	20 Fr.
Example	Abbott Hexi-Flo® tube	Abbott Hexi-Flo® Inverta PEG	Abbott Durapeg®

An LPGD can be inserted only into a well-developed tract between the skin and the stomach. The length of time required for the tract to heal varies among individuals, but it can take three months or more (Faller & Lawrence 1993). The tract can take longer to heal in certain individuals. These include people who (Kaufman, Faller & Lawrence 1995):

- have compromised nutritional status;
- have taken long-term steroids;
- are on chemotherapy; or
- have a thicker abdominal wall.

LPGDs have several advantages and disadvantages as compared with long tubes. These are listed in the Box on page 211.

Advantages and disadvantages of LPGDs

Advantages of LPGDs

Advantages of LPGDs include the following.

- The tube can be concealed.
- There is minimal alteration to body image and minimal negative effect on self-esteem.
- They are convenient for people who are active.
- They are less distressing for confused people, and less likely to be pulled out by agitated people.

Disadvantages of LPGDs

There are also disadvantages in using LPGDs. These include the following.

- A mature tract is needed.
- The tube's dimensions must be matched with stoma length and width.
- The size is fixed (which cannot be adjusted if the person's size changes).
- They have a fixed skin disc (which cannot be moved for cleaning).
- There might be increased risk of skin ulceration (due to the fixed skin disc).

Weight gain can cause the internal bumper of an LPGD to become embedded in the gastric mucosa (Faller & Lawrence 1993). The first signs of this might be a tight skin disc and difficulty in rotating the tube. To avoid the internal bumper becoming embedded, the LPGD is usually sized a little larger than needed—especially if the person is expected to gain weight (Faller & Lawrence 1993).

The two main types of LPGDs are obturated tubes and non-obturated tubes (see Figure 11.1, page 195). These are described below.

Obturated low-profile devices

The internal bumper of obturated tubes is an enlarged dome tip that acts as an internal stabiliser (Kaufman, Faller & Lawrence 1995). The tip is stretched with a special introducer—or *obturator*—to enable insertion and removal (Faller & Lawrence 1993).

The size of the internal bumper means that accidental removal is unlikely. These tubes are therefore used for people who might pull at the tube or try to remove it. The tube is made from silicone and has a fixed, oblong-shaped skin disc.

'Obturated LPGDs are used for people who might pull at the tube or try to remove it.'

An example of an obturated LPGD is shown in Figure 11.9 (below). This tube has a life-expectancy of about two years. It comes in an 18 Fr. or 20 Fr. size, and has three shaft lengths (the length between the internal bumper and the skin disc) for each size. This allows for an appropriate match to be made with the person's size.

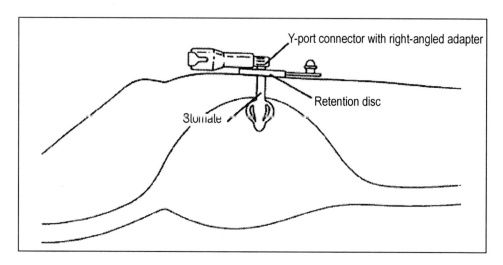

Y-port connector with right-angled adapter

Retention disc

Stomate

Figure 11.9 An example of an obturated LPGD: Abbott Flexi-Flo Stomate® tube

REPRODUCED WITH PERMISSION OF ABBOTT AUSTRALASIA PTY LTD

Changing obturated tubes

Obturated tubes are usually inserted and removed by stretching the internal bumper and elongating it sufficiently to allow it to be passed through the gastrostomy stoma. Because this process requires a degree of force, it must be performed by an appropriately trained health professional (Faller & Lawrence 1993; Kaufman, Faller & Lawrence 1995). In addition, the stoma must be measured to ensure that the replacement tube is of the correct size. This also requires specialist training.

Analgesia and sedation might be required because passing the tube through the muscle layers can be painful (Faller, Lawrence & Ferraro 1993).

Once the existing tube has been removed, the stoma is measured. The new tube is then inserted. Figure 11.10 (page 214) illustrates the process of inserting an obturated tube.

Non-obturated low-profile devices

A non-obturated LPGD does not require an obturator for insertion or removal. Non-obturated tubes usually have an internal balloon and do not require force for insertion (Kaufman, Faller & Lawrence 1995).

These tubes have a similar internal structure to long balloon tubes. They are used for people who are likely to benefit from a short tube and who are unlikely to try to remove the tube.

An example of a non-obturated LPGD is shown in Figure 11.11 (page 215). This tube is made of silicone and has a fixed, oblong-shaped skin disc. This tube comes in sizes 14 Fr., 16 Fr., 18 Fr., 20 Fr., and 24 Fr. The tube lasts about 6–12 months.

Changing non-obturated tubes

The process for changing a non-obturated LPGD is similar to that of a long balloon tube—that is, the balloon is deflated for removal. However, with an LPGD, it is important to ensure the correct sizing for the new tube—especially if the person has gained weight and the skin disc in now tight.

It is therefore preferable to have this tube changed by a gastroenterologist to ensure that the stoma length can be measured and that the new tube is the most appropriate size for the person's needs.

1. Insert balloon end of stoma-measuring device through stoma into stomach. Draw 3 mL of air into syringe and attach to stoma-measuring device.

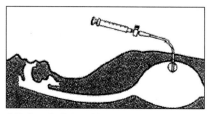

2. Inflate balloon. Close stopcock. Pull up on stoma-measuring device until balloon is seated gently against stomach wall.

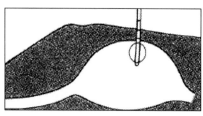

3. Note number of circumferential marks visible above skin to determine which length feeding device is needed. Open stopcock to deflate balloon. Withdraw stoma-measuring device.

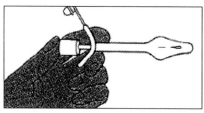

4. Place obturator into feeding device and elongate, pushing obturator down until disc back meets base of obturator.

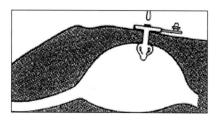

5. Insert elongated feeding device into stoma until disc reaches skin level. Withdraw obturator.

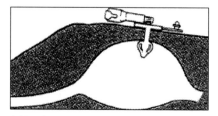

6. For feeding, attach Flexi-Flo Y-port connector with right-angle adapter and commence.

Figure 11.10 Insertion of an obturated tube: Abbott Flexi-Flo Stomate® tube

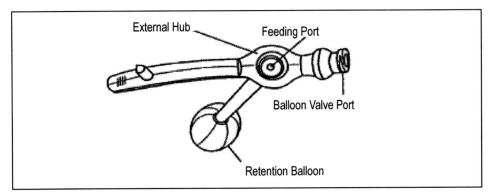

Figure 11.11 Example of a non-obturated low-profile balloon device: Abbott Hide-a-Port®
REPRODUCED WITH PERMISSION OF ABBOTT AUSTRALASIA PTY LTD

Summary of short tubes

Table 11.2 (below) presents a summary of the characteristics of short tubes. The table provides a guide to their uses, insertion, and removal.

Table 11.2 Gastrostomy short tubes
AUTHOR'S PRESENTATION

	Obturated tubes	**Non-obturated tubes**
Use	discreet replacement tubes (for people likely to try to remove tube)	discreet replacement tubes
Insertion	obturator	at bedside
Removal	obturator	balloon deflation
Made from	silicone	silicone
Skin disc	fixed	fixed
Internal bumper	soft dome (elongates when obturator used)	balloon
Approx. life-expectancy	2 years	6–12 months
Port	Y-port connector with right-angle adapter	Y-port connector with right-angle adapter
Size	18 Fr. (2.0/2.8/4.3 cm shaft) and 22 Fr. (1.7/2.8/4.3 cm shaft)	14, 16, 18, 20 and 24 Fr.
Example	Abbott Flexi-Flo Stomate® tube	Abbott Hide-a-Port® tube

Conclusion

This chapter has outlined some of the major categories of gastrostomy tubes and the procedures for changing them. Because of their individual characteristics, different tubes require different procedures for change.

The tubes described and illustrated here do not constitute an exhaustive list. But they are a representative sample of the options available. As the range of tubes continues to expand, it is important that health professionals keep abreast of the options available. This ensures that people with gastrostomy tubes have the best tube to meet their needs, that their care is appropriate, and that their safety is maximised.

'This ensures that people with gastrostomy tubes have the best tube to meet their needs, that their care is appropriate, and that their safety is maximised.'

Chapter 12
Selecting and Administering Medications

Jan Iskander

Introduction

Most people with a gastrostomy tube require medication at some time. For many people, medication is required on a regular basis, and health professionals and carers must therefore be aware of the potential problems that can be encountered and how to avoid such problems.

> 'Crushing tablets and removing the coating can alter the action of the drug and can place the person at risk of an adverse drug reaction.'

Crushing a tablet or removing the gelatine coating from a capsule might seem to be the easiest and most obvious way to administer a drug via a tube, but this is not appropriate for some drugs. Crushing tablets and removing the coating can alter the action of the drug and can place the person at risk of an adverse drug reaction.

It is also important to consider whether the medication is compatible with the nutrient formula and with other medications that might be administered at the same time.

Finally, it is important to ensure that the tube remains patent—to ensure that adequate nutritional support is maintained at all times.

Framework of the chapter

This chapter discusses various issues relating to the selection and administration of medications in tube-fed people. The chapter considers the following issues:

- dose form (page 218);
- alternative forms (page 221);
- drug–feed compatibility (page 223);
- drug–drug interactions (page 225); and
- tube patency (page 226).

Dose form

Preferred dose forms

The preferred dose forms for tube-fed people are syrups, suspensions, elixirs, mixtures, and effervescent tablets. These dose forms are preferred because:

- they can be given via the tube without being modified;
- there is minimal risk of the tube becoming blocked; and
- data are available to show that the products are stable and effective when given in this manner.

'It is always best to administer medications in the form supplied by the manufacturer.'

In most instances, data are not available about the effects of altering the dose form from the manufacturer's original presentation (for example, by crushing a tablet). It is therefore always best to administer medications in the form supplied by the manufacturer. Pharmaceutical manufacturers advise on the stability of the product and its absorption characteristics on the basis of tests carried out in the manufacturer's laboratory, and these characteristics cannot be guaranteed if the dose form of the product is altered before administration.

If the required medication is not available as a syrup, suspension, elixir, or liquid, it is important to ensure that modifying the available commercial product does not alter the potential clinical outcome for the person.

Capsules

Hard gelatine capsules

The contents of many hard gelatine capsules can be removed from the coating, mixed with water, and given via the tube. However, there are problems with this approach. If the pellets inside the capsule are 'enteric coated', crushing will damage the protective coating and render the drug ineffective when it reaches the stomach. (For more on enteric-coated medications, see 'Enteric-coated tablets', page 220.)

Soft gelatine capsules

Soft gelatine capsules are usually filled with liquid. These capsules can be pierced and the oily contents squeezed out. However, the total dose will not be delivered using this method, and it is therefore suitable only when the dose is not critical (McPherson 1994; Mitchell 1996). A more accurate method of administering the medication is to dissolve the soft gelatine capsule in warm water and give it as a solution.

Tablets

Uncoated, film-coated, and sugar-coated tablets

Uncoated tablets can usually be crushed. In addition, crushing film-coated and sugar-coated tablets is usually acceptable because these coatings do not affect the action of the drug. These coatings are designed only to improve the appearance of the medication or to mask an unpleasant taste.

Slow-release tablets

In contrast to uncoated, film-coated, and sugar-coated tablets, slow-release tablets should not be crushed. Such specialised forms of delivering medications are usually designed to enhance compliance—for example, slow-release forms that can be taken once a day instead of several times per day. If such a slow-release medication is crushed, the person receives the total dose immediately, rather than over an extended time as expected. This can result in an initial exaggerated clinical response followed by a loss of response for a large part of the dosing interval. For example, crushing an extended-release antihypertensive drug can cause an immediate and significant drop in blood pressure, followed by inadequate blood pressure control for the remainder of the dosing period.

'If a slow-release medication is crushed, the person receives the total dose immediately, rather than over an extended time as expected.'

Some drugs are presented as slow-release formulations to reduce side-effects (for example, potassium chloride slow-release tablets). If these tablets are crushed before administration, the person is at risk of experiencing unpleasant and potentially dangerous side-effects.

'Enteric-coated' tablets

Some medications have a protective 'enteric coating.' These coatings have two purposes:

- to protect the drug from exposure to gastric secretions; or
- to protect the person from the irritant effects of the drug on the stomach.

In the first case, the 'enteric coating' is designed to allow the drug to pass through the stomach without being destroyed by acidic gastric secretions. If such tablets are crushed, the drug is exposed to gastric secretions and can be rendered ineffective.

In the second case, 'enteric coatings' are used to protect the stomach from the irritant effect of some drugs (for example, aspirin). Crushing these products can increase the risk of gastric irritation and erosion.

Scored tablets

It is sometimes believed that scored tablets (a tablet with an indentation to make it easier to break) can be crushed. However, scoring does not necessarily mean that a tablet can be crushed. For example, although some slow-release tablets are designed to be cut across the centre, crushing can destroy the slow-release mechanism. Crushing such tablets can produce the same problems discussed above.

Sublingual tablets

Sublingual tablets (and sprays) can usually be used as intended. When administering a sublingual preparation it is important to ensure that the oral mucosa is moist because this encourages drug absorption.

Sublingual tablets are ineffective if swallowed and therefore should not be administered via a gastrostomy tube.

Cytotoxic, carcinogenic, and teratogenic drugs

Cytotoxic, carcinogenic, and teratogenic drugs should not be crushed because inhalation of any airborne powder might expose carers to unintended risks.

Alternative forms

If there is any doubt about the suitability of medication for administration via a gastrostomy tube, advice should always be sought from a pharmacist. In particular, pharmaceutical advice should always be sought:

- when a gastrostomy tube is first inserted; and
- if there is any change in a tube-fed person's medication regimen.

In both cases, the pharmacist can advise on the appropriate form of medication to be administered via the tube.

Carers should always make specific enquiries from their pharmacist before crushing any new medication. If possible, a liquid or effervescent formulation of the drug should be used instead. However, it should be noted that effervescent tablets usually have

'Pharmaceutical advice should always be sought when a gastrostomy tube is first inserted and if there is any change in a tube-fed person's medication regimen.'

a high sodium content and are not always suitable for people who have hypertension. In these cases, unmodified forms of medications can be used more frequently, or another route can be used. In summary, the following alternatives can be considered by the pharmacist:

- liquid and effervescent forms;
- unmodified forms administered more frequently; and
- using another route.

The Box below provides examples of appropriate substitutions.

Alternative forms of administration

Use liquid and effervescent forms

Examples of liquid and effervescent forms that might be suitable as replacements for other forms include the following:

- sodium valproate liquid (rather than sodium valproate 'enteric-coated' tablets);
- ferrous gluconate syrup (rather than ferrous sulphate slow-release tablets); and
- ranitidine effervescent tablets (rather than standard ranitidine tablets).

Administer unmodified forms more frequently

Because effervescent forms are unsuitable for some people (for example, those with hypertension), it might be possible to crush unmodified-release tablets and administer these more frequently. Examples include:

- diltiazem 60 mg tablets crushed and given three times a day (rather than using 180 mg slow-release tablets once a day); and
- verapamil 40 mg tablets crushed and given four times a day (rather than verapamil 160 mg slow-release tablets once a day).

Use another route

Another alternative is to give a drug by a different route. For example:

- glyceryl trinitrate can be given transdermally (by a patch) rather than by using slow-release oral nitrates; and
- prochlorperazine can be administered by suppositories (rather than tablets).

It is sometimes possible to use a different crushable drug with the same class action. For example, the calcium-channel blocker felodipine is currently marketed only as a slow-release preparation and is therefore unsuitable for crushing. Amlodipine, which can be crushed, has a similar pharmacological profile, and this might be a suitable alternative for some people.

Drug–feed compatibility

Limited data

There are limited data on the physical and chemical compatibility of most drugs with tube formulae. Most of the published data describe single case-study reports in which health professionals have observed a discrepancy between expected outcomes and actual outcomes.

This area is further complicated because of the broad range of tube formulae. The proportions and amounts of nutritional components in these various feeds differ widely.

Despite these difficulties, it can be assumed that any drug known to interact with food is also likely to interact with tube-feeding formulae. For example, a manufacturer's recommendation that an oral drug be given 30 minutes before food (because the presence of food in the stomach reduces drug absorption) indicates that drug absorption will also be adversely affected by the presence of formula in the stomach. Examples of such drugs include erythromycin and some penicillins. These drugs should not be given via the tube while feeding formula remains in the tube or in the stomach. Feeding should cease 30 minutes before giving such drugs, and feeding should not be recommenced for a further 30 minutes after administration.

Some known interactions

Despite the overall lack of data, incompatibility between drugs and tube formulae has been reported with certain drugs. These include:

- phenytoin (see page 224);
- warfarin (see page 225);

- theophylline;
- iron;
- methyldopa;
- sucralfate;
- norfloxacin and ciprofloxacin; and
- aluminium-containing antacids.

'No medication should ever be added directly to a tube-feeding formula—regardless of whether there is a known interaction.'

This list is by no means exhaustive, and the fact that a drug is not listed does not necessarily mean that it is compatible with all tube-feeding formulae. It is more likely to mean that possible interactions have not been investigated (Gilbar & Kam 1997).

Administration of these named drugs should be separated from feeding by two hours. The best advice is that no medication should ever be added directly to a tube-feeding formula—regardless of whether there is a known interaction.

Protein bound drugs

Phenytoin

Serum phenytoin levels are reduced by 70–80% when the drug is given with certain formulae (Bauer 1982).

It is thought that the reduced bioavailability of highly protein-bound drugs (such as phenytoin) occurs because the drug binds to the casein proteins in the formulae, thus reducing the amount of free phenytoin in the blood stream. The effect of high acidity in the gut associated with tube formulae could also reduce serum drug levels. Finally, it has also been suggested that phenytoin might bind to nasogastric tubing.

To minimise these effects, phenytoin should be given once a day, and feeding should be ceased two hours before administering the drug. Feeding should not be recommenced until two hours after the drug has been administered. If adherence to tubing is suspected as the cause of reduced drug levels, a different type of tubing should be considered.

It might be necessary to estimate serum drug levels more frequently to ensure that phenytoin levels remain within the therapeutic range.

Warfarin

Warfarin is another highly protein-bound drug that has been shown to interact with tube feeds. The interaction might be due to warfarin binding to the soy protein or the casein in the formulae.

Warfarin is a vitamin K antagonist and the high concentrations of this vitamin in certain tube feeds might have been the cause of reported warfarin resistance before 1980. The vitamin K content of formulae is now lower, but it is advisable to check the vitamin K content of all tube feeds before use. In general, formulae based on soy should be avoided in persons taking warfarin because these feeds usually have higher levels of vitamin K.

'Feeds based on soy should be avoided in persons taking warfarin because these feeds usually have higher levels of vitamin K.'

Tube-fed people taking warfarin will require more frequent monitoring of their international normalised ratio (INR). Particular attention should be given to monitoring the INR if the tube-feed formulation is changed or if oral feeding resumes.

Any change in the brand of the formula should alert staff to the possibility of altered bioavailability of phenytoin, warfarin, and other protein-bound drugs. Increased monitoring and vigilance are necessary to monitor for signs of toxicity or lack of efficacy. Good documentation is essential to ensure that any change in the person's clinical status is associated with changes in the tube-feeding regimen.

Drug–drug interactions

It should never be assumed that drugs are physically and chemically stable when mixed together, and the possibility of a chemical reaction should always be considered if two or more medications are administered at the same time.

Chemical interactions between drugs can be avoided if medications are always given individually—separated by a flush of water.

The Box below reports one such interaction.

A drug–drug interaction

An example of a drug–drug interaction is that between carbamazepine suspension and chlorpromazine solution.

A person who received this combination of drugs (orally) was reported as passing an orange rubbery mass in his stools the following day. Later laboratory testing confirmed a physical reaction between these two drugs.

Carbamazepine suspension should therefore be given separately from any other medication (ISMP 1998).

Tube patency

All tube-feeding formulae are suspensions and are therefore prone to settling. This can cause a blockage in any horizontal section of a gastrostomy tube. Because the bore of a nasogastric tube is finer than that of a gastrostomy tube, particular care is required with these tubes. Clogging seems to be a greater problem with silicone tubes than with polyurethane tubes.

Preventing blockages and unblocking tubes

Cola is commonly used to unblock tubes, but there are few published data to support this practice (Nicolau & Davis 1990). Cranberry juice and enzyme solutions have also been used with varying degrees of success.

'Frequent flushing with water is usually effective … in preventing clogging and facilitating declogging.'

Frequent flushing with water is usually as effective as carbonated beverages, and better than cranberry juice, in preventing clogging and facilitating declogging.

Feeds and blockages

As noted above, all tube-feeding formulae are suspensions and are therefore prone to settling. Formulae should be vigorously shaken before administration, and diluted if they are thick.

Medications and blockages

Administering inadequately crushed medication can also block the tube. It is advisable to use a commercial tablet crusher or a mortar and pestle to crush tablets. The pestle can be used to break the tablet into smaller pieces by crushing from directly above. Once the tablet has been reduced to small pieces, the pestle can be used to crush the pieces against the side of the mortar in a circular motion. Once a uniformly smooth powder has been formed, a small amount of water should be added to form a slurry. The slurry should be diluted with more water (unless the person is restricted to small volumes of fluid). The pestle should be rinsed with extra water to ensure that most of the drug is administered.

'Before administering the crushed tablets, the feed should be stopped and the tube flushed with water. The medication should then be administered and the tube flushed again with water before the feed is recommenced.'

Before administering the crushed tablets, the feed should be stopped and the tube flushed with water. The medication should then be administered and the tube flushed again with water before the feed is recommenced.

Best practice to avoid blockages

Best practice in avoiding blockages includes the following:
- administering medications in liquid form;
- adequately shaking formulae before administration;
- irrigating the tube with water after administering medication or formula; and
- frequently flushing the tube with water (every 4–6 hours).

Conclusion

Most people with a gastrostomy tube require medication at some time, and many require regular medication. This chapter has discussed some of the medication issues of which health professionals and carers should be aware.

A summary of the recommendations for administering medications to tube-fed people is presented in the Box below.

Summary of medication recommendations

- Whenever possible, choose a marketed liquid form of the drug.
- Consider alternative routes of administration (for example, rectal, transdermal, or parenteral).
- Consider alternative drugs that might be available in a form suitable for administration via a tube.
- Do not crush any medication until it is established that it is safe to do so.
- Do not crush any medication that has been formulated by the manufacturer to increase its duration of action.
- Do not crush any medication that is coated (except sugar or film coating).
- Ensure tablets are crushed to a very fine powder before adding water to form a slurry.
- Allow medications to flow through the tubing by gravity—do not use any force.
- Dilute viscous liquids (including tube formulae) with water before administration.
- Dilute hypertonic solutions (for example, potassium chloride, theophylline) with water to reduce gastric irritation.
- Do not add any medication directly to a tube-feeding formula.
- Heed information on drug–food interactions. Stop the feed 30 minutes before administering any drug that should be given on an empty stomach. Allow at least 30 minutes after the drug is administered before recommencing the formula.
- Any drug known to be incompatible with formula should be administered as a single daily dose (if possible). Stop the feed two hours before administering the drug and allow two hours before the feed is restarted.

(continued)

(continued)

- Give multiple medications separately. Flush with water before, between, and after each medication.

- Use the Y-port to administer medications using a syringe. If the system does not have a Y-connection, stop the feed, disconnect the giving set, and add the medication using a syringe (without a needle).

- Before changing a tube-feeding formula, consult a pharmacist about the potential for protein-binding changes with any drugs being administered.

- Monitor and document the feeding regimen to ensure that any drug-related problems are recognised and addressed.

- Always monitor and document the person's response to therapy to ensure that optimal clinical response is achieved and that adverse drug-related events are avoided.

Chapter 13
Nasogastric Tubes
Susan Camilleri and Catherine Barrett

Introduction

Although nasogastric tube feeding is not as common as gastrostomy tube feeding, the care of people who require nasogastric feeding is just as specialised.

This chapter presents an overview of the indications for using nasogastric tubes and the care of a person with a nasogastric tube. Much of the care for a person being fed via a tube is the same as that discussed elsewhere in this book, regardless of the location of the tube. This chapter therefore highlights the special issues to be considered when tube feeding is provided through a nasogastric tube.

Indications

Nasogastric tube feeding is usually used for:
- short-term tube feeding;
- longer-term tube feeding for people who are unable to tolerate a gastrostomy tube; or
- as a trial of tube feeding.

Each of these is discussed below.

Short-term tube feeding

Nasogastric tube feeding might be used as a short-term method of tube feeding for people who:

- are malnourished;
- have suffered an acute event that is expected to improve (for example, a stroke causing temporary dysphagia); or
- require tube feeding, but are waiting for a gastrostomy tube to be inserted.

The case study below illustrates a situation in which a short-term nasogastric tube was used effectively.

Mr Black

Mr Black was an 82-year-old man who had been admitted with a recent history of confusion, urinary incontinence, poor mobility, and weight loss.

An assessment by a speech therapist revealed that Mr Black had a poorly coordinated swallowing action and was at risk of aspiration pneumonia. After consultation with Mr Black and his wife it was agreed that his diet would be changed to puréed meals and thickened fluids.

Mr Black found these meals unappetising. Despite a number of strategies to stimulate his appetite, his food intake decreased significantly. A week after admission he was more lethargic, and a dietitian assessed his intake as being inadequate.

After discussion with Mr Black and his family it was agreed that his oral intake would be boosted with tube feeds delivered at night via a nasogastric tube. It was anticipated that tube feeding would be required for a period of 4–5 weeks. Night feeds would allow Mr Black the opportunity to attend daily therapy sessions and to eat small amounts during the day.

One-month after the nasogastric tube had been inserted Mr Black was less confused and his weight had increased by four kilograms. As his strength increased, his mobility and continence also improved. His swallowing improved as his recovery progressed and he was able to return to a normal diet.

Five weeks after it had been inserted, the nasogastric tube was no longer required.

Longer-term tube feeding

Longer-term nasogastric feeding is less common than short-term nasogastric feeding. However it can be useful for:

- people who are unable to have an anaesthetic; and
- people in whom there is limited abdominal access.

Anaesthetic concerns

Nasogastric tube feeding might be used in the longer term for people who are unable to tolerate an endoscopic procedure and light sedation—which are necessary to insert a gastrostomy tube.

Limited abdominal access

Nasogastric tube feeding might be required in the longer term for people who have abdominal pathology (such as fistulae or adhesions) that prevent the placement of a tube in the stomach.

Trials of tube feeding

As discussed in Chapter 2 (page 38), a trial usually involves the insertion of a nasogastric tube for a short time to ascertain whether tube-feeding goals can be achieved.

If the trial is successful and longer-term feeding is required, the possibility of a gastrostomy tube can be discussed with the person and his or her family. However, if the goals are not achieved, or if tube feeding is too burdensome, the trial is discontinued.

It should be noted that nasogastric feeding is associated with a higher mortality than is gastrostomy tube feeding (Norton et al. 1996).

Contraindications

Nasogastric tube feeding is unsuitable for some people. Nasogastric tube feeding is contraindicated in the following conditions (Fawcett 1995):

- complete intestinal obstruction;
- oesophageal reflux;
- oesophageal fistulae;

- gastric fistulae; and
- delayed gastric emptying.

Indications and contraindications

Indications

Nasogastric tube feeding is usually used for:

- short-term tube feeding;
- longer-term tube feeding for people who are unable to tolerate a gastrostomy tube; or
- as a trial of tube feeding.

Contraindications

Nasogastric tube feeding is contraindicated in the following conditions (Fawcett 1995):

- complete intestinal obstruction;
- oesophageal reflux;
- oesophageal fistulae;
- gastric fistulae; and
- delayed gastric emptying.

Complications

Nasogastric tube feeding is associated with a number of potential complications. In particular, incorrect insertion of the tube can cause perforation of the lungs or oesophagus.

'Nasogastric tube feeding is associated with a number of potential complications.'

Apart from the risk of such inadvertent perforation of major organs, the complications experienced by people with gastrostomy tubes also apply to nasogastric tubes. These include the complications discussed earlier in this book—such as diarrhoea, vomiting, tube blockage, aspiration pneumonia, altered body image, and so on.

Complications that are especially relevant to nasogastric feeding include:

- aspiration pneumonia;
- discomfort;
- displacement of the tube; and
- altered body image.

Each of these is discussed below.

Aspiration pneumonia

Aspiration pneumonia is, potentially, a life-threatening complication of nasogastric tube feeding. There is a lack of consensus as to whether the risk of aspiration is greater with a nasogastric tube than with a gastrostomy tube. However, some experts believe that there is an increased risk of reflux and aspiration with nasogastric tubes because they keep the oesophageal sphincter open (Eisenberg 1994).

'Aspiration pneumonia is, potentially, a life-threatening complication of nasogastric tube feeding.'

People who are particularly at risk of aspiration are those who:

- have large-bore nasogastric tubes;
- are heavily sedated;
- have delayed gastric emptying (Eisenberg 1994);
- have compromised gag or cough reflexes;
- have altered conscious state;
- are nursed in the prone position; and
- try to remove their tubes.

It is important to monitor the person for signs of aspiration—including changes in the colour and amount of sputum and changes in vital signs (Eisenberg 1994). Strategies to minimise aspiration are discussed in Chapter 10 (page 185).

Discomfort

Pressure from the nasogastric tube in the nasal passage, throat, and oesophagus can cause irritation and damage to tissues. Some people report that nasogastric tubes are uncomfortable. It is therefore not surprising that some people, especially those who cannot remember why they have the tube, pull them out.

Displacement of the tube

Accidental displacement

Unlike gastrostomy tubes, nasogastric tubes do not have an internal bumper to prevent their being accidentally removed.

Nasogastric tubes are usually taped to the person's face. However, the tape often loosens with sweating and bathing and it is therefore not uncommon for nasogastric tubes to be displaced. Once the tape has loosened, the tube can be easily removed if the person coughs or sneezes, or if it is accidentally pulled during a procedure.

'Accidental displacement is a burden to the person ... and there is a high risk of aspiration if the tube is dislodged during tube feeding.'

Accidental displacement is a burden to the person, because another tube has to be inserted. Furthermore, the person is at high risk of aspiration if the tube is dislodged during tube feeding.

Deliberate removal by person

As noted above (page 235), nasogastric tubes can be uncomfortable, and some people try to remove them.

Physical and chemical restraints are sometimes used to prevent deliberate removal of a nasogastric tube, but restraints can have significant adverse effects on physical and psychological well-being. It is not always possible to predict whether a person will require restraint, and the possibility that restraint might be needed should therefore be considered when making a decision to insert a nasogastric tube.

The sedative effect of *chemical* restraints can increase the risk of falls in older people, and can increase the risk of vomiting and aspiration by delaying gastric emptying (Eisenberg 1994).

Physical restraints, such as mittens and manacles, have been used to prevent people from removing a nasogastric tube. However, physical restraints can also have negative consequences. These include:

- injury while trying to remove restraints;
- increased frustration; and
- increased risk of complications associated with inactivity—such as thrombosis, pneumonia, and decubitus ulcer.

Careful consideration should be given to these potential adverse effects before using any form of chemical or physical restraint.

Altered body image

Many of the psychosocial issues discussed in Chapter 5 (page 97) with respect to gastrostomy tubes are also relevant to nasogastric tubes. Nasogastric tubes can have a significant effect on the person's body image.

'Nasogastric tubes can have a significant effect on the person's body image.'

Although gastrostomy tubes can be tucked into the person's clothing (and thus be hidden), a nasogastric tube is more obvious. For some people this can cause embarrassment. In some cases, there can be a significant alteration to the person's perception of his or her body image.

It is important that taping be as discreet as possible. If appropriate, a gastrostomy tube should be used in preference to a nasogastric tube.

Types of nasogastric tubes

The two main types of nasogastric tubes used are:

- fine-bore tubes; and
- Ryle's tubes.

These are discussed below. Table 13.1 presents a summary of the characteristics of the two types of tubes.

Table 13.1 Characteristics of nasogastric tubes
Authors' PRESENTATION

Characteristic	Fine-bore tube	Ryle's tube
Material	polyurethane	polyvinyl chloride (PVC)
Size	fine-bore	large-bore
Uses	manufactured for nasogastric tube feeding	usually used for stomach drainage
Duration of placement	up to 12 weeks (dependent on tube and person)	short-term use
Guide wire	usually provided	not provided
Aspiration	might not be possible	can be aspirated
Distal feeding port	at least one side-port through which medications can be administered	no side-port

Fine-bore tubes

Fine-bore nasogastric tubes are specifically manufactured for nasogastric tube feeding, and are more commonly used than Ryle's tubes. The characteristics of fine-bore tubes are listed in the Box below.

Characteristics of fine-bore nasogastric tubes

Fine-bore nasogastric tubes:

- are made from polyurethane, and are soft and flexible;
- are less likely to irritate the mucosa;
- do not deteriorate on contact with gastric juices (Montgomery 1987);
- have side-ports that allow medication to be administered;
- have an interlocking port to ensure secure connection to the giving set;
- are radiopaque so their position can be checked on X-ray;
- have a tungsten (weighted tip) that keeps them in place; and
- come with a guide wire to assist insertion.

Because they are of small size and made of soft material, fine-bore tubes are more comfortable. However, these attributes can also result in:

- increased risk of tube blockage;
- inability to aspirate the tube;
- rupture or kinking of the tube (Eisenberg 1994); and
- increased likelihood that misplacement will not be detected (Metheny et al. 1998).

Because polyurethane tubes are so soft, a guide wire is usually provided to make it easier to insert them. The guide wire must never be reinserted once the tube is in position (Rollins 1997).

After they have been inserted, polyurethane tubes can last from several weeks (Rollins 1997) to several months (Arrowsmith 1996). Manufacturers usually provide guidelines on the recommended frequency of changing the tube. However, it has been suggested that nasogastric tubes should be replaced every 5–10 days to prevent damage to the tissues with which they are in contact (Kennedy 1997).

Ryle's tubes

Wide-bore tubes, such as Ryle's tubes, were designed for gastric drainage (Rollins 1997), but are used in some facilities for nasogastric tube feeding. The general characteristics of Ryle's tubes are listed in the Box below.

Characteristics of Ryle's tubes

Ryle's tubes:

- are made from polyvinyl chloride (PVC);
- harden when they come in contact with gastric juices (Fawcett 1995);
- are usually larger than fine-bore tubes;
- have a radiopaque tip to allow their position to be checked by X-ray; and
- allow for aspiration to be performed through the tube.

Most Ryle's tubes do not have a side-port, interlocking port, or guidewire. They have been associated with discomfort, nasal ulceration, oesophageal erosion, and incompetence of the cardiac sphincter (Fawcett 1995).

The frequency of replacing a Ryle's tube depends on the manufacturer's guidelines. However, it has been recommended that they be changed after 10 days because the PVC hardens when it comes into contact with gastric juices (Arrowsmith 1996).

Choice of tube type

The needs of the person and the policy of the facility determine the choice of tube. However, a fine-bore tube should be used whenever possible (Fawcett 1995). These tubes are more comfortable, do not need to be changed as often, and do not deteriorate after coming into contact with gastric juices.

'A fine-bore tube should be used whenever possible.'

Inserting a nasogastric tube

Policies and guidelines

Inserting a nasogastric tube requires a significant level of clinical expertise. If health professionals are inexperienced in the technique of inserting nasogastric tubes, difficulties can be experienced. There is potential for the tube to be inserted into the person's airway, and there can be uncertainty about the correct position of the tube.

'If health professionals are inexperienced in the technique of inserting nasogastric tubes, difficulties can be experienced.'

Insertion of a tube can cause discomfort to the person, and he or she might move or gag during the procedure.

Policies for insertion of nasogastric tubes vary among facilities. A policy should state:

- which health professionals can insert nasogastric tubes;
- how staff competency is assessed and maintained;

- where the nasogastric tube should be placed;
- frequency of changing nasogastric tubes;
- a procedure for checking tube position; and
- principles of care.

Many tube-feeding companies have consultants and videos available to instruct health professionals on the procedure for inserting a nasogastric tube.

Preparation for tube insertion

Choosing the tube type

Before beginning the procedure, careful consideration should be given to selection of an appropriate tube type. The type of tube that is selected will influence how the position of the tube is to be checked, the equipment required for checking, and whether an X-ray will be required. (For more on this, see 'Checking the position of a nasogastric tube', this chapter, page 244.)

Explanation of procedure

Explaining the procedure to the person and his or her family helps them understand what to expect. Having families present during the procedure can help to reduce anxiety and minimise discomfort.

Chapter 3 (page 43) discussed the importance of familiarising the person and his or her family with the tube and feeding equipment before the procedure. Those comments were made with respect to gastrostomy feeding, but similar comments apply to nasogastric feeding.

'Explaining the procedure, and having families present during the procedure, can help to reduce anxiety and minimise discomfort.'

Discussing the tube-feeding regimen with the person and his or her family will help them to understand what to expect.

Finally, in preparing for the procedure, a nasal toilet can facilitate the insertion of a nasogastric tube.

The procedure

The tube is inserted through the person's nose, passed down the oesophagus, and positioned in the stomach. The best way to learn how to insert a nasogastric tube is by observing and learning from an experienced clinician. Advice on the correct procedure can also be obtained from the facility's guidelines and policies (if these exist) or from instructional videos. Several companies that produce tube feeding equipment have instructional videos on how to insert nasogastric tubes.

'The best way to learn how to insert a nasogastric tube is by observing and learning from an experienced clinician.'

It is important that the person does not feel rushed and that the health professional has sufficient support to enable the tube to be inserted successfully.

Once the tube is inserted and the position verified, the tube should be marked with a pen at the level of the tip of the nose. This mark assists in monitoring possible tube migration. It also allows for a measure to be taken of the length of tube required for future tube insertions. An alternative is to measure and record the external length of the tube.

Securing a nasogastric tube

Removing or dislodging a nasogastric tube is dangerous because it exposes the person to aspiration. Furthermore, a dislodged tube has to be reinserted—which is uncomfortable for the person and time-consuming for staff.

Nasogastric tubes can become dislodged if the person tugs at the tube, or as a result of coughing, sneezing, or vomiting. Tubes can also be accidentally removed by staff. Securing the tube is therefore important.

One useful method of securing a nasogastric tube is described in the Box on page 243. The taping technique can be practised by first taping a pen to the office desk. Alternatively, there is a range of commercially available products specifically manufactured for securing nasogastric tubes.

Securing a nasogastric tube

A useful method for securing a nasogastric tube involves the following steps.

- Take a piece of tape about 10 cm long (after ensuring that the person is not allergic to the tape).
- Cut the middle of the tape lengthwise to half-way along the tape (see Figure 13.1, below).
- Apply the uncut end along the bridge of the person's nose (see Figure 13.2, page 244).
- Wrap the cut ends around the nasogastric tube.
- Place a second piece of tape across the person's nose, horizontal to the first piece of tape, to form a cross across the bridge of the nose (see Figure 13.2).
- Attach a rubber band (or piece of tape) to the external end of the tube.
- Secure the tube to the person's clothing with a safety pin through the rubber band.
- Ensure that enough slack is left to allow the person to move his or her head freely.

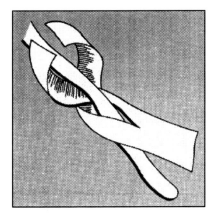

Figure 13.1 Cutting the tape to secure a nasogastric tube

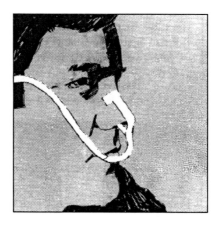

Figure 13.2 Securing the tube to the nose with tape
REPRODUCED WITH PERMISSION OF ABBOTT AUSTRALASIA PTY LTD

Checking the position of a nasogastric tube

It is important to check the position of a tube immediately after it has been inserted—and on an ongoing basis thereafter.

The frequency of checking is dependent on the needs of individuals and on the policy of each facility. Many facilities require the position of the tube to be checked before administration of each feed. A person who frequently pulls at the tube will obviously require more frequent checks.

Common methods used to check the position of nasogastric tubes include:

- X-rays;
- auscultation; and
- assessing the colour and/or pH of aspirated fluid.

Each of these is discussed below.

X-rays

X-rays are effective in checking the position of nasogastric tubes, especially if the tube has a radiopaque tip. However, there are potential problems in using X-rays.

Checking the position of a nasogastric tube

Common methods used to check the position of nasogastric tubes include:

- X-rays;
- auscultation; and
- assessing the colour and/or pH of aspirated fluid.

Each of these is discussed in this section of the text.

Having an X-ray might be inconvenient or distressing for the person. X-rays can also be costly in terms of the direct cost of the X-ray and the indirect costs of transporting and escorting the person to the radiology department. Repeated X-rays expose the person to unnecessary radiation.

Auscultation

The auscultation method of checking the position of a nasogastric tube involves injecting air into the nasogastric tube with a syringe and listening over the stomach area with a stethoscope. The air should be heard gurgling in the person's stomach.

Although health professionals commonly use this method, it is considered to be unreliable (Eisenberg 1994; Kennedy 1997). The problems with the method are as follows:

- air can be heard whether the tube is in the stomach, lungs, or intestine;
- bowel sounds can be mistaken for air in the stomach;
- due to the narrowness of fine-bore tubes it might not be possible to inject sufficient air into the nasogastric tube (Eisenberg 1994); and
- abdominal obesity can distort sounds (Viall 1996).

Colour and pH of the aspirant

To improve accuracy in assessing tube position, the colour and numerical pH value of tube aspirant can be tested (Metheny et al. 1998). This process involves taking a small sample of fluid from the nasogastric tube. However, it is not suitable in all cases because, as previously described, some tubes cannot be aspirated.

Several studies have been conducted into the colour and pH of aspirants from the stomach, duodenum, and tracheobronchial tree. The colour of these aspirants can be summarised as follows (Metheny et al. 1994; Metheny et al. 1998):

- *tracheobronchial tree aspirant:* off-white, heavily tinged with mucus;

- *gastric aspirant:* 'grassy green', tan to off-white, bloody or brown;

- *duodenal aspirant:* medium-to-deep golden yellow.

However, the colour of an aspirant, on its own, is not conclusive. Tracheobronchial fluid and gastric fluid can both be off-white, bloody, or brownish; and intestinal and pleural fluid can both be yellow (Metheny et al. 1998). Because of this potential confusion in identifying the source of aspirant, colour is usually considered in combination with pH. The pH of aspirant is measured with a pH meter (or with a testing paper that covers a pH range between 0 and 14).

'Although the combined method of assessing colour and pH does not definitively prove that a nasogastric tube is in the stomach, it is a more accurate method than auscultation.'

The pH values of aspirants vary—depending on the origin of the aspirant. For example, a pH reading between 0 and 4 means that the aspirant definitely comes from the stomach, whereas aspirant from the pulmonary tree has a pH reading of 6 or greater (Metheny et al. 1998). However, 20% of gastric aspirates actually have a pH higher than 6, and the pH of the stomach alters with tube feeding and with the administration of certain medications (such as antacids and acid inhibitors) (Metheny et al. 1998).

Although the combined method of assessing colour *and* pH does not definitively prove that a nasogastric tube is in the stomach (Metheny et al. 1998), it is a more accurate method than auscultation.

Care plan

After the tube has been inserted, a care plan should be developed. An example of a care plan for managing nasogastric tubes is shown in Figure 13.3 (page 248).

Case study

The case study (below) outlines the distress that a nasogastric tube can cause.

Mr White

Mr White was a 72-year-old man who had been admitted for assessment of renal failure, poor nutrition, and acute confusion. Two weeks after admission it was apparent that his oral intake was inadequate. It was therefore decided to insert a nasogastric tube.

A medical officer inserted the initial nasogastric tube. Insertion was difficult because Mr White did not appear to understand the procedure and was clearly distressed throughout.

Mr White reported that the tube was uncomfortable and he was often found pulling at the tube or picking at the tape used to secure the tube to his cheek. Despite frequent reminders of why a nasogastric tube was required he did not appear to understand its significance. As Mr White's agitation increased he was commenced on a small dose of a sedative.

Mr White stopped eating any food and began complaining that there was 'something at the back of my throat'. The sedation appeared to have contributed to an increase in the frequency of falls.

In the first week after the initial tube was inserted Mr White removed his tube on three occasions. Each time that the tube was replaced several staff members were required because Mr White became very distressed and tried to hit out. The procedure left Mr White agitated and bleeding from the nose.

It was therefore decided to insert a PEG tube. Mr White made no attempt to remove the PEG tube and became less agitated. Sedation was ceased and Mr White began to take an interest in eating and drinking again.

Two weeks later Mr White was transferred to a nursing home.

NASOGASTRIC TUBE CARE PLAN	NAME:

Instructions for inserting the tube (include person's preferences)

. . . .

. . . .

Record of tubes inserted

Tube type	Size	Date inserted	Date to be changed	Nostril used	Inserted by	External tube length	Comments

Position check

Frequency . . . .

Method . . . .

Securing the tube . . . .

. . . .

Nasal toilet (check skin integrity) . . . .

. . . .

Checking residual volumes (include frequency of checks and limit to be reported to dietitian/medical officer) . . . .

. . . .

Medical administration (special instruction to include flush amount) . . . .

. . . .

Tube-feeding regimen

Delivery rate	Formula type	Formula volume	Water added	Times given	Flushes	Position

Completed by: Designation: Date:

Figure 13.3 Example of care plan for managing a nasogastric tube
AUTHOR'S PRESENTATION

Conclusion

The case study at the beginning of the chapter shows the benefits that can be obtained from the insertion of a nasogastric tube when short-term tube feeding is required. However, the case study at the end of the chapter highlights some of the complexities of choosing the nasogastric route for tube feeding. Nasogastric tube feeding has its place, but it can be uncomfortable, complicated, and distressing for all involved.

If staff members care for a person with a nasogastric tube on an infrequent basis, it can be difficult for them to maintain their skills in this area. Given the potential complications and the complexity

'Nasogastric tube feeding has its place, but it can be uncomfortable, complicated, and distressing for all involved.'

of care required to manage nasogastric tubes, as discussed in this chapter, it is crucial that health professionals maintain their skills. If the facility does not have staff experienced in the care and insertion of nasogastric tubes, or if it lacks policies to guide staff, training must be provided.

Chapter 14

Transferring Care

Jacqui Bailey

Introduction

After a person has been started on gastrostomy feeds and is tolerating the prescribed regimen, he or she can usually be discharged home or to another care facility. This chapter discusses this transition of care. In transferring care, the following matters require attention:

- transfer of information and documentation;
- education required before discharge;
- practicalities of gastrostomy feeding at home;
- supplies of formula and equipment; and
- monitoring.
    The chapter considers these matters under two broad headings:
- transfer to another institution; and
- transfer to home.

Transfer to another institution
Timely communication

When a person who is tube fed is to be transferred to another institution, timely and detailed information about his or her nutritional care should be provided in writing and by telephone. The charge nurse and dietitian are the most appropriate people with whom to communicate. Contact with the facility should be initiated as soon as possible to allow staff to prepare to receive the person and acquire the necessary supplies for tube feeding.

If adequate notice of the person's transfer to another institution cannot be provided, it is courteous to provide enough formula and/or equipment to ensure continuity of care until the new facility can reasonably source its own.

The transfer letter

A letter should be written advising the new facility of the person's transfer. This letter should contain all relevant information that might be required by the receiving institution. The Box on page 253 lists the information that should be included.

Transfer to home

Benefits of home tube feeding

Tube feeding at home gives people an opportunity to participate in home and community activities while ensuring that their nutritional needs are met. For some people, the comforts of home assist in further recovery before they resume their usual activity levels. In addition, the cost/benefits of discharging people to their homes can be significant for the healthcare system. However, tube feeding at home is not suitable for everyone.

'Tube feeding at home gives people an opportunity to participate in home and community activities while ensuring that their nutritional needs are met.'

Team involvement before discharge

If a decision is made to proceed with home tube feeding, all relevant team members need to be notified to allow them to prepare for the person's discharge and follow-up care. The team members who should be notified about a pending discharge include the person's dietitian, nurse, stomal

Transfer letter

A transfer letter to a receiving institution should contain the following information:

- *personal details:* the person's name and date of birth;
- *timing:* the anticipated date of transfer;
- *health history:* the person's medical and nutritional history, and current issues that need to be addressed and monitored;
- *tests and measurements:* anthropometry and biochemistry (and trends in these);
- *drug therapy:* current medication list (including administration times and routes);
- *commencement of tube feeding:* the date on which tube feeding was first commenced, and the name of the facility where the gastrostomy tube was inserted or replaced;
- *current tube:* (i) the size, brand, and type of tube now in use; (ii) manufacturer's information about the tube (such information is usually provided with the insertion kit and should stay with the person); and (iii) how the tube should be removed (for example, traction or endoscopic removal only);
- *current feeding regimen:* current formula (including the correct name and manufacturer) and current regimen (including the prescribed volume to be administered per day, and the times and rate of feeds);
- *oral intake:* type and amount of oral intake (if appropriate); and
- *contacts:* the name and contact details of medical practitioner(s), charge nurse, speech pathologist, and dietitian involved in the person's care before transfer.

therapist, general practitioner, gastroenterologist, occupational therapist, and speech pathologist.

Suitability for home tube feeding

When determining a person's suitability for tube feeding at home, certain criteria need to be carefully considered. The Box on page 254 lists these criteria.

Criteria for home tube feeding

In assessing whether a person is suitable for home tube feeding, the following criteria should be carefully considered.

Personal criteria

Personal criteria to be considered include the following:

- that the person and carer are willing and able to continue tube feeding at home; and
- that the person's quality of life will be maintained or improved by discharge to home with nutritional support.

Health criteria

Health criteria to be considered include the following:

- that the person is otherwise ready for discharge home;
- that the inpatient tube-feeding experience was successful and uncomplicated (that is, that nutritional needs were met and that the person accepted the tube-feeding regimen well); and
- that the cognitive ability, manual dexterity, and independent function of the person and/or carer are satisfactory to undertake home tube feeding (including demonstrated understanding and capability with respect to safe use and care of the tube, formula, and other equipment).

Environmental criteria

Environmental criteria to be considered include the following:

- that the home environment is appropriate for the safe and effective use of nutritional support;
- that financial arrangements have been discussed and accepted by the person and carer; and
- that appropriate support and follow-up care are available to the person and carer.

Feeding regimens

Before the person is discharged, due consideration must be given to his or her usual activity patterns at home. If possible, tube-feeding times should be compatible with the person's usual lifestyle and activity pattern.

The home environment is obviously different from that in an institution. Nursing shift times and ward routines are not relevant in the home situation. Medications might change, or be ceased altogether. These factors obviously affect the options that are available to a person in considering a feeding regimen at home.

When designing an optimal feeding regimen for home, the following factors should be considered:

- the person's usual sleep pattern;
- the person's usual meal times;
- medications that are needed, and the times at which they must be taken;
- regular family, work, and social commitments;
- other practical care issues (such as bathing, toileting, or physiotherapy);
- storage space and refrigeration available for formula and equipment; and
- the availability of an intravenous (IV) pole or an alternative.

If possible, a trial of the proposed home feeding regimen should take place before discharge—under supervision of staff. If this is not possible, a new regimen can be introduced incrementally at home under close supervision by a community based dietitian and/or nurse. The purpose of the trial is to monitor the person's tolerance of the feeds and his or her ability to manage the regimen.

'If possible, a trial of the proposed home feeding regimen should take place before discharge.'

The case study presented in the Box on page 256 describes several alternative tube-feeding regimens. Each of these takes into account the particular circumstances of the person involved.

Formulae and equipment

When selecting formulae and equipment for home feeding, product availability and cost are important considerations. Equipment such as pumps and IV poles might need to be purchased or borrowed. The local

Home feeding regimens

Health status and lifestyle

Robyn was a 44-year-old married woman who worked four 8-hour days per week as a telephonist. Robyn had developed achalasia—a condition in which the sphincter between the oesophagus and stomach does not allow food to pass readily into the stomach. This condition meant that Robyn was unable to tolerate sufficient food and drink by mouth to maintain her weight. A PEG tube had therefore been inserted.

Robyn was independent in all other areas of her life. She shared her home with her partner who worked full time.

Robyn was able to take very small quantities of food and drink by mouth during the day. She enjoyed this limited oral intake. In addition, Robyn required 1500 mL of formula each day via her PEG tube. She was able to connect her pump set to her gastrostomy tube while working. Robyn liked to be in bed by 10.30 pm, and she usually woke at 6.00 am.

Possible regimens

Robyn's requirements could be met in several ways—by continuous feeding, intermittent feeding, or bolus feeding. Suggested regimens for each of these options are presented below.

Continuous feeding

The following regimen is suggested, with the feed running via a pump at a set rate to administer Robyn's required 1500 mL per day:

- 65 mL/hr continuously, 24 hours per day (other than showering times).

Intermittent feeding

Three options are suggested:

- *Option 1:* 125 mL/hr over 12 hours a day (for example, from 6.00 pm to 6.00 am); or
- *Option 2:* 150 mL/hr over 10 hours a day (for example, from 8.00 pm to 6.00 am); or
- *Option 3:* 215 mL/hr over 7 hours a day (for example, from 8.00 am to 12.00 noon, disconnected during a break from the office, and then reconnected between 1.00 pm and 5.00 pm).

(continued)

(continued)

(Note re Option 2: Because Robyn's feed containers can hold a maximum of 1200 mL, she could run a 300 mL bag between 8.00 pm and 10.00 pm and then connect a 1200 mL bag to run for eight hours overnight without having to wake to change bags.)

Bolus feeding:

Two options are suggested:

- *Option 1:* six volumes of 250 mL each, administered at intervals throughout the day (for example, at 7.00 am, 10.00 am, 1.00 pm, 4.00 pm, 5.00 pm, and 11.00 pm); or
- *Option 2:* five volumes of 300 mL each, administered at intervals throughout the day (for example, at 8.00 am, 11.00 am, 2.00 pm, 5.00 pm, and 8.00 pm).

Mixed regimen:

The following regimen is suggested to avoid Robyn having to change bags of formula during the night:

- two bolus feeds of 250 mL at 12.00 noon and 6.00 pm, then 1000 mL overnight at 100 mL/hr.

hospital or district nursing service is likely to know where to procure such equipment. If the person needs to borrow equipment from the facility, a loan agreement (and payment of a deposit) might have to be arranged.

Staff should investigate whether the person qualifies for any subsidies or entitlements from government or other agencies. Depending on the local jurisdiction, various subsidies for the cost of home tube-feeding formula and equipment are usually available—particularly if the person is in financial hardship. It is worth asking local government bodies, health departments, welfare agencies, and charitable organisations whether the person qualifies for any such subsidy. This is especially important if a person requires an expensive specialty formula. Some people might not be aware of these subsidies unless staff members discuss them with them.

Sometimes cost-effective alternatives can be arranged for a minimal financial outlay. For example, a plant hanger hook placed in an appropriate position in the home can be substituted for an IV pole.

Proper care and maintenance of equipment can also reduce the expense of home tube feeding for a person.

Education

Comprehensive education about managing tube feeding should be provided to the person and his or her carer by a registered nurse and a dietitian before discharge to home. It is preferable if such education begins before the gastrostomy tube is inserted. Written material should be provided for the person and/or carer on key issues. The issues that should be included are listed in the Box below.

'Comprehensive education about managing tube feeding should be provided to the person and his or her carer before discharge to home.'

Education for person and carer

In providing comprehensive education about managing tube feeding before discharge to home, the following issues should be covered:

General issues
- the rationale for tube feeding;
- the length of time that tube feeding is likely to be required (months, years, or indefinitely); and
- any change in the structure or function of the gut due to surgery or medical conditions.

Tube
- the name, brand, size, and type of tube inserted;
- monitoring the position of the tube;
- routine tube maintenance; and
- how the tube (or parts) will be replaced or changed.

(continued)

(continued)

Formula
- the exact name and required daily volume of formula;
- correct storage, preparation, and administration of formula (and the importance of hygienic practices);
- administering medications (if necessary); and
- ordering and obtaining formula.

Other equipment
- the names of different pieces of equipment;
- the safe use and care of all equipment; and
- ordering and obtaining equipment.

Lifestyle and daily activities
- discussion regarding lifestyle changes (especially with respect to oral intake, see Chapter 6, page 119);
- discussion regarding altered body image, and sensual and sexual health (see Chapter 5, page 97);
- advice regarding bathing and swimming with tube in situ; and
- preventing and recognising complications (such as infection, aspiration, occlusion of tube, and displacement of tube).

Costs
- the cost of supplies and equipment; and
- availability of entitlements or subsidies.

Support
- contact details for 24-hour support;
- what to do if the tube falls out;
- other troubleshooting tips; and
- arrangements for follow-up care.

Practical aspects of going home

It is important to consider what equipment and supplies the person needs to take home, and how it will be transported. Consideration should be given to how much formula and equipment will be provided on discharge, where

'It is important to consider what equipment and supplies the person needs to take home, and how it will be transported.'

the person will collect the equipment and formula, and whether assistance is required to transport it to home. It should be noted that boxes of formula can be quite heavy. Once home, the person might need assistance to move formula and equipment inside the house.

Another consideration is whether the person will be given a spare gastrostomy tube to take home. If not, it might be necessary to provide a urinary catheter of the same size to use in the short term in an emergency— such as dislodgment of the initial tube. Instructions should be given to the person about the steps to take if the tube is accidentally dislodged.

It should be explained that some tubes can be repaired if any problems arise. It some cases it might be appropriate to send a person home with an extra Y-port connection or extension tube(s).

For more information on tube replacement, see Chapter 11 (page 193).

Team involvement after discharge

General practitioner

The person's general practitioner (GP) will appreciate a letter that outlines the nutritional care of the person. The letter should also include the information outlined in the transfer letter described on page 253. The doctor should be asked to contact the nurse and dietitian caring for the person if any new medical issues arise that have relevance to tube feeding (such as gastrointestinal signs or symptoms, new medications, or an infection of the stoma site).

Other health professionals

Follow-up care should be arranged with a nurse (and/or stomal therapist) and a dietitian. A speech pathologist and gastroenterologist can also be involved in ongoing monitoring and review as needed. Occupational therapists can assist the person to create practical and safe alternatives for feeding equipment.

If healthcare reviews are going to occur in another facility, the relevant health professionals should contact their counterparts to inform them of the person's history and needs.

Readmission and emergency care

If the person is to be managed primarily through the original healthcare facility, his or her potential readmission in future should be considered. Arrangements should be made regarding contact with the facility in an emergency, and whether 24-hour access is available if problems arise. Enquiries should be made about making the person's notes readily available to an after-hours duty nurse.

'Arrangements should be made regarding contact with the facility in an emergency, and whether 24-hour access is available if problems arise.'

Home support

Dietitian's review

It is important to ensure that the person's nutritional requirements continue to be met. Regular follow-up by a dietitian should be arranged to review the person's progress after discharge. Such a review should consider the matters listed in the Box on page 262.

Team review

As indicated above (page 260), involvement of the whole team is important in supporting a person who is receiving tube feeding at home. The person should be reviewed by the person's GP, a nurse (or stomal therapist), and a dietitian. Speech therapists, social workers, and gastroenterologists might also be required.

It should be possible for all necessary monitoring to be undertaken at home by the local GP, or at a community health centre, or at an outpatient clinic. The team should initially review the person within six weeks of

Dietitian's home review

Regular follow-up by a dietitian should be arranged to review the person's progress after discharge. Such a review should include:

- monitoring of the person's nutritional status;
- monitoring of the person's tolerance of the regimen;
- monitoring of the person's ability to swallow and the adequacy of oral intake (if relevant);
- provision of ongoing support and information;
- adjustment of the feeding regimen (if necessary);
- assessment of the person's psychosocial adjustment;
- monitoring of routine biochemistry;
- observation of the stoma site and tubing; and
- review of current medication.

discharge from hospital. If all is well, review should take place at least every six months thereafter.

Good communication among team members is essential. If optimal care is to be provided at home, all team members should be aware of the roles of other team members, and all should feel comfortable about their own roles when some aspects of care overlap. This is particularly important if the person lives in a remote area or if coordination of team members is difficult for other reasons. One health professional should be the key care coordinator for home tube-feeding issues. This person might be a dietitian, a nurse, or a GP—depending on individual circumstances.

'Good communication among team members is essential . . . One health professional should be the key care coordinator for home tube-feeding issues.'

Monitoring weight and energy balance

Weight and general well-being should be monitored to ensure that the goals of tube feeding are being achieved, and that the feeds are not adversely affecting other aspects of the person's life.

Weight loss (or a lack of desirable weight gain) indicates that insufficient energy is being administered. Conversely, undesired weight gain shows that excessive energy is being provided. Formula volume or type can be adjusted accordingly—taking care not to compromise other nutrient needs. The person should be advised to check his or her weight at least once a month to monitor energy balance. Weight should be measured at the same time of day, wearing the same clothing, and on the same set of scales. A good time to take a weight measurement is first thing in the morning—before breakfast, but after toileting. The weight should be recorded on a calendar or in a diary. Results should be compared with the previous month's weight, noting any increase or decrease.

'Weight loss indicates that insufficient energy is being administered. Conversely, undesired weight gain shows that excessive energy is being provided.'

The significance of weight loss can best be gauged in terms of percentage weight loss. Percentage weight loss can be calculated as follows (Blackburn et al. 1977):

Percentage weight loss = (usual weight – actual weight) x 100 / usual weight

Every person's weight fluctuates somewhat over time. Changes in lifestyle, seasonal activity, and eating patterns can all affect weight. Some people also have significant fluid shifts—for example, with conditions such as renal disease and congestive heart failure. All of these factors must be taken into account when interpreting weight gain or loss.

Allowing for the variable factors described above, a judgment on whether a percentage weight loss is *significant* depends on the time over which the weight has been lost. The Box on page 264 lists some convenient 'rules of thumb'.

Managing weight loss prevents or slows functional decline and other negative effects of weight loss on quality of life. A significant loss (or gain) in any two consecutive months should be reported to the dietitian—particularly if the change is undesirable.

Significant weight loss

The following 'rules of thumb' can be applied:

- *after one week:* weight loss of 1–2% is significant;
- *after one month:* weight loss of 5% is significant;
- *after three months:* weight loss of 7.5% is significant; and
- *after six months:* weight loss of 10% is significant;

The significance of any weight change must be seen in the context of the goal of tube feeding in any given individual. In some cases, it might be impossible to arrest weight loss completely—for example, in some hypermetabolic conditions (such as cancer cachexia). However, in circumstances such as these the provision of extra energy can minimise or slow the loss of weight.

The case study presented in the Box below illustrates some of these weight-monitoring issues.

Nancy

Nancy commenced tube feeds after developing Parkinson's disease. She was no longer able to take food by mouth due to a high risk of aspiration. Nancy had lost a lot of weight before having a gastrostomy tube inserted.

Before commencing tube feeds, Nancy weighed 43 kg. One week later she weighed 42.1 kg. The weight loss of 0.9 kg therefore represented a percentage weight loss of 2.1% (over one week). This is significant.

Nancy's significant weight loss was addressed immediately by increasing the energy content of her tube-feeding formula.

Suppliers

Arrangements for the collection of home tube-feeding supplies vary among different countries and regions. Some areas use local hospitals to provide formula and equipment; others use pharmacies, nutritional companies, or support groups.

Commercial home-delivery services are provided in some areas. Further information can be obtained from the local hospital, pharmacy, or phone directory. The Internet is also a useful source of information, and is now being used to take orders for such businesses.

Nutritional companies are becoming more involved in delivering supplies direct to homes. Some also provide home-care professionals such as nurses and dietitians to customers. Some companies also provide 24-hour contact phone lines for advice. Such information lines are a valuable source of information. They can also act as a support service by putting people in contact with other people in the local area who are having tube feeds at home, or by providing advice about existing community support groups.

Terminating home tube feeding

It is important to continue to monitor the suitability of the person for home tube feeding—using the selection criteria applied at the time of discharge (see page 254). If any of those factors have changed, the desirability of current home tube feeding arrangements should be reviewed. In particular, if a person (or carer) becomes unable to administer feeds independently, or if the person's quality of life is not being maintained, discontinuation of tube feeds should be seriously considered.

The possibility that home tube feeding might be discontinued at some future time should be discussed with the person before he or she is discharged from the facility. When education for discharge home is being undertaken (see page 258), the person should be reminded that tube feeding remains a *choice*. He or she should feel free to discuss treatment options at any time. Health professionals should always be aware that, for various personal and cultural reasons, many people are reluctant to speak openly about their medical and nutritional treatment.

'Tube feeding remains a choice. The person should feel free to discuss treatment options at any time.'

In considering whether to discontinue tube feeding, the psychological and social dynamics of the person, family, and friends must be acknowledged. People who are being tube-fed sometimes wish to withdraw from active tube-feeding support, but say nothing because they feel under pressure to continue. Despite their feeling that tube-feeding is not enhancing their own quality of life (or, indeed, that it is worsening their quality of life), they feel reluctant to say so. Health professionals need to be aware of these psychological and social dynamics.

If possible cessation of treatment is addressed early—especially with palliative-care patients and their families—the issue is likely to be less confronting when it does arise.

References

Preface

Department of Human Services (Victoria) 1997, Ministerial Working Party on Home Enteral Nutrition in Victoria, July, Department of Human Services, Melbourne.

DHS, see Department of Human Services (Victoria).

Chapter 1 Indications for Tube Feeding

Anderson, T. 1991, *Much Ado About Swallowing*, South Western Sydney Area Health Service, Sydney.

Britton, J., Lipscomb, G., Mohr, P., Rees, W. & Young, A. 1997, 'The use of percutaneous endoscopic feeding tubes in patients with neurological disease' *Journal of Neurology*, 244, 431–4.

Bucholz, D.W. & Neumann, S. 1998, 'Recent dysphagia literature', *Dysphagia*, 13, 191–2.

Callahan, C.M., Haag, K.M. & Weinberger, M. 2000, 'Outcomes of percutaneous endoscopic gastrostomy among older adults in a community setting', *Journal of the American Geriatrics Society*, 48 (9), 1048–54.

Campbell-Taylor, I. & Fisher, R. 1987, 'The clinical case against tube feeding in palliative care of the elderly', *Journal of the American Geriatrics Society*, 35, 1100–4.

Chouinard, J. Lavigne, E. & Villeneuve, C. 1998, 'Weight loss, dysphagia and outcome in advanced dementia', *Dysphagia*, 13, 151–5.

Ciocon, J.O. 1990, 'Indications for tube feeding in elderly patients', *Dysphagia*, 5, 1–5.

Dharmarajan, T., Unnikrishnan, D. & Pitchumoni, C. 2001, 'Percutaneous endoscopic gastrostomy and outcome in dementia', *The American Journal of Gastroenterology*, 96 (9), 2556–63.

Feinberg, M., Knebl, J., Tully, J. & Seagall, L. 1990, 'Aspiration and the elderly', *Dysphagia*, 5: 61–71.

Fernandez-Viadero, C., Pena Sarabia, N., Jimenez Sainz, M. & Verduga Velez, R. 2002, 'Percutaneous endoscopic gastrostomy: better than nasoenteric tube?', *Journal of the American Geriatrics Society*, 50 (1), 199–200.

Gilbar, P. & Kam, F. 1997, 'Guidelines for drug administration in the elderly', *Australian Journal of Hospital Pharmacy*, 27 (3), 214–20.

Groher, M.E. 1994, 'Determination of the risks and benefits of oral feeding', *Dysphagia*, 9, 233–5.

Kyle, H. 1996, 'PEG-percutaneous endoscopic gastrostomy', *British Journal of Theatre Nursing*, 6 (4), 27–30.

Logemann, J.A. 1983, *Evaluation and Treatment of Swallowing Disorders*, College-Hill Press, Boston.

Nicholson, F., Korman, M. & Richardson, M. 2000, 'Percutaneous endoscopic gastrostomy: A review of indications, complications and outcome', *Journal of Gastroenterology and Hepatology*, 15, 21–5.

O'Brien, B., Davis, S. & Erwin-Toth, P. 1999, 'G-tube site care: a practical guide', *Registered Nursing*, 62 (2), 52–6.

Peck, A., Cohen, C. & Mulvihill, M. 1990, 'Long-term enteral feeding of aged demented nursing home patients', *Journal of the American Geriatrics Society*, 38, 1195–8.

Robbins, J., Levin, R., Wood, J., Roecker, E. & Luschie, E. 1995, 'Age effects in lingual pressure generation as a risk factor for dysphagia', *Journal of Gerontology Medical Services*, 50A (5), m257–m262.

Sonies, B. 1992, 'Oropharyngeal dysphagia in the elderly', *Clinics in Geriatrics Medicine*, 8 (3), 569–77.

Chapter 2 Making Decisions on Tube Feeding

Ackerman, T. 1996, 'The moral implications of medical uncertainty: tube feeding demented patients', *JAGS*, 44 (10), 1265–7.

BMA. see British Medical Association.

British Medical Association 1998, 'Withholding and withdrawing life-prolonging medical treatment: guidance for decision making', <www.bmjpg.com/withwith/chapters/3d_3.thm>.

Brockett, M. 1999, 'Substitute decision-making for cognitively impaired older people', *CMAJ*, 160 (12), 1721–3.

Callahan, C., Haag, K., Buchanan, N. & Nisi, R. 1999, 'Decision-making for percutaneous endoscopic gastrostomy among older adults in a community setting', *JAGS*, 47 (9), 1105–9.

Cartwright, C. & Steinberg, M. 2000, 'PEG feeding, dementia and the need for policies and guidelines', *Australasian Journal on Ageing*, 19 (3), 106–7.

Darzins, P., Molloy D. & Strang, D. (eds) 2000, *Who Can Decide? The Six Step Capacity Assessment Process*, Memory Australia Press, Alzheimer's Association (SA), Adelaide.

Department of Human Services (Victoria) 1997, *Ministerial Working Party on Home Enteral Nutrition in Victoria*, July 1997. DHS, Melbourne, Victoria.

DHS, see Department of Human Services (Victoria).

Finucane, T., Christmas, C. & Travis, K. 1999, 'Tube feeding patients with advanced dementia', *JAMA*, 282 (14), 1365–70.

Gillick, M. 2000, 'Rethinking the role of tube feeding in patients with advanced dementia', *The New England Journal of Medicine*, 343 (3), 206–10.

Goodhall, L. 1997, 'Tube feeding dilemmas: can artificial nutrition and hydration be legally or ethically withheld or withdrawn?', *Journal of Advanced Nursing*, 25 (2), 217–22.

Guido, M., Van Rosendaal, M., Verhoef, M. & Kinsella, T. 1999, 'How are decisions made about the use of percutaneous endoscopic gastrostomy for long-term nutritional support?', *The American Journal of Gastroenterology*, 94 (11), 3225–8.

Herrmann, V. & Norris, P. 1998, 'Ethical issues in instituting and discontinuing enteral feeds', *Gastrointestinal Endoscopy Clinics of North America*, 8 (3), 723–31.

Hodges, M. & Tolle, S. 1994, 'Tube-feeding decisions in the elderly', *Clinics in Geriatric Medicine*, 10 (3), 475–88.

Kowalski, S. 1996, 'Withdrawal of nutritional support: a family's choice', *Gastroenterology Nursing*, 19 (1), 25–8.

McCann, R. 1999, 'Lack of evidence about tube feeding—food for thought', *JAMA*, 282 (14), 1380–1. *Ministerial Working Party on Home Enteral Nutrition in Victoria*. July 1997, Department of Human Services, Melbourne.

McNabney, M., Beers, M. & Siebens, H. 1994, 'Surrogate decision-makers' satisfaction with the placement of feeding tubes in elderly patients', *JAGS*, 42 (2), 161–8.

Meisel, A. 1995, 'Barriers to forgoing nutrition and hydration in nursing homes', *American Journal of Law and Medicine*, XXI (4), 336–82.

Mitchell, S. & Lawson, F. 1999, 'Decision-making for long-term tube-feeding in cognitively impaired elderly people', *CMAJ*, 160 (12), 1705–9.

Mitchell, S., Berkowitz, R., Lawson, F. & Lipsitz, L. 2000, 'A cross-national survey of tube-feeding decisions in cognitively impaired older persons', *JAGS*, 48 (4), 391–7.

Mitchell, S., Keily, D. & Lipsitz, L. 1998, 'Does artificial enteral nutrition prolong the survival of institutionalized elders with swallowing problems?', *Journal of Gerontology*, 53A (3), 207–13.

Rabeneck, R., McCullough, L. & Wray, N. 1997, 'Ethically justified, clinically comprehensive guidelines for percutaneous endoscopic gastrostomy tube placement', *The Lancet*, 349 (15), 496–8.

Rabeneck, L., Wray, P. & Petersen, N. 1996, 'Long-term outcomes of patients receiving percutaneous endoscopic gastrostomy tubes', *JGIM* 11, 287–93.

Tealey, A. 1994, 'Percutaneous endoscopic gastrostomy in the elderly', *Society of Gastroenterology Nurses and Associates*, February, 151–7.

Van Rosendaal, G. & Verhoef, M. 1999, 'Difficult decisions for long term tube-feeding', *CMAJ*, 161 (7), 798–9.

Wilson, D. 1992, 'Ethical Concerns in a long term tube feeding study', *IMAGE: Journal of Nursing Scholarship*, 24 (3), 195–9.

Chapter 3 Inserting a Gastrostomy Tube

Department of Human Services (Victoria) 1997, Ministerial Working Party on Home Enteral Nutrition in Victoria, July, Department of Human Services, Melbourne.

DHS, see Department of Human Services (Victoria).

Fawcett, H. 1995, 'Nutritional support for hospital patients', *Nursing Standard*, 9 (48), 25–8.

Gauderer, M., Ponsky, J. & Izant, R. 1998, 'Gastrostomy without laparotomy: a percutaneous endoscopic technique', *Nutrition*, 9 (14), 736–8.

Kulling, D., Sonnenberg, A., Fried, M. & Bauerfeind, P. 2000, 'Cost analysis of antibiotic prophylaxis for PEG', *Gastrointestinal Endoscopy*, 51 (2), 152–6.

Shike, M. 1995, 'Percutaneous endoscopic stomas for enteral feeding and drainage', *Oncology*, 9 (1), 1–10.

Thompson, L. 1995, 'Taking a closer look at percutaneous endoscopic gastrostomy', *Nursing*, 95, 63.

Vargo, J. & Ponsky, J. 2000, 'Percutaneous endoscopic gastrostomy: clinical applications', <www.medscape.com/viewarticle/407957?sec=search>.

Chapter 4 Nutritional Assessment and Tube Feeding

Abbott Australasia nd, 'Tube feeding at home: For gastrostomy or jejunostomy tube feeding', Abbott Australasia.

Crook, M., Hally, V. & Panteli, J. 2001, 'The importance of the refeeding sydrome', *Nutrition*, 17: 632–7.

McNeill, G. 2000, 'Energy Intake and Expenditure', in Garrow, J., James, W. & Ralph, A. (eds), *Human Nutrition and Dietetics*, 10th edn, Churchill Livingstone, London.

Chapter 5 Living with a Gastrostomy Tube

Gastrostomy Information Support Service 1992, *Newsletter No 14*, Gastrostomy Information Support Service, Melbourne.

GISS, *see* Gastrostomy Information Support Service.

Goodhall, L. 1997, 'Tube feeding dilemmas: Can artificial nutrition and hydration be legally or ethically withheld or withdrawn?', *Journal of Advanced Nursing*, 25(2), 217–22.

Quandt, S., Arcury, T., Bell., R., McDonald, J. & Vitolins 2001, 'The social and nutritional meaning of food sharing among older rural adults', *Journal of Aging Studies*, 15(12), 145.

Ruark, J. 1999, 'Place at the table: scholars of cultural meanings of food', *Chronicle of Higher Education*, July 6, 46 (44), pA 17 (3).

Van Rosendaal, G. & Verhoef, M. 1999, 'Difficult decisions for longterm tube-feeding', *CMAJ*, 161 (7), 798–9.

Chapter 6 Reintroducing Meal Choices

Barkan, L. 1999, 'Feasts for the eyes, food for the thoughts', *Social Research*, Spring, vol. 66, issue 1, p. 225.

Department of Health and Family Services 1998, *Standards and Guidelines for Residential Aged Care Services Manual*, Aged and Community Care Division, Department of Health and Family Services, Canberra.

DHFS, see Department of Health and Family Services.

Kaplan, E. 2000, 'Using food as a metaphor of care: middle school children talk about family, school and class relationships', *Journal of Contemporary Ethnography*, vol. 29, issue 4, 474 (36).

Lupton. D. 1994, 'Food, memory and meaning: the symbolic and social nature of food events', *The Sociological Review*, vol. 42, no. 4, 664 (22).

Quandt, S., Arcury, T., Bell, R., McDonald, J. & Vitolins 2001, 'The social and nutritional meaning of food sharing among older rural adults', *Journal of Aging Studies*, vol. 15, issue 2, p. 145.

Ruark, J. 1999, 'A Place at the Table (scholars of cultural meanings of food)', *The Chronicle of Higher Education*, July 6, vol. 46 issue 44, p. A17 (3).

Chapter 7 Stomal Care

Arrowsmith, H. 1996, 'Nursing management of patients receiving gastrostomy feeding', *British Journal of Nursing*, 5 (5), 268–73.

Bowers, S. 2000, 'All about tubes: your guide enteral feeding devices', *Nursing 2000*, 30 (12), 41–7.

Duszak, J. 2002, 'Percutaneous gastrostomy and jejunostomy', <www.emedicine.com/radio/topic798.htm>.

Hess, C.T. 1999, 'Managing a fistula', *Nursing 99*, January 18, 29 (1).

Lee, G. & Bishop, P. 1999, *Microbiology and Infection Control for Health Professionals*, Prentice Hall, Australia.

Liddle, K. 1995, 'Making sense of percutaneous endoscopic gastrostomy', *Nursing Times*, 91 (18), 32–3.

O'Brien, B., Davis, S. & Erwin-Toth, P. 1999, 'G-Tube site care: a practical guide', *RN*, 62 (2), 52–6.

Taylor, C., Lillis, C. & Lemone, P. 1997, *Fundamentals of Nursing: The Art and Science of Nursing Care*, Lippincott-Raven, Philadelphia.

Chapter 8 Care of the Gastrostomy Tube

Arrowsmith, H. 1996, 'Nursing Management of patients receiving gastrostomy feeding', *British Journal of Nursing*, 5 (5), 268–73.

Bowers, S. 1996, 'Tubes: a nurse's guide to enteral feeding devices', *MedSurg Nurs*, 5, 313–24.

Broscious, S.K. 1995, 'Preventing Complications of PEG Tubes', *Dimensions of Critical Care Nursing*, 14 (6), 37–41.

Eisenberg, P.G. 1994, 'Gastrostomy and jejunostomy tubes', *RN*, November, 54–9.

Guenter, P. 1989, 'Percutaneous endoscopic gastrostomy feeding tube in neuroscience patients', *Journal of Neuroscience Nursing*, 21 (2), 122–4.

Guenter, P. & Silkroski, M. 2001, *Tube Feeding Practical Guidelines and Nursing Protocols*, Aspen Publishers Inc., Maryland.

Klang, M.G. 1996, 'Medicating tube-fed patients', *Nursing*, 96, January, 13.

Kohn-Keeth, C. 2000, 'How to keep feeding tubes flowing freely', *Nursing 2000*, March, 58–9.

Krupp, K.B. 1998, 'Going with the flow: preventing clogged feeding tubes', *Nursing 98*, April, 54–5.

McMeekin, K. 2000, 'Replacing PEG tubes', *NT PLUS*, 96 (8), 9–10.

Metheney, N., Eisenberg, P. & McSweeney, M. 1988, 'Effect of feeding tube properties and three irrigants on clogging rates', *Nursing Research*, 37 (3), 165–9.

Ricciardi, E. & Brown, D. 1994, 'Managing PEG Tubes', *American Journal of Nursing*, October, 29–31.

Smeltzer. S. & Bare, G. (eds.) 1992, *Brunner and Suddarth's Textbook of Medical-Surgical Nursing*, J.B. Lippincott, Philadelphia.

Chapter 9 Mouth Care

Ebersole, P. & Hess, P. 1994, *Toward Healthy Aging: Human Needs and Nursing Response*, 4th edn, Mosby, St Louis.

Fuller, J. & Schaller-Ayers, J. 1994, *Health Assessment, A Nursing Approach*, J.B. Lippincott Company, Philadelphia.

Joshipura, K.J., Rimm, E.B., Doulas, C.W., Trichopoulos, D., Ascherio, A. & Willett, W.C. 1996, 'Poor oral health and coronary heart disease', *Journal of Dental Research*, 75, 1631–6.

Miller, M. & Kearney, N. 2001, 'Oral care for patients with cancer', *Cancer Nursing*, 24 (4), 241–54.

Walton, J., Miller, J. & Tordecilla, L. 2001, 'Elder assessment and care', *MedSurg Nursing*, 10 (1), 37–44.

Chapter 10 Troubleshooting

Bass, J., Forman, L., Abrams, S. & Hsueh, A. 1996, 'The effect of dietary fibre in tube-fed elderly patients', *Journal of Gerontological Nursing*, 22 (10): 37–44.

Bliss, D. & Lehmann, S. 1999, 'Tube feeding: Administration tips', *RN*, 62 (8): 29–32.

Bliss, D., Johnson, S., Savik, K., Clabots, C., Willard, K. & Gerding, D. 1998, 'Acquisition of *Clostridium difficile* and *Clostridium difficile*-associated diarrhoea in hospitalised patients receiving tube feeding', *Annals of Internal Medicine*, 129 (12): 1012–19.

Bockus, S. 1991, 'Troubleshooting your tube feedings', *American Journal of Nursing*, May: 24–8.

Bockus, S. 1993, 'When your patient needs tube feeding, making the right decisions', *Nursing*, July: 34–43.

Burns, E. & Jairath, N. 1994, 'Diarrhoea and the patient receiving enteral feedings: a multifactorial problem', *Journal of the Wound, Ostomy and Continence Nurses Society*, 21 (6): 257–63.

DeLegge, M. & Rhodes, B. 1998, 'Continuous versus intermittent feedings: slow and steady or fast and furious?', *Support Line*, XX (5): 11–15.

Drickamer, M. & Cooney, L. 1993, 'A geriatrician's guide to enteral feeding', *Journal of the American Geriatric Society*, 41: 672–9.

Dunning, T. 2003, *Care of People with Diabetes: A Manual of Nursing Practice*, 2nd edn, Blackwell Publishing, Oxford.

Edes, T., Walk, B. & Austin, J. 1990, 'Diarrhoea in tube-fed patients: feeding formula not necessarily the cause', *The American Journal of Medicine*, 88: 91–3.

Keohane, P., Attrill, H., Love. M., Frost, P. & Silk, D. 1984, 'Relation between osmolality of diet and gastrointestinal side effects in enteral nutrition', *British Medical Journal*, 288: 678–80.

Marcuard, S.P., Stegall, K.L. & Trogdon, S. 1989, 'Clearing obstructed feeding tubes', *Journal of Parenteral and Enteral Nutrition*, 13 (1): 81–3.

Thomas, B. 2001, *A Manual of Dietetic Practice*, Blackwell Publishing, Oxford.

Chapter 11 Changing a Gastrostomy Tube

Abbott Australasia Pty Ltd 2002, 'Removal of PEG Tube: Endoscopic PEG; Non-endoscopic Inverta-PEG'.

Faller, N. & Lawrence, K. 1993 'Comparing low-profile gastrostomy', *Nursing*, 93, December, pp 46–8.

Faller, N., Lawrence, K. & Ferraro, C. 1993, 'Gastrostomy, replacement, feeding tubes: The long and the short of it', *Ostomy/Wound Management*, 39(1), pp 26–33.

Hall, J.C., Brennan, K. & Heximer, B. 1996, 'Trouble-shooting G-tubes: Balloon deflation problems', *RN*, July, 25–8.

Kadakia, S., Cassaday, M, & Shaffer, R. 1994, 'Comparison of Foley catheter as a replacement gastrostomy tube with commercial replacement gastrostomy tube: a prospective randomized trial', *Gastrointestinal Endoscopy*, 40(1), pp 188–93.

Kaufman, M,. Faller, N. & Lawrence, K. 1995. 'Low-profile gastrostomy devices', *Gastroenterology Nursing*, 18(5), pp 171–6.

Marshall, J. & Barthel, J. 1994, 'Early accidental dislodgment of PEG tubes', *Journal of Clinical Gastroenterology*, 18(3), pp 210–2.

O'Dell, K., Gordon, R. & Becker, L. 1991, 'Gastrostomy tube transmigration: A rare cause of small bowel obstruction', *Annals of Emergency Medicine*, 20:7, July, pp 165–7.

O'Keefe, K., Dula, D. & Varano, V. 1990, 'Duodenal obstruction by a nondeflating Foley catheter gastrostomy tube', *Annals of Emergency Medicine*, 19: 12 December, pp 131–4.

Pereira, M. & Mersich, K. 1991, 'Foley catheter gastrostomy tube migration: Small bowel obstruction relieved by percutaneous balloon aspiration', *Gastrointestinal Endoscopy*, 37(3), pp 372–4.

Chapter 12 Selecting and Administering Medications

Bauer, L.A. 1982, 'Interference of oral phenytoin absorption by continuous nasogastric feedings', *Neurology*, 32: 570–2.

Gilbar, PJ. and Kam, FSF. (1997): Guidelines for drug administration during enteral feeding. *Aust J Hosp Pharm*, 27: 214–220.

Institute of Safe Medication Practices, 'Medication Safety Alert', 25 March 1998.

ISMP, *see* Institute of Safe Medication Practices.

Kuhn, T.A., Garnett, W.R., Wells, B.K. & Karnes, H.T. 1989, 'Recovery of warfarin from an enteral nutrient formula', *American Journal of Hospital Pharmacy*, 46: 1395–9.

McPherson, M.L. 1994, 'Don't crush that tablet', *Journal of the American Pharmacists Association*, NS34 (5): 57–8.

Mitchell, J.F. 1996, 'Oral solid dosage forms that should not be crushed: 1996 revision', *Australian Journal of Hospital Pharmacy*, 31: 27–37.

Nicolau, D.P. & Davis, S.K. 1990, 'Carbonated beverages as irrigants for feeding tubes', *Drug Intelligence & Clinical Pharmacy*, 24: 840.

Chapter 13 Nasogastric Tubes

Arrowsmith, H. 1996, 'Nursing management of patients receiving gastrostomy tube feeding', *British Journal of Nursing*, 5 (5), 268–73.

Eisenberg, P. 1994, 'Nasoenteral tubes', *RN Journal*, October 62–70.

Fawcett, H. 1995, 'Nutritional support for hospital patients'. *Nursing Standard*, 9 (48), 25–8.

Kennedy, J. 1997, 'Enteral feeding for the critically ill patient', *Nursing Standard*, 11 (33), 39–43.

Metheny, N., Reed, L., Berglund, B, & Wehrle, M.A. 1994, 'Visual characteristics of aspirates from feeding tubes as a method for predicting tube location', *Nursing Research*, 43(5), 282.

Metheny, N., Smith, L., Werhle, M., Wiersema, L. & Clark, J. 1998, 'pH, colour, and feeding tubes', *RN*, 61 (1), 25–7.

Montgomery, P. 1987, *Enteral Tube Feeding*, Home Nutrition Service, Melbourne.

Norton, B., Homer-Ward, M., Donnelly, M., Long, R. & Holmes, G. 1996, 'A randomised prospective comparison of percutaneous endoscopic gastrostomy and nasogastric feeding after dysphagic stroke', *British Medical Journal*, 312 (7022), 13–16.

Rollins, H. 1997, 'A nose for trouble', *Nursing Times*, 93 (49), 66–7.

Viall, C.D. 1996, 'Location, location, location', *Nursing*, 96, September, 43–5.

Chapter 14 Transferring Care

Blackburn, G., Bistrain, B., Maini, B., Schlamm, H. & Smith, M. 1977, 'Nutritional and metabolic assessment of the hospitalised patient', *Journal of Parenteral and Enteral Nutrition*, 1 (11), 11–22.

Index

From the extensive list of books from Ausmed Publications, the publisher especially recommends the following as being of interest to readers of *Gastrostomy Care: A Guide to Practice*.

All of these titles are available from the publisher: Ausmed Publications, 277 Mt Alexander Road, Ascot Vale, Melbourne, Victoria 3032, Australia.
website: <www.ausmed.com.au>; email: <ausmed@ausmed.com.au>

Dementia Nursing: A Guide to Practice
Edited by Rosalie Hudson

Dementia is one of the major health problems of our ageing society and dementia nursing is one of the most important and highly skilled of nursing specialities. As another volume in Ausmed's growing 'Guide to Practice' series, this is the definitive textbook on dementia nursing. The chapters are written primarily by nurses for nurses. But dementia nursing is essentially an exercise in teamwork, and valuable contributions and insights are offered by other health professionals, carers, artists, and relatives from a variety of backgrounds and countries. The result is a comprehensive international volume on all aspects of dementia nursing. Available as textbook alone or as audiobook–textbook package.

Nurse Managers: A Guide to Practice
Edited by Andrew Crowther

This book addresses the core issues associated with nurse management, and is thus an essential primary text for all nurses as they develop their managerial skills. This book is an innovative and practical text that fulfils a previously unmet need. It provides the evidence-based, practical advice that nurse managers require to undertake their important role with growing confidence and expertise. The book covers such issues as promotion, leadership and motivation, moral management, dealing with unhelpful staff, occupational health and safety, budgets, information technology, and many other vital issues in modern nurse management. In all these areas, the reader is offered a range of solutions and coping strategies for the issues that confront nurse managers every day. Available as textbook alone or as audiobook–textbook package.

Ageing at Home: Practical Approaches to Community Care
Theresa Cluning

Most older people prefer to live independently in their own homes. But to do this they often need community support—even if they remain relatively healthy into very old age. *Ageing at Home* is written for professionals and other interested people who care for the frail elderly who choose to remain at home. The book is easy to read and provides practical ideas for helping ageing persons and those who care for them. The wide range of contributing authors includes geriatricians, community-based professionals, and academics. From their practical experience these authors have provided informative text, prompt sheets, assessment tools and tables on diverse topics. If you are a professional or family carer, this book is for you.

From the extensive list of books from Ausmed Publications, the publisher especially recommends the following as being of interest to readers of *Gastrostomy Care: A Guide to Practice*.

All of these titles are available from the publisher: Ausmed Publications, 277 Mt Alexander Road, Ascot Vale, Melbourne, Victoria 3032, Australia.
website: <www.ausmed.com.au>; email: <ausmed@ausmed.com.au>

Aged Care Nursing: A Guide to Practice
Edited by Susan Carmody and Sue Forster

The aged population has grown markedly throughout the world, but there is a shortage of experienced nurses with expertise in the holistic care of the elderly. This book is written to inspire and empower such nurses. *Aged Care Nursing: A Guide to Practice* is written by clinicians for clinicians. The inclusion of evidence-based and outcome-based practices throughout the book ensures that all readers, be they novices or experts, will have a reliable and comprehensive reference to guide their practice. Each author is a recognised expert in his or her subject area, and all present their topics with a focus that is practical, rather than academic. Available as textbook alone or as audiobook–textbook package.

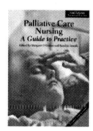

Palliative Care Nursing: A Guide to Practice (2nd edn)
Edited by Margaret O'Connor and Sanchia Aranda

This second edition of Palliative Care Nursing has been totally revised, rewritten, and redesigned. The result is a comprehensive handsome volume that builds upon the successful formula of the popular first edition. All nurses and other health professionals with an interest in this vital subject will welcome this new edition as an essential addition to their libraries. This is the definitive textbook on palliative-care nursing.

Nursing Documentation in Aged Care: A Guide to Practice
Edited by Christine Crofton and Gaye Witney

The title of this book is carefully chosen. All of the contributors to *Nursing Documentation in Aged Care: A Guide to Practice* firmly believe that nursing documentation in aged care—if performed with pride and professionalism—is truly a *guide to practice*. Documentation is a wonderful opportunity to record and reflect upon all that is good in nursing. In addition to their ethical and professional responsibilities, caring nurses are aware of the personal satisfaction to be gained from documenting their holistic and reflective nursing practice. This book shows how nursing assessments, care plans, and progress notes can allow nurses to share their knowledge, observations, and skills. This is more than a 'how-to-do-it' workbook. With contributions from a range of experts, this comprehensive evidence-based textbook explores the issues surrounding documentation and reveals the importance of professional communication within multidisciplinary teams. Available as textbook alone or as audiobook–textbook package.

Printed in the United Kingdom
by Lightning Source UK Ltd.
121199UK00001B/9